Motivation, Autonomy and Emotions in Foreign Language Learning

PSYCHOLOGY OF LANGUAGE LEARNING AND TEACHING
Series Editors: **Sarah Mercer,** *Universität Graz, Austria* **and Stephen Ryan,** *Waseda University, Japan*

This international, interdisciplinary book series explores the exciting, emerging field of Psychology of Language Learning and Teaching. It is a series that aims to bring together works which address a diverse range of psychological constructs from a multitude of empirical and theoretical perspectives, but always with a clear focus on their applications within the domain of language learning and teaching. The field is one that integrates various areas of research that have been traditionally discussed as distinct entities, such as motivation, identity, beliefs, strategies and self-regulation, and it also explores other less familiar concepts for a language education audience, such as emotions, the self and positive psychology approaches. In theoretical terms, the new field represents a dynamic interface between psychology and foreign language education and books in the series draw on work from diverse branches of psychology, while remaining determinedly focused on their pedagogic value. In methodological terms, sociocultural and complexity perspectives have drawn attention to the relationships between individuals and their social worlds, leading to a field now marked by methodological pluralism. In view of this, books encompassing quantitative, qualitative and mixed methods studies are all welcomed.

All books in this series are externally peer-reviewed.

Full details of all the books in this series and of all our other publications can be found on http://www.multilingual-matters.com, or by writing to Multilingual Matters, St Nicholas House, 31-34 High Street, Bristol, BS1 2AW, UK.

PSYCHOLOGY OF LANGUAGE LEARNING AND TEACHING: 27

Motivation, Autonomy and Emotions in Foreign Language Learning

A Multi-Perspective Investigation in Hungary

Kata Csizér, Dávid Smid,
Anna Zólyomi and Ágnes Albert

MULTILINGUAL MATTERS
Bristol • Jackson

DOI https://doi.org/10.21832/CSIZER2750
Library of Congress Cataloging in Publication Data
A catalog record for this book is available from the Library of Congress.
Names: Csizér, Kata, author. | Smid, Dávid, author. | Zólyomi, Anna, author. | Albert, Ágnes, author.
Title: Motivation, Autonomy and Emotions in Foreign Language Learning: A Multi-Perspective Investigation in Hungary/Kata Csizér, Dávid Smid, Anna Zólyomi, Ágnes Albert.
Description: Bristol, UK; Jackson, TN: Multilingual Matters, 2025. | Series: Psychology of Language Learning and Teaching: 27 | Includes bibliographical references and index. | Summary: 'This book highlights the roles of individual difference variables on the language learning process, exploring them from both the students' and the teachers' perspectives. The contrastive analysis of these two datasets yields interactional results that have the potential to shape classroom learning in the future' – Provided by publisher.
Identifiers: LCCN 2024021408 (print) | LCCN 2024021409 (ebook) | ISBN 9781800412743 (paperback) | ISBN 9781800412750 (hardback) | ISBN 9781800412767 (pdf) | ISBN 9781800412774 (epub)
Subjects: LCSH: Languages, Modern – Study and teaching – Psychological aspects. | Individualized instruction. | Motivation in education.
Classification: LCC PB36 .C75 2025 (print) | LCC PB36 (ebook) | DDC 418.0071 – dc23
LC record available at https://lccn.loc.gov/2024021408
LC ebook record available at https://lccn.loc.gov/2024021409

British Library Cataloguing in Publication Data
A catalogue entry for this book is available from the British Library.

ISBN-13: 978-1-80041-275-0 (hbk)
ISBN-13: 978-1-80041-274-3 (pbk)

Multilingual Matters
UK: St Nicholas House, 31-34 High Street, Bristol, BS1 2AW, UK.
USA: Ingram, Jackson, TN, USA.

Website: https://www.multilingual-matters.com
X: Multi_Ling_Mat
Facebook: https://www.facebook.com/multilingualmatters
Blog: https://www.channelviewpublications.wordpress.com

Copyright © 2025 Kata Csizér, Dávid Smid, Anna Zólyomi and Ágnes Albert.

All rights reserved. No part of this work may be reproduced in any form or by any means without permission in writing from the publisher.

The policy of Multilingual Matters/Channel View Publications is to use papers that are natural, renewable and recyclable products, made from wood grown in sustainable forests. In the manufacturing process of our books, and to further support our policy, preference is given to printers that have FSC and PEFC Chain of Custody certification. The FSC and/or PEFC logos will appear on those books where full certification has been granted to the printer concerned.

Typeset by Riverside Publishing Solutions.

We dedicate this book to all the participants of our research. Thank you for your time.

Contents

Tables	ix
Acknowledgments	xi
1 Introduction	1
1.1 The Structure of the Volume	2
2 The Context and the Research Study	3
2.1 A Brief Introduction to Hungary	3
2.2 The L2 Proficiency of Hungarians	4
2.3 L2 Instruction in Hungarian Secondary Schools	7
2.4 Pre-Service L2 Teacher Education in Hungary	10
2.5 The Working Conditions of In-Service L2 Teachers in Hungary	12
2.6 The Implications for Our Study	14
3 The Theoretical Background of the Study	15
3.1 Language Learning Motivation	15
3.2 Perceived Importance of Contact	19
3.3 Language Learning Autonomy	20
3.4 Emotions	21
3.5 Self-Confidence and Self-Efficacy	32
3.6 The Interrelationship of Motivation, Emotions, Autonomy and Self-Efficacy	34
4 Methods	38
4.1 Brief Overview of the Research Program	38
4.2 Overview of the Research Design	40
4.3 The Participants	40
4.4 The Instruments	42
4.5 Data Collection	45
4.6 Data Analysis	46
4.7 Ethical Considerations and Quality Control	48

5 Results and Discussion: Dispositions and Views of Participants — 50
   5.1 Students' Individual Difference Characteristics — 50

6 Results and Discussion: Teachers' Views of the Individual Difference Variables Measured in the Study — 66
   6.1 Individual Differences Taken into Consideration by Teachers — 66
   6.2 Motivation — 67
   6.3 Emotions — 68
   6.4 Self-Efficacy and Self-Confidence — 72
   6.5 Autonomy — 74

7 Results and Discussion: Student Profiles — 78
   7.1 L2 Learning Motivation-Based Student Profiles — 78
   7.2 L2 Learner Autonomy-Based Student Profiles — 84
   7.3 Positive Emotions Profiles — 90
   7.4 Negative Emotions Profiles — 93
   7.5 Results of Cross-Tabulations: Analyzing the Interrelationships of the Different Learner Profiles — 96

8 Results and Discussion: The Comparative Analysis of Student and Teacher Perspectives — 105
   8.1 Motivation — 105
   8.2 Autonomy — 108
   8.3 Self-Confidence and Self-Efficacy — 111
   8.4 Emotions — 112

9 Conclusion — 117
   9.1 The Main Results of Our Study — 117
   9.2 The Limitations of Our Research Project — 121
   9.3 Future Research Directions — 123
   9.4 Final Remarks — 128

Appendix A: Constructs in the Student Questionnaire in English and Hungarian — 129
Appendix B: Teacher Interview Guide in English and Hungarian — 138
Appendix C: Paired Samples *t*-tests — 143
References — 144
Index — 161

Tables

2.1	L2 instruction in Hungarian public education since the 1990s	5
2.2	Results of the national secondary school leaving exams in Hungary in the past two decades	6
4.1	Overview of the full research program	39
4.2	Summary of the participating teachers' background information	41
4.3	The final round of the reliability analysis	47
4.4	Categories, codes and the number of coded segments in the qualitative data	49
5.1	Results of the descriptive statistical analysis	51
5.2	Gender differences	54
5.3	Differences regarding attendance of extracurricular English classes	56
5.4	Differences regarding the order of L2 acquisition for English	58
5.5	Differences with respect to students' weekly number of English lessons	59
5.6	Differences according to school year	61
5.7	Differences according to region	63
5.8	Differences regarding the time of data collection	64
7.1	Results of the ANOVA in L2 learning motivation-based student profiles: The scales used for the construction of the clusters	79
7.2	The number and percentage of the participants belonging to each cluster in L2 learning motivation-based student profiles	79
7.3	Results of the ANOVA: Group performance on the rest of the measures in L2 learning motivation-based student profiles	81
7.4	Stepwise multiple linear regression controlling for motivated learning behavior in L2 learning motivation-based student profiles	83
7.5	Results of the ANOVA in L2 learner autonomy-based student profiles: The scales used for the construction of the clusters	85
7.6	The number and percentage of participants belonging to each cluster in L2 learner autonomy-based student profiles	85

7.7	Results of ANOVA analyses for L2 learner autonomy-based student profiles: Group performance on the rest of the measures	86
7.8	Stepwise multiple linear regression controlling for the two autonomy constructs in the L2 learner autonomy-based student profiles	88
7.9	The ANOVA of each cluster on the clustering scales in the positive emotions profiles	90
7.10	The number and percentage of the participants belonging to each cluster in the positive emotions profiles ($N = 1152$)	90
7.11	The ANOVA of each cluster on the remaining scales in the positive emotions profiles	91
7.12	The ANOVA of each cluster on the clustering scales in the negative emotions profiles	93
7.13	The number and percentage of the participants belonging to each cluster in the negative emotions profiles ($N = 1152$)	93
7.14	The ANOVA of each cluster on the remaining scales in the negative emotions profiles	94
7.15	Cross-tabulation of the motivational clusters and the autonomy clusters ($N = 1152$)	97
7.16	Cross-tabulation of the motivational clusters and the positive emotions clusters ($N = 1152$)	98
7.17	Cross-tabulation of the motivational clusters and the negative emotions clusters ($N = 1152$)	100
7.18	Cross-tabulation of the autonomy clusters and the positive emotions clusters ($N = 1152$)	101
7.19	Cross-tabulation of the autonomy clusters and the negative emotions clusters ($N = 1152$)	102
7.20	Cross-tabulation of the positive emotions clusters and the negative emotions clusters ($N = 1152$)	103
Appendix C1 Paired samples *t*-tests		143

Acknowledgments

First of all, we would like to thank our co-researchers in this project: Katalin Piniel and Brigitta Dóczi. We could not have completed this project and written this book without their invaluable help during our work. They helped with data collection, analyzed various parts of the data and also read and commented on the present volume at manuscript stage. We would like to thank our (former) PhD students, most notably Dávid Smid and Anna Zólyomi, for their work. Life is considerably easier with smart and hard-working PhD students! Why do you have to finish your studies so quickly? We would like to thank Enikő Öveges for her work in the initial phases of this study and Ádám Lajtai for his support in collecting data. We also want to thank the work of our mentors who have helped us in our careers: Zoltán Dörnyei, Edit Kontra, Marianne Nikolov and Judit Kormos. We are trying to pay forward whenever we can.

This study was supported financially by the National Research, Development and Innovation Office in Hungary (grant number NKFIH – 129149); we thank the work of the agency and the reviewers who deemed this project worthy as well as the work of the administrative staff at our faculty, most notably Ágnes Sipos.

We are grateful to the editors at Multilingual Matters for their work; this publishing house truly feels like home. The manuscript could not have been finalized without the work of James Griffin: thank you for your continuous help with our writing. We also thank our respective families for tolerating our spending so much time in front of our screens and on the phone when writing this book (and beyond). Finally, we owe a great debt to our research participants: heads of schools, teachers and students. To show our appreciation we dedicate our book to them.

Kata and Ágnes

In addition to all those who have contributed in some way to the success of the research project and the book itself, most importantly we would also like to thank our supervisors, Professor Kata Csizér and Professor Ágnes Albert, for their continuous support, help and guidance, and we would like to express our sincere gratitude for the opportunity to write up this book together. We have learned a lot in the process and look forward to working on many more projects.

Dávid and Anna

1 Introduction

Our motivation to study processes pertaining to foreign language (L2) learning in Hungary has been fueled by the fact that over the past decades various surveys have shown that the foreign language knowledge of the Hungarian population lags behind that of other European Union countries (Eurobarometer, 2012; European Statistics, 2016, 2021). Our expertise lies in the investigation of individual difference (ID) variables – i.e. why some students learn an L2 seemingly without any difficulties and relatively quickly, while other students struggle. Since there are several IDs that are believed to be at least partially responsible for variation in language learning success, in this research project we decided to focus on a number of these and we set out to investigate students' characteristics in concert (Ryan, 2019). We selected three groups of ID variables. First: motivational variables. These are thought to be important, as motivation is one of the key ID variables shaping the learning process (Dörnyei & Ushioda, 2021). Second, we included variables about L2 learning autonomy, as this seems to be an important variable in the Hungarian context in the sense that frontal teaching is still often prevailing (Öveges & Csizér, 2018) and autonomy is strongly linked to L2 motivation (Kormos & Csizér, 2014). Third, self-efficacy – i.e. the individual's beliefs of being able to complete tasks necessary to L2 learning – was included not only because of its close link to motivation and, possibly, autonomy, but also for the fact that in a formal instructional context, such as the context of the present investigation, it influences students' goals, motivation and emotions (Bandura, 1993).

We regard the main novelty of our study to be the systematic investigation of various emotions intertwined in the L2 learning processes. Accordingly, as part of this project, we standardized a questionnaire measuring four positive emotions and five negative ones.

We would like to argue that students' dispositions towards these variables measured quantitatively only provide a partial picture, and in a context where classroom teaching of a L2 is prevalent the views of teachers cannot be neglected. Therefore, we also planned an interview study to map the way teachers think about the ID variables outlined above. We were interested in understanding in what ways English teachers in

Hungary perceive the workings of these variables and what they think they can do to enhance positive effects and mitigate negative influences. As it is challenging to analyze quantitative and qualitative data in parallel, the analytical framework used here is facilitated by students' data. Teachers' views are seen to complement student-related results; therefore, qualitative data are presented after discussing the descriptive aspects of the quantitative data.

1.1 The Structure of the Volume

First, we present some important contextual issues to our study. We briefly introduce Hungary as a monolingual Central European country, then touch upon the L2 proficiency of Hungarians. L2 instruction in Hungarian secondary schools, pre-service L2 teacher education and the working conditions of L2 teachers are also seen as providing important information, helping to establish the background and to delineate the setting of our study. We see this volume as the direct continuation of Dörnyei *et al.* (2006) and the interested reader can find more historical information on Hungary and Hungarians in that book.

Next, the relevant literature is synthesized to provide validity to our study and, thus, we concentrate on the ID variables and previous empirical studies of their interrelationships. Our methods chapter (Chapter 4) begins with a brief overview of the full research program. We then provide information on the studies presented in this volume in order to establish the most important quality-control characteristics. We have organized our results into several chapters, starting from description to inferencing relationship-related results. As explained above, the descriptive quantitative data are presented in concert with our teacher-based qualitative findings. The final chapter intends to pull all the strings together by comparing and contrasting student- and teacher-related results as well as outlining future research directions.

2 The Context and the Research Study

2.1 A Brief Introduction to Hungary

Hungary is a country situated in Central Europe with a population of some 9.7 million people and an area of 93,028 km² (Central Intelligence Agency, 2023). Urbanization has grown steadily since the turn of the millennium, with 72% of the total population living in urban areas in 2020 (World Bank, n.d.). The capital and most populous city is Budapest, which is the economic, political, cultural and technological center of the country. It numbered 1.752 million residents in 2019 (Hungarian Central Statistical Office, 2019), approximately one-fifth of the total population of Hungary. Administratively, the country is made up of 19 counties and the capital city (Hungarian Central Statistical Office, n.d.a). These, in turn, are grouped into eight regions (Hungarian Central Statistical Office, n.d.b): For the sake of simplicity we divide Hungary into four parts. We refer to Budapest and Pest as the central part of Hungary; Northern Hungary and the Northern Great Plain as the eastern part of Hungary; the Southern Great Plain as the southern part of Hungary; while Central Transdanubia, Western Transdanubia and Southern Transdanubia are referred to as the western part of Hungary. Apart from Budapest, there are seven settlements with a population of more than 100,000 people: Debrecen, Szeged, Miskolc, Pécs, Győr, Nyíregyháza and Kecskemét (Hungarian Central Statistical Office, 2019).

In our study, we collected data from three of the earlier-mentioned four parts of Hungary: namely, from Central, Eastern and Western Hungary. Our rationale for this was the contrasts between them both with reference to economic measures as well as measures of well-being. The central part of Hungary, especially Budapest, has long been known as the richest part of the country (OECD, 2018b, 2020); the capital city alone accounted for 54% of the growth in national GDP between 2000 and 2016 (OECD, 2018b). In addition, Central Hungary tends to occupy the top rank in most measures of well-being. In 2020, these were education, health, income and access to services (OECD, 2020).

In stark contrast, the eastern part of Hungary consistently fares not only as the poorest (OECD, 2018b, 2020) but also as the least favorable place in terms of measures of well-being, such as education, health, income and jobs (OECD, 2020). As regards the western part of Hungary, it is relatively rich (OECD, 2018b, 2020), and fares favorably on well-being indicators (OECD, 2020), albeit overall remaining behind Central Hungary.

Hungary has a history of more than a thousand years. During its past, the Hungarian nation has endured several turbulent periods. The country was originally founded as a Christian kingdom in 1000; however, later, it was occupied by the Ottomans, then ruled by the Austrian Habsburgs and, subsequently, by Soviet communist forces (*Columbia Encyclopedia*, 2019). With the conclusion of World War I, under the Treaty of Trianon Hungary lost a significant portion of its territory and population to the present-day countries of Austria, Slovakia, Ukraine, Romania, Serbia, Croatia and Slovenia (*Columbia Encyclopedia*, 2019). The country progressed into a democratic governance in 1989, which marks the beginning of its current era. Since then, it has increasingly become affiliated with Western countries, joining the North Atlantic Treaty Organization in 1999 and the European Union in 2004 (Central Intelligence Agency, 2023).

Hungary's integrative approach has resulted in the country's gradual accession to the international scene. This, in turn, has evoked a significant rise in foreign visitors. According to the United Nations World Tourism Organization (UNWTO, 2021), Hungary had around 17.2 million foreign visitors in 2018, which is almost a 200% increase compared to the 9.5 million tourist arrivals in 2010. These numbers not only make Hungary one of the top three tourist destinations within Central and Eastern Europe but also a popular European target among international visitors (UNWTO, 2021). Given its historical and cultural significance, Budapest has been foreign tourists' favorite destination in Hungary (Hungarian Central Statistical Office, 2021). In recent pre-pandemic years, the overwhelming majority of visitors has tended to come from the UK, the USA, France, Italy and Russia (Hungarian Central Statistical Office, 2021). In addition, Hungary's exposure to the global sphere has also been reflected in the education sector. More specifically, the number of foreign students studying in the country at a tertiary level doubled between 2008 (16,916 students) and 2019 (36,090 students; Hungarian Educational Authority, n.d.b).

2.2 The L2 Proficiency of Hungarians

Hungary is predominantly a monolingual country, which cannot be overlooked when it comes to Hungarians' L2 acquisition. The official language is Hungarian, which was the mother tongue of 98.9%

Table 2.1 L2 instruction in Hungarian public education since the 1990s

School year	Type of school	Total number of learners L2					
		Russian	English	German	French	Italian	Spanish
1990/1991	ES	485,002	130,663	186,017	9,928	n.d.	n.d.
	HS	166,688	124,388	113,951	25,530	7,424	2,049
2001/2002	ES	3,538	336,642	275,652	5,575	1,456	315
	HS	5,032	308,075	267,051	30,142	13,234	4,978
2011/2012	ES	658	372,231	153,641	2,222	613	451
	HS	3,778	374,730	222,096	23,241	16,619	11,060
2018/2019	ES	553	431,654	125,299	1,998	608	1,046
	HS	4,337	327,869	173,695	17,585	13,373	12,264

Note: Based on *Statistical Yearbook of Public Education 2018/2019* (Ministry of Human Capacities, 2020).
ES = elementary schools; HS = high schools; n.d. = no data.

of the population in 2011 (Central Intelligence Agency, 2023). In the same year, Hungarians were the largest ethnic group (85.6%; Central Intelligence Agency, 2023). What these data indicate is that, in general, most Hungarians acquire L2s in instructed learning environments. Between 1949 and 1989 Russian was the only L2 that was taught in public education on a compulsory basis. The fall of communism ended this tradition, and the role of Russian began to be replaced by Western languages (Medgyes, 1992; see Table 2.1). Since the turn of the millennium, the three most widely taught L2s in Hungarian public education have been English, German and French (for more information, see Table 2.1).

As regards the L2 proficiency of the Hungarian population, the situation is far from being ideal. According to the statistics representing the adult (working-age) population (i.e. those aged between 25 and 64 years), there has been a slight improvement in the past two decades: i.e. in 2007 some 74.8% of the people in question did not speak a L2 at all, while in 2011 this number was 63.2% and, by 2016, it had decreased further to 57.6% (European Statistics, 2021). Regarding the young adult population of Hungary (i.e. those aged between 25 and 34 years), the statistics were more promising in all three years of the data collection: namely, 60.6%, 42.3% and 40.4%, respectively (European Statistics, 2021). This might be attributed to the impact of the various governmental initiatives aimed at the improvement of L2 instruction in Hungarian public education from the turn of the century onwards (e.g. World – Language; see, for example, Fischer & Öveges, 2008; Kapitánffy, 2001). Nevertheless, the results presented are less favorable when subjected to international comparison. More specifically, as opposed to the 57.6% of the total adult (working-age) population and the 40.4%

of the young adult population of Hungary who did not know any L2s in 2016, across the whole EU, the numbers were only 31.8% and 21.3%, respectively (European Statistics, 2021).

When it comes to the English proficiency of Hungarian secondary school students – the target population of our study – the available data paint an ambivalent picture. We have selected the results of the national secondary school leaving exams as an indicator of L2 proficiency. All students in Hungary take these exams in at least five different school subjects, one of which must be an L2. Since English is the most widely taught L2 (*Statistical Yearbook of Public Education 2018/2019*; Ministry of Human Capacities, 2020), it is no wonder that most students choose to be examined in it (Hungarian Educational Authority, n.d.c). The successful completion of the intermediate-level exam corresponds to a B1-level proficiency and that of the advanced-level exam to a B2-level proficiency (Council of Europe, 2001; Hungarian Educational Authority, n.d.a).

As Table 2.2 shows, the general trend is that it is the intermediate exam that is taken by the majority of students, although the number of those taking the advanced exam has been on the rise. According to governmental policies (Decree no. 5/2020), secondary school leavers should ideally possess a B1-level proficiency (Council of Europe, 2001) in their first L2. While there are no available data on the linguistic background of the exam takers, assuming that English is the first L2 of those who take an intermediate-level exam in it, the results shown in Table 2.2 appear to indicate that, in general, students meet the expectations adequately. Nevertheless, the results also suggest that there might be differences in students' quality of English proficiency across

Table 2.2 Results of the national secondary school leaving exams in Hungary in the past two decades

Intermediate-level exam				Advanced-level exam			
No. of exam takers	Average score (%)			No. of exam takers	Average score (%)		
	Whole country	Budapest	Sz-Sz-B county		Whole country	Budapest	Sz-Sz-B county
May/June 2006							
38,315	52.38%	55.20%	48.60%	3,530	62.98%	63.17%	59.19%
May/June 2010							
56,302	61.65%	66.17%	57.07%	4,510	68.20%	68.55%	61.41%
May/June 2015							
52,487	61.35%	65.81%	54.81%	9,113	69.32%	69.99%	66.51%
May/June 2020							
33,889	58.34%	62.06%	53.67%	14,311	69.28%	71.04%	66.32%

Note: Sz-Sz-B county = Szabolcs-Szatmár-Bereg county (part of Eastern Hungary).

the country. The fact that students in the eastern part of Hungary (e.g. Szabolcs-Szatmár-Bereg county; Sz-Sz-B county) consistently score lower than those in the capital city (Table 2.2) is in line with the regional disparity between Central and Eastern Hungary outlined above.

In connection with Hungarian secondary school students' English proficiency, it is also worth highlighting that the Hungarian education system is heavily exam-centered (Öveges & Csizér, 2018). This means that the results of students' school-leaving exams can have significant weightings in their chances of continuing their education at the tertiary level and, thus, of pursuing their choice of career (Tartsayné Németh et al., 2018). Moreover, the possession of a state-accredited language exam can also be an important asset when it comes to university or job applications (Fekete & Csépes, 2018). In support of this, in a representative survey Albert et al. (2018b) found that about one-fifth of secondary school students already had a language exam by grade 11, and 67% of those not yet possessing one were planning to obtain it. Nonetheless, this trend might change in the near future given the recent introduction of a law that abolishes the language exam requirement for university graduates in Hungary (Act no. 59/2022, 2022). One important implication of the exam-centeredness is that L2 education in Hungary emphasizes language form and correctness over function and practical language use. As such, no matter how high the students' L2 proficiency is based on the different exam results, they might possess a low level of self-efficacy to use the L2 in real-life situations (Csizér & Illés, 2020; Csizér et al., 2020).

2.3 L2 Instruction in Hungarian Secondary Schools

In Hungary, secondary education is part of compulsory public education, which is regulated by the Public Education Act (Act no. 190/2011, n.d.). There are two main types of secondary education programs, general and vocational, which can last from four to eight years. In addition, secondary schools might also choose to organize one-year preparatory programs for new entrants who would like to boost their L2 proficiency before starting their studies in grade 9; this is known as the year of intensive language learning (YILL), 'a special program to rocket Hungarian students' foreign language proficiency' (Öveges, 2017: 150). In the school year 2018/2019, the number of students pursuing secondary education in Hungary was 501,300 (*Statistical Yearbook of Public Education 2018/2019*; Ministry of Human Capacities, 2020). Within the same period, most students (i.e. 45.1%) attended a general secondary school program, while 54.9% were enrolled in one of the various types of vocational school programs (e.g. vocational grammar school, vocational secondary school, etc.; *Statistical Yearbook of Public Education 2018/2019*; Ministry of Human Capacities, 2020).

In light of this trend, we aimed primarily to recruit students attending a general secondary school program for our study, so as to increase the generalizability of our results.

Secondary public education in Hungary is regulated by a 3-layer policy system, which is set forth in Decree no. 5/2020 and Decree no. 20/2012. At the top level, there is the National Core Curriculum, which prescribes four important things with respect to secondary school students' L2 instruction: the number of languages learned; the starting year of instruction of each L2; the weekly number of L2 classes; and the outcome requirements. According to the regulations, students must learn two L2s between grades 9 and 12. This approach is evocative of the concept of the ideal plurilingual speaker promoted by the Council of Europe (2001). Instruction in students' first L2 should start no later than grade 4 and that for their second L2 should start in grade 9. The number of weekly L2 classes in secondary school programs can be 3–4 per L2 in the case of the standard format of L2 instruction, but at least 5 in the case of the intensive format of L2 instruction. As noted earlier, students must take a school-leaving exam in one of their L2s: they are expected to attain B1-level proficiency (Council of Europe, 2001) in their first L2 by the time of their graduation; for those who receive intensive L2 instruction, however, the requirement is B2-level proficiency (Council of Europe, 2001).

With regard to the other two levels of the policy system – the frame curricula and the local curricula – the frame curricula entail the main content areas that students must be taught in the L2 in each grade as well as the goals of L2 instruction, while the local curricula contain more detailed specifications as to the various facets of L2 instruction in a given institution (e.g. course requirements, assessment methods).

We can argue that the quality of L2 instruction in Hungarian secondary schools would benefit from development. More specifically, we identified several potentially problematic areas in need of attention. The first is the size of L2 classes. Currently, policymakers' advice is that L2 classes should be smaller than the regular class of 26–34 individuals (Act no. 190/2011, n.d.). Öveges (2018) found L2s to be taught typically in groups of 11–15 students or even smaller in grade 11 in 2017, which adheres to the earlier mentioned recommendation. Nevertheless, there is reason to think that inadequate L2 group size may still be an issue across secondary schools in Hungary based on the results of some further studies (Illés & Csizér, 2018; Kálmán & Tiboldi, 2018; Tartsayné Németh *et al.*, 2018), which involved such stakeholders in instructed L2 learning in Hungary as school leaders, L2 teachers and L2 consultants, respectively.

Another problem concerns the possibility of continuing the L2 that the student already started in primary school at the appropriate level when students enter secondary education. Albert *et al.* (2018b) found that almost 31% of 11th graders claimed that they were unable to continue their first L2 at their current level when finishing their primary education. Reasons for this included the learners' unwillingness to continue the L2 they had already started (2%) and the lack of opportunity to continue the language they started in primary school (2%). However, in the majority of cases the opportunity to continue the language they had started was there, but students reported the inadequacy of the level of the group they were assigned to (27%).

A related matter is the method of grouping students in L2 classes. The general trend that Öveges's (2018) research showed was that secondary school students in grade 11 were not streamed according to their achievement on a placement test but to some other method (e.g. alphabetically). While there is no official recommendation from Hungarian policymakers as to the ideal grouping method, homogeneous grouping has long been held more favorable (Öveges, 2018) than heterogeneous grouping (Scrivener, 2011).

As with L2 group size, the opportunity to continue, and the grouping method, the state of affairs regarding the quality of L2 teachers' professional competences and practices appears to be ambivalent as well. Illés and Csizér (2018), using a representative sample of 1118 participants, found that L2 teachers in Hungary were likely to perceive themselves to be competent in areas such as motivating the students, the application of differentiation strategies, and adapting lesson plans to the needs of students. These findings are supported by Kálmán and Tiboldi's (2018) research in that it showed that L2 consultants working in Hungarian public education tended to have a favorable opinion of L2 teachers' work. Still, despite teachers' self-confidence, when it comes to professional training, almost everyone, including teachers and other stakeholders as well, agreed that there is a need for further training in differentiation in teaching (Illés & Csizér, 2018; Kálmán & Tiboldi, 2018; Tartsayné Németh et al., 2018).

A further problem in relation to teachers concerned the frequent changes in the staff teaching the L2 class. In Hungary the first four grades are usually taught by class teachers who do not necessarily specialize in subjects, but from grade 5 upwards students are assigned subject teachers who usually teach them throughout the remaining years they spend in the primary school. Since the teaching of L2, which according to the regulations starts in grade 4, is assigned to subject teachers, the expectation is to have the same teacher from this subject through the primary years as well. In reality, 7th graders reported having an average of 2.74 teachers in a nationwide survey (Albert et al., 2018a), which meant that only around 18% of the students reported having the same L2 teacher throughout their primary years, 33% had 2, 25% had 3, while the remaining 24% had 4 or more teachers, indicating that they had a new L2 teacher every single year. A similar trend can be observed in high schools. Here 46% of the students reported having 1 teacher,

30% reported having 2, while the remaining 24% reported having 3 or more teachers from the first L2 they were learning in their high school (Albert *et al.*, 2018b). In an educational system where the expectation is to have stability in terms of the teachers instructing the different school subjects over the years, this level of fluctuation is perceived as unfavorable by the students.

Coursebook use also seems to pose difficulties for the quality of L2 instruction in Hungarian secondary education. The given practice is subject to governmental regulations: the official list is made public by the Hungarian Educational Authority. Despite the fact that a relatively large number of course books are featured every year in the case of English as a school subject (Hungarian Educational Authority, 2021), the L2 teachers participating in Illés and Csizér's (2018) study expressed their dissatisfaction with the available list. Furthermore, Öveges's (2018) investigation revealed that teachers sometimes used course books that were not in line with the level of the group they taught. For example, in the case of a group at the B1 proficiency level (Council of Europe, 2001), they sometimes used the pre-intermediate, the intermediate, or the advanced course book from the course book series. What these results suggest is that the featured course books do not serve every purpose and, thus, there is a need for more relevant and up-to-date course materials (Öveges & Csizér, 2018).

Another issue pertaining to the quality of L2 instruction in Hungarian secondary schools is the availability of material resources. By this, we mean primarily the information and communications technology (ICT) equipment (e.g. smart boards, computers, projectors) of schools, which has been consistently found to be inadequate (Illés & Csizér, 2018; Kálmán & Tiboldi, 2018; Tartsayné Németh *et al.*, 2018). This finding contradicts current curricular regulations set by policymakers, according to which the fostering of students' digital competence must be one of the aims of instructed L2 learning in Hungarian public education.

2.4 Pre-Service L2 Teacher Education in Hungary

Since our study includes in-service English teachers, we think it is necessary to shed light on the main features of the training they received as it can have an impact on their professional practices as well as on their students' learning. Due to space limitations, we chose the early 1990s as the starting point for our critical analysis. During the given time frame, we are able to distinguish three types of frameworks for initial English teacher education in Hungary.

One such framework is the three-year-long single-major program, which lasted between 1990 and the early 2000s and emerged as a solution to the sudden demand for English teachers in public education after Soviet rule ended in Hungary and the country began its transition to Western policy

(Medgyes, 1992). It had two variants. One was the so-called re-training, aimed at teachers already possessing a qualification in teaching Russian as an L2, which lost its status as a compulsory school subject in 1989. The re-training meant a curriculum specially designed for the applicants in question: the number of contact hours was reduced, and the courses were held in a block format (Bárdos, 2009; Medgyes, 1992). While, eventually, this variant solved the English teacher shortage in Hungary to some extent, it has also received criticism for not equipping teachers with a sufficient amount of subject-specific knowledge, a potential corollary of the fast-track format (Bárdos, 2009; Medgyes, 1992).

The other variant of the three-year-long single-major framework is the English language teacher supply program (ELTSup). Its graduates received teaching qualifications both for primary and secondary education, which was not the case with the earlier-mentioned fast-track version of the framework (Bárdos, 2009; Kontra, 2016). Another noteworthy difference between the two variants was that the ELTsup placed a greater emphasis on the practical aspects of English language teaching (ELT), which was implemented in a logical manner. In the first year of the program, the focus was on L2 development, in the second year on L2 teaching methodology, while, in the third year, students did an intensive, supervised teaching practice (Kontra, 2016; Medgyes, 2011). This approach ensured the preparation of highly competent ELT professionals (Bárdos, 2009; Kontra, 2016).

The second framework for pre-service English teacher education in Hungary during the examined period is the two-cycle system. It can be divided into two phases: at the end of the three-year-long first cycle, students obtained a bachelor's degree, while the pursuit of the two-and-a-half-year-long second cycle (including a half-year-long teaching practice) resulted in a master's degree with a teaching qualification (Bárdos, 2009; Sáska, 2015). This framework was in effect between 2006 and 2013. The reason behind its emergence was the need to transform Hungarian higher education in harmony with EU policies (Crosier & Parveva, 2013), a result of Hungary's accession to the EU in 2004. One strength of the two-cycle system was that prospective primary school and secondary school English teachers received the same education (Bárdos, 2009; Sáska, 2015); thus, students had the chance to decide the level of public education they wanted to teach at as late as their graduation from the second cycle. In addition, the type of framework in question also increased the chances of graduates being more competent and dedicated to the ELT profession given that they underwent two admission procedures.

Nevertheless, the two-cycle system also had its drawbacks. One was that it required students to choose the two school subjects they desired to teach in the future already upon their enrollment to the first-cycle program, which can be challenging for an 18-year-old (Bárdos, 2009). Additionally, graduates did not have the same level of knowledge in the two school subjects, because the two specializations (i.e. major and minor) received unequal weightings during the first cycle (Bárdos, 2009). As such, graduates needed to compensate for their possible deficiencies in one of their school subjects during their professional lives.

Finally, the third framework for pre-service English teacher education is the undivided one. It has been in effect since 2013 following the introduction of Decree no. 8/2013, with some of its original practices being reformed in 2022 as a result of Decree no. 538/2021. The recent reform has affected both the structure of the framework as well as that of the curriculum and, in many ways, can be regarded as a positive development in light of the critiques received of the original version of the framework. The hierarchical differences regarding the duration of the program and the number of credits were abolished, resulting in a system that prepares all prospective teachers, during the course of 10 semesters, for teaching in both elementary and high schools. Therefore, students are not required to decide about the level of public education in which they wish to pursue their careers before starting their professional lives, only about the two school subjects they would like to teach. Regarding the curriculum, changes were introduced in 2022. These included increasing the emphasis placed on the teacher training module – which now has a new knowledge domain dedicated to educational technology, collaboration spaces and artificial intelligence – and the compulsory teaching practices that occur throughout the duration of the program. These changes can also be recognized as positive developments given that research involving L2 consultants (Kálmán & Tiboldi, 2018), pre-service English teachers and L2 teacher educators (Smid, 2022) pointed to the need for progress in these areas. L2 teacher educators have called for ascribing a higher priority to prospective English teachers' L2 methodological knowledge and skills (e.g. ICT use, differentiation) development in Hungary.

In sum, pre-service English teacher education in Hungary has had a turbulent history. This is attested to by the fact that, in the past 30 years, it has been reformed four times and that three types of frameworks have emerged. As such, there seems to be no agreement among ELT professionals, researchers and policymakers as to what makes an ideal framework for an initial English teacher education program in Hungary. While the latest reform introduced in 2022 seems promising in several respects, its long-term effects remain to be seen. Without doubt, the field would benefit from more research, especially evaluative studies.

2.5 The Working Conditions of In-Service L2 Teachers in Hungary

Given the posited interrelationship between L2 learner attributes and the surrounding social context (e.g. Dörnyei & Ushioda, 2011; Sulis et al., 2023), we find it important to include the working conditions of

Hungarian in-service L2 teachers in the present discussion. The pertinent and most current regulations can be found in the Public Education Act (Act no. 190/2011, n.d.), which reformed the teaching profession considerably by launching a teacher career management system. This act regulates the professional life of teachers working in Hungarian public education in four major respects. First, it classifies teachers into five ranks (i.e. apprentice; teacher I; teacher II; master teacher; and teacher–researcher) according to their professional experience and qualification. Second, it determines the salary a teacher is entitled to based on their rank. Third, it prescribes that the work of teachers must undergo external as well as internal school evaluations on a continuous basis. Fourth, it stipulates that teachers take part in training aimed at their professional development every seven years.

While the introduction of the career management system was meant to improve the quality of teachers' professional work and, thus, that of the public education system in Hungary (Antalné Szabó et al., 2014), in practice the situation has been far from ideal. This is because, as several large-scale investigations have shown (e.g. Horváth, 2020; Paksi et al., 2015; Sági, 2015), teachers are more inclined to think of the regulations unfavorably given the excessive number of administrative tasks they come with. To illustrate, an OECD (2018a) report found that elementary and secondary school teachers in Hungary spend about two-thirds of their total working time (i.e. 1664 hours) on non-teaching tasks. In light of the statistics, it is not surprising that teachers tend to attribute their being overburdened and stressed to the reform (Csizér, 2020; Paksi et al., 2015), which, in turn, is likely to undermine the efficiency of their work.

In addition to work overload, inadequate financial remuneration is another concomitant of the introduction of this latest Public Education Act (Act no. 190/2011), which has the potential to detract from the quality of teaching professionals' work in Hungary. Low teacher salary has been a salient theme in research involving both pre-service (Smid, 2022) and in-service teachers (Csizér, 2020; Horváth, 2020; Paksi et al., 2015). This has also been supported by economic reports. For example, in a cross-country analysis of wages, Hajdu et al. (2019) found that practicing teachers holding a master's degree received 40% less salary than people in Hungary employed in a different field albeit with the same level of qualification. Taking an international perspective, this means that Hungary was the fourth most disadvantageous place in the EU in 2017 when it came to the differences between the salaries of teachers and other professionals with a university degree (Hajdu et al., 2019). Unfortunately, the situation is not expected to change for the better in the near future, since the law introducing a new career management system for teachers, which came into effect on 15 July 2023 (Act no. 52/2023), has been heavily criticized by both teachers and students as well as by teachers' unions, and there are fears that it may lead to even more teachers leaving the profession.

2.6 The Implications for Our Study

In this chapter, we have sought to provide an overview of the main characteristics of L2 instruction in Hungarian public education. The contextual variables presented influenced our research methodological choices to a great extent. We selected high school English as a foreign language (EFL) learners as the target population of our study because, as recent reports have revealed (e.g. Öveges & Csizér, 2018), the quality of L2 instruction at the secondary level in Hungarian public education is especially exposed to challenges (e.g. in terms of student grouping, L2 teachers' professional competences and material resources). In addition, we aimed for a nationwide sample so as to be able to examine general trends as well as detect possible differences across the target population.

Our research context also had an impact on the constructs that we chose to investigate. First, we regarded motivation as a crucial aspect of Hungarian secondary school students' L2 learning processes given the compulsory nature of L2 learning in public education from the age of 10 onwards and that of the secondary school leaving exams. Second, students' L2 learner autonomy also lent itself for inquiry. This is because, by default, learners are not necessarily directly exposed to the English language outside formal educational contexts due to Hungary being a monolingual country. This unique background setting is the reason we chose to target L2 learning emotions as well, which are known for their context-sensitivity (Keltner *et al.*, 2014). Finally, the rationale for including the construct of L2 learner self-efficacy is the fact that the L2 proficiency of Hungarians has consistently proved to be unfavorable when compared to the population of other European countries (European Statistics, 2021).

3 The Theoretical Background of the Study

3.1 Language Learning Motivation

Motivation as a concept needs no introduction in applied linguistics: it has been consistently researched over decades as one of the most important contributing variables to success in language learning. One generally accepted definition states that motivation 'concerns the direction and magnitude of human behavior, that is: the choice of a particular action, the persistence with it, the effort expended on it' (Dörnyei, 2001: 8). The theoretical and practical importance of this concept is attested to by the fact that numerous theories attempt to conceptualize L2 motivation. In the most recent comprehensive overview of the field, Dörnyei and Ushioda's (2021) volume contains an increasing number of theories and conceptualizations of the dynamics of L2 motivation, taking focus, time and context into consideration in varying degrees. Apart from theoretical work, empirical studies also abound, and a recent handbook also summarized the state-of-the-art (Lamb *et al.*, 2019a). In the present overview we will focus only on those concepts that we included in various forms in our data collection instruments and discuss their relevance here to the Hungarian context.

When selecting the main theoretical approach to our data collection, we focused on the fact that various ID variables were to be measured in concert; therefore, we needed a well-established and versatile theory that could provide different points of connections to the additional ID variables. Hence, we decided to include Dörnyei's (2005, 2009) L2 motivational self system as the basic L2 motivation theory. The reason for this was that earlier studies in the Hungarian context showed that this theory captures the essence of secondary school language learning with the juxtaposing effects of external and internal motivation as well as the importance of the language learning experience. What is even more interesting is that the L2 motivational self system has its genesis in a large-scale Hungarian study by Dörnyei *et al.* (2006), which produced comprehensive results. What proved to be challenging to explain in the Hungarian context at the time was the emerging importance of the

Gardnerian notion of integrativeness in an environment where there were no visible L2 communities into which students could actually strive to integrate. Drawing on motivational work in Japan (Yashima, 2000) as well as psychological self and self-discrepancy theories (Higgins, 1987; Markus & Nurius, 1986), the L2 motivational self system was defined by three constructs: the ideal L2 self, the ought-to L2 self and the L2 learning experience. The ideal L2 self intends to measure the extent to which the learner can imagine themselves as highly proficient users of the L2; the ought-to L2 self conceptualizes the external pressures that the individual is aware of during the learning process; and lastly, the L2 learning experience encapsulates situated motives that relate to the immediate learning environment and includes attitudes toward classroom processes (Dörnyei, 2005, 2009). It needs to be mentioned here that the internal and external aspects of selves relate well to self-determination theory and its notions of external and internal motivation (Noels et al., 2003, 2016).

A series of studies on the L2 motivational self system was started by Kormos and Csizér (2008) in Hungary. They have investigated the components of the L2 motivational self system in three different age groups: secondary school students, university students and adult language learners. While the ideal L2 self and L2 learning experiences (labeled as language learning attitudes) proved to be reliable constructs, it has been necessary to exclude the ought-to L2 self scale from the analysis due to its low Cronbach's alpha values. Secondary school students scored significantly lower on both measured components – ideal L2 self and L2 learning experiences – than the other two groups. In addition, these two constructs proved to affect motivated learning behavior in a significant way. This initial study was followed by several investigations in the Hungarian context with various focuses.

As secondary students in Hungary often learn two L2s simultaneously, the first follow-up study investigated the differences concerning students' dispositions towards English and German (Csizér & Lukács, 2010). The main results not only indicated the effect of the order in which English/German were learnt but also revealed that students' ideal German self impacted their ideal English self in a positive way, yet the same students' ideal English-speaking selves had a negative impact on their ideal German-speaking selves when German was their first L2 and they started learning English later on. This line of research has blossomed in recent years, and researchers have offered ideas to reconceptualize the L2 part of the theory into multilingual approaches (Henry, 2017). Indeed, the European ideal is to have citizens who speak two additional languages besides their mother tongue (European Commission, 2005). Hence, motivation models should consider students' desire to be multilingual speakers (Henry, 2017; Ushioda, 2017), and both the focus of the research and that of language teaching should consider learners' ideal multilingual selves. In fact, Henry (2017) showed the interaction among self-guides related to various languages and how the multilingual self appears as a result of positive interactions. This idea is furthered by Thorsen *et al.* (2017), who identified the distinct function of the ideal multilingual self as generating effort to learn languages other than English.

Another follow-up study investigated students' perceptions of the extent to which teachers' and parents' views and behavior shaped the components of the L2 motivational self system (Csizér & Galántai, 2012). The results of this study indicated that it was only L2 learning experiences that were shaped by teachers' views, while parents' views had significant influences on each aspect of the L2 motivational self system, indicating that both selves and experiences are socially constructed and that for secondary school students the role of parental encouragement seems to be indispensable.

In addition, the dynamic nature of L2 motivation cannot be ignored either, because it is in fact the long process of language learning that is being investigated; therefore, we integrated the elements of the L2 motivational self system into a longitudinal study. Piniel and Csizér (2015) explored a slightly older cohort than secondary school students and followed English major university students during a semester by measuring their dispositions towards motivation at regular intervals. The changes measured indicated that the most stable component of the L2 motivational self system was students' ideal L2 selves, while L2 learning experiences and ought-to L2 selves showed more variation. These results indicated that having a strong future vision about being a proficient speaker of English often failed to counteract negative outside expectations and learning experiences.

The L2 motivational self system quickly gained international recognition and became the leading theory in our field (Boo *et al.*, 2015). This is attested to by the fact that the editors of *The Palgrave Handbook of Motivation for Language Learning* (Lamb *et al.*, 2019a) decided to devote an entire chapter to the L2 motivation self system and thus further underline its importance in our field. The chapter in their book underlines the fact that the theory received its fair share of criticism over the years both in terms of conceptual concerns as well as measurement weaknesses (Csizér, 2019b; see also Al-Hoorie, 2018). As international research efforts continued, the emerging results obviously informed our efforts in Hungary, and the most relevant issues are summarized here.

It became apparent early on that contextual variation is to be expected. Lamb (2012), for example, differentiated between urban and rural settings in his study in Asia and mapped the role of the ideal L2 self varying, with its prominence only being significant in urban settings. In addition, Islam *et al.* (2013) found a relationship between the role of English at a national level and the construction of an ideal English-speaking self.

A further contextual issue was found to be relevant for components of the L2 motivational self system: students' socioeconomic status, with students in lower socioeconomic groups experiencing more challenges in developing their ideal L2 selves. These issues led us to include a fairly homogenous sample in the present investigation in terms of students' age and schooling, but we have sampled schools from various parts of the country with varying socioeconomic status.

This overview has concentrated on student-related research thus far, but it needs to be mentioned that the L2 motivational self system has been employed to investigate language teachers' characteristics as well. In terms of the international research scene, Kubanyiova needs to be mentioned as pioneering this line of investigation. Kubanyiova's (2009) interest in teacher professional development led her to investigate teachers' possible selves. Feared and ideal selves were conducive to teacher cognition and professional development. Kubanyiova (2015) then moved to the classroom context and explored the way in which teachers' selves influenced classroom interaction and students' behavior. Negative influences were also uncovered in relation to teachers' possible selves and lack of learner autonomy. These two studies focused on teachers' selves but not the L2 experience component of the model.

When considering teacher experiences, what comes to mind first is Lortie's (1975) idea of apprenticeship of observation (see also Borg, 2003). In many contexts, by definition, teachers have been language learners, and both their cognition and behavior might be influenced by their learning experiences. Indeed, this is what Thompson and Vásquez (2015) investigated as they explored how experiences shaped selves. They found that influences exerted impact through influential individuals in the teachers' milieu. In a different vein, Sahakyan *et al.* (2018) showed how teachers' early-in-their-career ideal selves changed into feasible selves through moving from concentrating on one's learning experiences to teaching experiences.

There is one fairly large-scale Hungarian study that investigated teacher selves and experiences (for a summary see Csizér, 2020). First, long interviews were employed to explore teacher experiences (Csizér, 2018, 2019a; Csizér & Kálmán, 2019). It was found that teacher experience was a complex notion but that its core components included language learning success and intercultural contact experiences. These experiences indeed seemed to impact in a complex way upon the manner in which teachers were teaching. Positive influences included specific teaching methods and techniques as well as ways of being engaged in learning; negative influences included past experiences that teachers did not want to relive.

Second, quantitative data were collected in which both selves and experiences were conceptualized in various manners only loosely linked to ideas presented by the L2 motivational self system (Csizér, 2020).

In terms of the conceptualization of selves, successful teacher self was measured, while the notion of experience was operationalized as four different scales: L2 learning experiences; L2 teaching experiences; experiencing students' successes; and experiencing professional development. These scales played various roles in the models that Csizér (2020b) explored. Starting with the earliest experiences of L2 learning, these still had a negative impact on teachers' motivation to develop professionally, interestingly enough for the highly motivated teachers. Concerning a more concurrent type of experience, L2 teaching experiences affected teachers' motivation to develop professionally in a positive way. Successful teacher self and experiencing professional success impacted motivated teaching behavior in a positive way. Remarkably, experiencing students' successes did not contribute to teacher motivation in the quantitative phase of the study. These results indicate an intricate interplay of selves and experiences in relation to motivation, which motivated us to investigate students' ID variables from the perspective of the teachers as well.

3.2 Perceived Importance of Contact

Intercultural contact research has been established in various Hungarian settings. The research takes into consideration social psychological results on the attitude–contact relationships (Allport, 1954; Pettigrew, 1998; Pettigrew & Tropp, 2006) as well as Richard Clément's pioneering work on L2 contact and self-confidence. Clément's studies showed that frequent and pleasant contact increased students' motivated behavior when it came to learning and speaking L2s (Clément, 1980; Clément & Kruidenier, 1983; Clément et al., 2001). This in turn led MacIntyre and colleagues to relate increased contact to increased willingness to communicate (WTC) (MacIntyre et al., 1998; see also Sampasivam & Clément, 2014). More recently the negative effects of contact have also been highlighted when language-based rejection is experienced in intercultural contact (Sisk et al., 2018) as well as the intricate relationship of contact to contextual variables (Yim et al., 2019). In sum, intercultural contact cannot be ignored, as Lamb et al. (2019b: 4) so aptly wrote:

> Globalization, advances in communication technology and increasing geographical mobility have brought languages into contact on an unprecedented scale, confronting people with the challenge of learning other languages, and teachers and institutions with the challenge of facilitating and encouraging that learning.

Accordingly, a broader conceptualization of contact also appears in various L2 motivational theories, such as self-determination theory and its interaction with contextual variables (Noels, 2001b; Noels et al., 2016). The importance of this line of research is highlighted in

Csizér (2020), who reasons: the ultimate aim of language learning is communication; therefore, language contact and contact with speakers of other languages is unavoidable for modern languages. In relation to this, language use contributes to language learning; thus, contact is both a means and an end in learning processes. It is not only through language use that learning processes are shaped, but dispositions and attitudes towards speakers and their culture are also formed, refined and maintained (Allport, 1954; Pettigrew, 1998; Pettigrew & Tropp, 2006).

When it comes to the Hungarian context, research efforts have generally begun with a qualitative interview study that maps the type of contact experiences students actually report (Kormos & Csizér, 2007). The results showed that primary school students aged 13–14 experienced both direct and indirect contact that included native and/or non-native speakers of the language. Based on these findings, quantitative exploratory studies were designed taking into account English as a lingua franca as well as German, a regionally important language. One of the most important results is that it is not only the contact experiences that shape students' intended effort/motivated learning behavior but also the perceived importance pertaining to these contact experiences (Csizér & Kormos, 2008a, 2009b). The perceived importance of contact experiences is especially important for those students who reported a generally low level of direct contact with the languages.

These research endeavors were completed by confirmatory quantitative studies showing the impact of contact experiences on L2 motivation (Csizér & Kormos, 2008b, 2009b). The results indicated that, for the German language, it was the students' attitudes towards the target language and its speakers, and students' experiences about speaking German with visitors to Hungary, as well as the perceived importance of these contact situations, that had a direct effect of shaping L2 motivation. In the case of English, the results were somewhat different: the students' attitudes towards the target language and its speakers and the perceived importance of contact contributed significantly to L2 motivation.

3.3 Language Learning Autonomy

Language learning autonomy has been researched in applied linguistics for decades, with Little (1999) setting the scene by defining autonomous language learning as students taking responsibility for their own learning that includes several aspects of the process from planning to execution. This definition has been elaborated upon by Hungarian researcher Éva Illés (2012), who suggests that the definition of language learning autonomy should consider that learners are language users who have to 'negotiate meaning and solve problems stemming from the international use of English' (2012: 507). In addition, the learning process is not linear, and its sub-processes relate to one another in different ways. Moreover, classroom learning is teacher-led and Illés convincingly argues that some elements of this process should be informed by the pedagogical knowledge of the teacher. Hence, Illés defined learner autonomy as 'the capacity to become competent speakers of the target language who are able to exploit the linguistic and other resources at their disposal effectively and creatively' (2012: 509).

Despite definitional disagreements, there seems to be a consensus that language learning autonomy can be developed through training (Benson, 2011; Little *et al.*, 2017). Some examples are offered by Illés (2012), such as including problem-solving activities and presenting different varieties of English in teaching in order to increase learners' language awareness. Illés (2012) suggests that teaching students literature and setting them translation tasks are suitable challenges for students in the classroom (see also Csizér & Illés, 2020).

Several studies carried out in Hungary informed the present investigation: most importantly, a series of studies that set out to map the interrelationship between L2 motivation and autonomy. Csizér and Kormos (2012, 2014; Kormos & Csizér, 2014) were researching how aspects of L2 motivation contributed to students' using self-regulatory strategies through which their autonomous learning behavior developed as well. Their results not only corroborated that motivation and autonomy were strongly interlinked when it comes to L2 learning (Csizér & Kormos, 2012) but, using structural equation modeling, it was also shown that the effort learners invested into L2 learning in general had wide-ranging implications for learner autonomy and related strategy use (Kormos & Csizér, 2014). As for the most important strategies, three seem to be decisive: active involvement in using the L2 outside the classroom; time management related to learning; and the capacity of counteracting boredom during the learning process (also known as satiation control; see Tseng *et al.*, 2006).

Following Benson's (2001, 2007, 2011) work on language learning autonomy, it is important to point out that language learning autonomy is a complex notion; therefore, any research conceptualization needs to take into account the effects of this complexity on the level of measurement as well. In the present study, we planned to juxtapose two different conceptualizations of English language learning autonomy. One related to the classroom use of the language and to learner autonomy related to classroom processes, while the second construct set out to measure English language learning autonomy outside the classroom through various technology-enhanced learning practices.

3.4 Emotions

Although emotions have not been as widely researched, and their investigation within the field of applied linguistics also started later than that of motivation, there is now a growing interest in the affective aspects of language learning (see for example, Albert, 2022; Dewaele, 2015; MacIntyre & Gregersen, 2012) due to the realization that affective and cognitive processes are inseparable, and they mutually influence each other (Oxford, 2015; Swain, 2013). Emotions are usually conceptualized as part of the larger category of affects or affective variables (Oatley, 2004), which also comprise moods, dispositions, sentiments and traits. According to Keltner *et al.* (2014), when people talk about their emotions, they usually refer to those affective states that they currently experience and that are relatively shortlived, lasting potentially for a few hours, whereas they use the term mood to talk about longer-lasting affects. The terms sentiments, dispositions and traits are used to characterize the affective aspects of people's personalities, and these are expected to be relatively stable characteristics.

In the same way as the generic term *affect* covers a range of phenomena, the term *emotion* is often interpreted in various ways by different scientists (Izard, 2010). In an attempt to arrive at a common understanding of the construct that could form the basis for creating a universally accepted definition, Izard (2010) tried to harmonize the views of his fellow researchers. What he managed to establish when summarizing different definitions was that all definitions of emotions described them as multi-componential, and that the majority recognized the following three components as basic aspects of emotions: '(a) neural circuits and neurobiological processes, (b) phenomenal experience or feeling, and (c) perceptual-cognitive processes' (Izard, 2010: 368).

Indeed, Keltner *et al.*'s definition (2014: 27), which states that emotions are 'multifaceted responses to events that we see as challenges or opportunities in our inner or outer world, events that are important to our goals', also draws attention to the multi-componential nature of emotions while also highlighting their evolutionary role. Although it is relatively easy to see how the fight-or-flight reactions that are often triggered by negative emotions might have an adaptive value, the evolutionary advantage ensured by positive emotions is much less obvious.

It was Fredrickson (2003, 2008) who, in her influential *broaden-and-build theory*, proposed the theoretical foundations supporting the usefulness of positive emotions. According to this theory, negative emotions can be described as focusing or narrowing, since they lead to very characteristic thought patterns and actions: for example, fear urges the individual to leave a dangerous situation, while anger makes them prone to attack. In contrast, 'positive emotions all share the ability to broaden people's momentary thought-action repertoires and build their enduring personal resources, ranging from physical and intellectual resources to social and psychological resources' (Fredrickson, 2003: 219). Positive emotions are believed to encourage exploration, play and experimenting with new behaviors, instead of insisting on tried-and-tested routines, which appears to assist in the building of a range of potentially beneficial new resources.

Clearly, novel physical, psychological, intellectual and social resources can prove useful in all contexts, including educational ones. However, in an educational context – or more precisely in our own language learning context – defining emotions as 'affective experiences that are directly tied to language learning activities and resulting learning outcomes, a dynamic process which is determined by appraisals of socio-culturally shaped L2 learning tasks' (Shao *et al.*, 2019: 2) might appear more appropriate. This definition points out the connection between the learners' language learning experiences and learners' emotions, besides drawing attention to their cognitive aspects when mentioning appraisals. Although this definition might seem somewhat limited, as it does not include reference to language use, our research aimed to focus on the emotions that learners experience specifically in connection with their English classes, so this was the definition we adopted in our study.

The claim that cognitive and affective processes are inseparable (Oxford, 2015; Swain, 2013) is clearly supported by the fact that all three definitions of emotion cited above (Izard, 2010; Keltner *et al.*, 2014; Shao *et al.*, 2019) contained reference to some form of cognition or cognitive processes. A possible way these processes might interact while shaping emotions was proposed by Lazarus (1991). He argued that individuals evaluate events affecting them according to their own priorities during a so-called appraisal process, consisting of two phases. Primary appraisal happens first, which is a reflex-like and automatic process. This is followed by secondary appraisal, during which the individual's cognitions – also referred to as attributions (Keltner *et al.*, 2014) or schemas (Izard, 2007) – have a decisive role in shaping the quality of the emotion experienced and, ultimately, the emotion label attached to it.

Whatever the processes involved, the relationship between affective and cognitive factors appears to be reciprocal, and is supported by a number of findings. For example, people are more likely to perceive those events and objects that are congruent with their current emotions; and, with regard to memory functions, emotionally loaded events are easier to remember and tend also to be recalled more frequently (Keltner *et al.*, 2014). It appears that emotions have a crucial role in setting priorities for the individual, since emotions direct people's attention to what is perceived or recalled as the most relevant through their emotions. These amplifying effects of emotions have also been highlighted by Oxford (2015) in connection with language learning: she claimed that since emotions act as amplifiers, they tend to either enhance or disrupt the learning process.

Although emotions are indisputably important, not only their definition but their categorization poses difficulties as well. The words that label emotions are part of our vernacular, our everyday language use, which means that these words are too fuzzy and lack scientific rigor. The emotion that would be labeled shyness in one culture might have a different label in another, and perhaps even people from the same cultural background might label different people shy. A possible solution for this classification problem might be concentrating on affective dimensions rather than distinct emotions. Russell's (1980) circumplex model adopted this approach, proposing two dimensions: arousal/activation and valence/pleasantness. These dimensions serve as the two axes in the model, and emotions are arranged on the circumference of the circle drawn around them. This model appears to make defining and comparing emotions easier, since only a limited number of factors needs to be taken into consideration, but it is clearly not very refined and tends to blur fine distinctions. Moreover, an important argument of those proposing a categorical rather than a dimensional view of emotions is that 'discrete emotion variables have different predictors and contribute to different behavioral outcomes' (Izard, 2007: 267) – that is, they appear to serve different functions. Furthermore, the fact that emotion labels exist, which signals that people talk about their emotions as distinct entities, lends support to the psychological reality of distinct emotions (Field, 2003).

Additionally, distinct emotions seem problematic not only because of their above-mentioned fuzziness but also because of the sheer number of emotion labels that exist. Therefore, finding a way to reduce the number might actually make the problem more manageable. Identifying basic emotions upon biological bases that are more or less universal across cultures can be considered such an attempt, and a number of researchers have adopted this approach according to Reeve (2009). This has usually resulted in describing 4–6 primary or first-order emotions – for example, in Izard's (2010) case: (a) interest, (b) enjoyment/happiness/contentment, (c) sadness, (d) anger, (e) disgust and (f) fear. Although this looks like a manageable list, researchers claim that these first-order emotions are rarely experienced by people except perhaps in their early childhood because of the increasing influence of appraisal processes, in other words cognitions, as people mature (Lazarus, 1991). Thus, in the case of adults, using the term 'emotion schemas' instead of 'emotions' would be more appropriate. These can be defined 'in terms of the dynamic interaction of emotion and cognition' (Izard, 2007: 265). These emotion schemas have influential cognitive aspects besides the feelings derived from primary emotions. Since considerable variation is to be expected in adults' appraisals contributing to their emotion schemas, it is probably not surprising that there will be differences in the way they conceptualize their emotions, which might serve as an explanation for the lack of uniformity even within the same culture as described above.

Emphasizing the unique features of distinct emotions, i.e. adopting the categorical view rather than the dimensional one, also means going beyond the approach where one negative and possibly one positive emotion, serving as examples of positive and negative emotions, are measured, and their relationship with other ID variables or language learning achievements is investigated. A true adoption of the categorical view would require examining a range of emotions, since they are expected to lead to different outcomes. For such research, it is necessary to establish the list of emotions that are relevant in the context of education. In a UNESCO publication, Pekrun (2014) argued that there are four groups of emotions that are relevant in academic settings: achievement emotions; epistemic emotions; topic emotions; and social emotions. The first group includes shame and anxiety, which are relevant for failure; hope and pride, which are related to success; and enjoyment of the learning process itself; these all belong to the group of achievement emotions. Emotions arising in response to cognitive challenges or difficulties belong to the group of epistemic emotions. Examples include curiosity, surprise, frustration and confusion. The content of the material to be learnt can also arouse emotions; interest, enjoyment, anxiety and disgust are all examples of topic emotions. Finally, learning in the classroom setting has unavoidable social aspects, like the presence of the teacher and peers. In some cases they might evoke contempt, envy, anger or social anxiety; in others, love, sympathy, compassion or admiration. These are all social emotions.

In educational research, it is the group of achievement emotions that has received considerable attention lately. Pekrun *et al.* (2007) claim that 'individuals experience specific achievement emotions when they feel in control of, or out of control of, achievement activities and outcomes that are subjectively important to them, implying that control appraisals and value appraisals are the proximal determinants of these emotions' (2007: 16), which is the main tenet of the control-value theory of achievement emotions. In this theory the quality of the emotion experienced is therefore determined by control and value appraisals. Control appraisals refer to the extent to which learners feel that they control the learning situation and their achievements, including attributions of failure and success to their own abilities or efforts. The other important determinant is the value that learners attach to the activity, which can be positive (in the case of success) or negative (in the case of failure).

According to the three-dimensional taxonomy of achievement emotions (Pekrun *et al.*, 2023), specific achievement emotions can be described along three basic dimensions: valence; arousal; and object focus. While this third dimension refers to achievement activities and their success and failure outcomes in the case of achievement emotions, object focus can be further differentiated by (1) the temporal relation between the person and the object at the time of the emotional experience and (2) the object type. The temporal relation can refer to the past, present or future while the type of object can be achievement activities and achievement outcomes. Out of the six possible combinations of temporal aspect and object type, three categories appear particularly important according to Pekrun and colleagues: concurrent activity emotions, which are experienced in sync with an activity; prospective outcome emotions, which refer to future outcomes; and retrospective outcome emotions, which are linked to past achievement or failures.

Within this framework enjoyment, relaxation, anger and boredom are all activity focused (i.e. in the category concurrent activity emotions), where enjoyment and anger are both activating but with opposing valences, while relaxation and boredom are both deactivating but positive and negative, respectively. The category of prospective outcome emotions comprises hope, assurance, anxiety and apathy, where hope and anxiety are activating emotions with opposing valences, while assurance and apathy are deactivating and also opposing in valence. Finally, pride, relief, disappointment and shame are retrospective outcome emotions. Pride and shame are both activating although their valences are opposite, while relief and disappointment are deactivating, again with opposing valences.

Investigations in academic contexts revealed that, in line with intuitive expectations, apathy and boredom were in general found to be linked to academic achievements in a negative way, while the relationship between school results and hope and pride was mostly positive (Pekrun et al., 2002, 2023). Nevertheless, the picture was less clear in the case of negative activating emotions like anger, anxiety and shame and positive deactivating emotions like relaxation (Pekrun et al., 2002, 2007, 2023). Thus, it might be hypothesized that the effects of these emotions might be more prone to contextual factors.

As regards the language learning context, studies initially were concerned with mapping the terrain, i.e. identifying the range of emotions that are experienced by language learners besides anxiety. This has led to identifying language learning enjoyment (Boudreau et al., 2018; De Smet et al., 2018; Dewaele & Alfawzan, 2018; Dewaele & Dewaele, 2020; Dewaele & MacIntyre, 2014, 2016; Resnik & Schallmoser, 2019), followed by other emotions like joy, shame and guilt (Teimouri, 2017, 2018), hope and frustration (Ross & Rivers, 2018), pride (Ross & Stracke, 2016), love (Pavelescu & Petrić, 2018) and boredom (Kruk et al., 2021, 2022; Pawlak et al., 2020a, 2022b, 2021). Emotions have also been investigated in relation to different language skills, such as speaking, listening, reading and writing (Piniel & Albert, 2018; Pishghadam et al., 2016). Linking emotions to language learning motivation has been attempted by a number of researchers (MacIntyre & Vincze, 2017; Saito et al., 2018) but attempts to connect emotions to language achievements are still relatively recent (Li et al., 2020; Shao et al., 2020).

Since our empirical investigations are aimed at nine distinct emotions, we attempted to provide a brief summary of the empirical research carried out in connection with them in language learning contexts, specifically in Hungary. In cases where such studies could not be located, we drew on research findings from general education. The emotions to be discussed in this section comprise anxiety, shame, boredom, confusion, apathy, enjoyment, curiosity, hope and pride.

Anxiety is an affective state that has been investigated in connection with language learning for quite some time. For example, Krashen (1976) hypothesized that it contributes to the affective filter in a way that prevents the intake of comprehensible input and thereby makes language learning unsuccessful. Although the trait and state interpretations of anxiety (for an overview see Csizér & Albert, 2022) have both been investigated within applied linguistics (MacIntyre & Gardner, 1989), language learning anxiety was finally conceptualized as a situation-specific emotion. Characteristically emerging in language learning situations (Horwitz et al., 1986, 1991), it was defined as 'the feeling of tension and apprehension specifically associated with second language contexts, including speaking, listening, and learning' (MacIntyre & Gardner, 1994: 284). As regards its effects on language learning, although facilitative effects of anxiety had been proposed earlier (Chastain, 1975; Kleinmann, 1977), language learning anxiety has been found to be detrimental in all phases – input, processing and output – of the learning process (MacIntyre & Gardner, 1994). Moreover, there seems to be evidence for a reciprocal relationship between anxiety and language performance, in the sense that in certain cases a result of poor L2 performance can also arise from anxiety (Sparks & Ganschow, 1991). More recently, it has been highlighted that contextual factors impact learners' feelings of anxiety, resulting in dynamic changes in the process that may occur both over relatively short (Gregersen et al., 2014) and also longer time frames (Piniel & Csizér, 2015). Anxiety might also be systematically linked to different learning contexts: in their qualitative study involving English major university students in Hungary, Piniel and Albert (2018) found that anxiety was the most frequently mentioned emotion in connection with the classroom context. Another recent finding from Hungary lent support to gender differences in connection with this emotion: schoolgirls, both in the 7th and 11th grade, were found to exhibit higher levels of anxiety than boys (Albert et al., 2018a, 2018b), similar to studies conducted by Dewaele et al. (2016) and Donovan and MacIntyre (2004).

In the field of language teaching and learning, studies of shame are notably fewer compared to anxiety, and research interest in this emotion appears to be relatively recent. However, this emerging interest extends beyond individual experiences, as demonstrated by Liyanage and Canagarajah's (2019) investigation into the social and political dimensions of shame. Shame as an ID variable appears to be quite closely associated with anxiety, especially social anxiety, which is anxiety experienced in relation to other people (Galmiche, 2018). When attempting to characterize shame, Teimouri (2018) emphasized that those experiencing this feeling focus on their self (rather than just an action, which is typical in the case of guilt) and perceive that their whole self is judged negatively by others, resulting in feelings of worthlessness and powerlessness. He argued that, unlike guilt, which tends to evoke reparative actions, shame is likely to be purely detrimental, as it harms learners' feelings of self-worth. Indeed, in his studies Teimouri (2017) was able to find empirical support suggesting that feelings of shame are related to others' expectation and that shame has a motivation-reducing effect on learners. Interview findings also seem to suggest that feelings of shame are relatively frequent among language learners, although the results need to be corroborated by quantitative studies (Cook, 2006; Galmiche, 2017).

As is the case with shame, boredom has begun to attract researchers' attention only recently. This attention has led to the publication of a large number of articles using both quantitative approaches (Pawlak *et al.*, 2020a, 2020b, 2022b) and qualitative approaches (Pawlak *et al.*, 2020a, 2022a; Zawodniak *et al.*, 2017), investigating boredom both inside and outside the classroom, mainly in the Polish university context. When describing boredom, the words 'disengagement, dissatisfaction, attention deficit, altered time perception and decreased vitality' are used (Pawlak *et al.*, 2020b: 2), and the authors emphasize disengagement and disaffection as the main characteristics of this emotional state. With the help of their Boredom in Practical English Language Classes Questionnaire, the authors (Pawlak *et al.*, 2020b) identified two main factors of boredom: (1) disengagement, monotony and repetitiveness and (2) lack of satisfaction and challenge, interpreting the first as a reactive and the second as a proactive aspect of boredom (Pawlak *et al.*, 2020b). Their results showed that less successful learners tended to be more bored than more successful ones, but that the difference in the group averages was only significant in the case of the reactive factor of boredom. This was hypothesized as a sign of possible resilience to boredom in the case of high achievers.

The negative relationship between boredom and performance has also been confirmed in other studies (Shao *et al.*, 2020). In the Hungarian context, gender differences have been identified in connection with boredom: in a study involving 7th and 11th graders, boys reported significantly higher levels of boredom than girls (Albert *et al.*, 2018a, 2018b), which seems to be in line with the higher levels of boredom-proneness found among males in general (Vodanovich *et al.*, 2011). When comparing boredom across the grades, 11th graders were found to report significantly higher levels of boredom than 7th graders (Albert *et al.*, 2018a, 2018b).

When trying to locate studies on the emotion of confusion within applied linguistics, we realized that it does not appear to be the main focus in any major study published within our field. Turning to the field of general education, confusion is 'hypothesized to be the affective signature of cognitive disequilibrium and is expected to be highly relevant to both the processes and products of learning' (D'Mello & Graesser, 2014: 290). Pekrun (2014) also considered confusion an academically relevant emotion and placed it in the group of epistemic emotions, which typically arise in response to cognitive challenges or difficulties. Experiencing confusion appears to be directly linked to interpreting something as new: according to Silvia (2010), if a novel stimulus can be understood, then it is likely to evoke interest but, if it cannot, it will lead to confusion; and this hypothesis was confirmed in his study investigating the understanding of poems. Consequently, the valence of this emotion is considered negative, as it is evoked when a person comes across new information that is for some reason incongruent with their previous knowledge structures, so this tension is likely to give rise to uncomfortable feelings. Despite this, D'Mello and Graesser (2014) argue that confusion is actually beneficial for learning, as it signals the detection of an anomaly or discrepancy and urges the individual to engage in active problem-solving so that, having resolved the problem, equilibrium can be restored. Although D'Mello *et al.* (2014) were successful in demonstrating that confusion can indeed be evoked in an experimental setting by providing incongruent information to the participants, Arguel *et al.* (2019) warn about the dangers of unresolved confusion, since it can lead to harmful consequences like frustration or boredom.

Finding studies focusing on apathy or hopelessness (which we considered a synonym of apathy) also proved to be difficult within applied linguistics, so we again turned to the field of general education and psychology for a general overview of this construct. Csíkszentmihályi (1990) claimed that apathy arises when an individual with low skills faces unchallenging tasks, i.e. low skills are paired with low challenges; thus, apathy together with boredom and anxiety represent anti-flow experiences (Csíkszentmihályi, 1975). Liu (2021), while also emphasizing the lack of research in connection with hopelessness, defines it as 'negative feeling and anticipation about one's future which takes roots from his/her negative attributional styles and experiences' (2021: 5). In Pekrun's (2006) control-value theory framework, the outcome-oriented emotion of hopelessness is characterized by attribution of a lack of control and negative valence. Shao *et al.* (2020), who tested predictions of the control-value theory on L2 learning, found that, in line with the theory, hopelessness was negatively correlated with both control and value appraisals as well as test performance. Through structural modeling, it was also revealed that hopelessness acted as a mediator regarding the association between perceived control and value and performance. Although Shao *et al.*'s (2020) study was not solely concerned with hopelessness, it provided support for the detrimental effect of hopelessness on language performance. In the Hungarian context, relatively low levels of apathy were found among learners attending the 7th and 11th grades, although the level of hopelessness increased significantly over the years (Albert *et al.*, 2018a, 2018b). Moreover, in the 11th grade, girls were found to report significantly more apathy than boys.

The growing popularity of positive psychology within our field (MacIntyre & Gregersen, 2012; MacIntyre *et al.*, 2016; Mercer & MacIntyre, 2014) has raised interest in positive emotions; thus, research into enjoyment has gained impetus. In their seminal article, instead of offering a definition for enjoyment Dewaele and MacIntyre (2014) claim that 'enjoyment is a defining component of Csíkszentmihályi's (1990) concept of flow, a positive state where challenges and skills to meet them are aligned well. Enjoyment is indicative of a state in which psychological needs are being met' (2014: 242). They also argue that enjoyment is related to the core emotion of joy. Their empirical data revealed that enjoyment is a frequently occurring emotion in the L2 classroom, and although it has a negative correlation with anxiety, these two emotions should not be thought of as opposite ends of the same dimension. The absence of enjoyment does not necessarily signal the presence of anxiety, and vice versa, and it is even possible to experience both emotions more or less at the same time. Further investigations into enjoyment revealed that females tend to experience more enjoyment than males, which is the same pattern that was found in the case of anxiety (Dewaele *et al.*, 2016). Enjoyment seems to vary with numerous background variables and contextual factors. For example, primary school learners seemed to enjoy language learning more than high school students, and students also found more enjoyment when learning English compared to Dutch (De Smet *et al.*, 2018); furthermore, unlike anxiety, language learning enjoyment was found to be linked to specific teachers instructing a course (Dewaele & Dewaele, 2020). Also, in a study involving multilinguals, higher levels of multilingualism and higher levels of self-perceived proficiency were found to be associated with more enjoyment (Botes *et al.*, 2020b). Moreover, Jin and Zhang (2021) found evidence that higher levels of enjoyment were associated with better performance on a mid-term test.

In the Hungarian context, enjoyment was one of the most frequently reported emotions in connection with learning English among English major university students, but this emotion was more closely associated with out-of-classroom contexts rather than with classroom learning (Piniel & Albert, 2018). Students involved in public education were also found to enjoy their English lessons, although their level of enjoyment was lower in grade 11 than in grade 7 (Albert *et al.*, 2018a, 2018b). In the same study, gender differences were only found among 7th graders; in this age group girls reported enjoying their English lessons more.

Compared to enjoyment, there are considerably fewer studies conducted on the emotion of curiosity in language learning, which should probably be surprising in light of the fact that the construct of interest, which is strongly linked to the feeling of curiosity, is included in the self-determination theory of motivation (Noels *et al.*, 2003), and it is also considered to be one of the main drives of autotelic activities (Csíkszentmihályi *et al.*, 2005). Indeed, the drive to explore the environment is of fundamental evolutionary importance (Gottlieb *et al.*, 2013), so it is difficult to understand why the role of curiosity in language learning has not attracted more attention as a research topic. In the field of psychology, curiosity is generally defined as the desire for 'new knowledge and new sensory experiences that motivate exploratory behavior' (Litman & Spielberger, 2003: 75). Within applied linguistics, it was Mahmoodzadeh and Khajavy (2019) who developed a questionnaire – the Language Learning Curiosity Scale (LLCS) – to measure two aspects of language learning curiosity. One sub-scale – language curiosity as a feeling-of-interest (LCFI) – aims to map curiosity related to interest, which is an emotion that often motivates the subject to communicate (communicative curiosity). The other sub-scale – language curiosity as a feeling-of-deprivation (LCFD) – captures the desire to reduce knowledge deficit; in other words, it reflects curiosity to acquire linguistic knowledge (linguistic curiosity). Although these two types of curiosity clearly stem from different sources – one is the joyful desire to discover, while the other is the desire to overcome the discomfort of lack of knowledge – their existence is not mutually exclusive and they can be present simultaneously in any language learner. The authors did not find gender differences in levels of curiosity, but they did report a strong positive correlation with enjoyment and a more moderate correlation with anxiety. Moreover, language learning curiosity was identified as a significant predictor of WTC along with enjoyment.

Although studies explicitly targeting hope are not numerous within our field, a hopeful orientation towards the future is undoubtedly present in Dörnyei's (2005, 2009) L2 motivational self system, more specifically in the concept of the ideal L2 self, which has been reviewed in the section on motivation. Snyder *et al.* (1991), who created a psychometric scale for measuring hope, claimed that although the everyday definition of hope simply reflects the possibility of something desired happening, from the cognitive perspective of goal-setting, hope should be defined 'as a cognitive set that is based on a reciprocally derived sense of successful (a) agency (goal-directed determination) and (b) pathways (planning of ways to meet goals)' (1991: 571). Although this definition clearly emphasizes the cognitive appraisal processes that are inherent in this emotion, positive feelings also contribute to it. This is why Pekrun (2006) categorized it as an outcome-oriented emotion with positive valence and medium level of control.

In their qualitative interview study, which focused on the out-of-class emotional experiences of learners in the Australian English as a second language (ESL) setting, Ross and Rivers (2018) identified hope as one of the most prominent positive emotions besides enjoyment. They claimed that although hope can originate in the classroom or beyond, the future outcomes or goals that are judged desirable and are hoped for almost exclusively referred to out-of-class contexts; moreover, hope often appeared linked to the learners' future selves. Recently Ghadyani *et al.* (2022) developed a questionnaire to measure Hope for Learning English as a Foreign Language (HLEFL). They identified seven categories that influence HLEFL – interpersonal relationship, social purpose, goal setting, emotion, certainty, source and anticipated effort – and they drew up various paths for activating HLEFL through these. Based on their findings, they attributed lower significance to goal-setting than Snyder *et al.* (1991) and they emphasized interpersonal relationship, certainty and anticipated effort as main factors in their model. Although these authors offer a complex conceptualization of the construct of HLEFL, using their model is not viable in a study that aims to measure a range of different emotions influencing language learning.

Finally, according to control-value theory, pride is also an outcome-oriented emotion with positive valence, where control attributions are directed at the self; in this sense, therefore, it is the positive counterpart or the opposite of shame (Pekrun, 2006). This emotion, which often accompanies important achievements, was the focus of investigation in an interview study conducted by Ross and Stracke (2016), involving 12 students studying English at an Australian university. The authors drew on psychology when they distinguished two types of pride: authentic and hubristic (Tracy & Robbins, 2007). Authentic pride means that someone is proud of their accomplishments, so the focus is on the person's actions. In hubristic pride, it is the self or actor who is in focus, which is clearly the same distinction that has already been described in connection with guilt and shame (Teimouri, 2018). Ross and Stracke (2016) identified four main themes in relation to learners' pride. The first theme involved pride experienced over classroom and learning-based achievements, the second was related to successful communication outside the classroom environment, the third was concerned with making significant others proud, while the fourth reflected a lack of pride in situations when the respondents should normally have felt proud. This last theme involved instances when learners felt pressured into achieving something, when they perceived no challenge, and when they judged the situation unauthentic or unrealistic, an example of which was the English classroom.

3.5 Self-Confidence and Self-Efficacy

When considering the role of self-efficacy, we need to start by establishing the differences between self-efficacy and self-confidence. Self-confidence is a socially constructed ID variable that describes students' generalized perceptions concerning their coping potentials, which might be relevant to various tasks (Csizér, 2020). Self-efficacy, on the other hand, is an entirely cognitive variable that is linked to specific tasks or skills (Bandura, 1997; Dörnyei & Kormos, 2000), and it often results from mastery experiences, social modeling, social persuasion and psychological responses (Bandura, 1997). As for learners, these constructs might characterize them to different degrees: for example, one learner might have general self-confidence towards speaking English but lack self-efficacy when it comes to particular writing tasks.

The role of self-efficacy in L2 motivation research was established relatively early with Richard Clément conducting some of the pioneering work concerning the role of linguistic self-confidence in L2 motivation in particular and language learning processes in general (Clément, 1980; Clément et al., 1977). Self-confidence and self-efficacy are closely related, as both are conceptualized as learners' beliefs concerning their abilities in relation to a number of tasks, goals and subject domains with varying degrees of cognitive and socially grounded components (cf. Bandura, 1997) as well as with a different level of specificity (e.g. Dörnyei & Kormos, 2000).

Canadian research activities had a direct impact on Hungarian studies through the close collaboration between Zoltán Dörnyei and Richard Clément, which resulted in an impactful study in the Hungarian context about the role of linguistic self-confidence in a monolingual society (Clément et al., 1994). Based on the results of this study, the direct impact of linguistic self-confidence as well as integrativeness and the appraisal of the classroom environment on L2 motivation was proven. The important role of self-confidence led Dörnyei to include the concept in his large-scale, longitudinal study spanning the 1990s and early 2000s. As detailed in Dörnyei et al. (2006), primary school students' general linguistic self-confidence not only correlated with their milieu, i.e. the supportive role of friends and family, but also impacted L2 specific cultural interest, an indirect contact measure of students' engagement of various L2 cultural products as presented by the media.

Measuring linguistic self-confidence in a more specific setting, Kormos and Dörnyei (2004) found strong correlations between students' self-confidence and a number of different output measures related to task completion and task motivation. In a more specific vein, Piniel and Csizér (2013) investigated the interrelationship of L2 motivation, anxiety and self-efficacy; and one particular strength of this study was that circular relationships were tested with structural equation modeling. The results indicated that learning experiences had a direct impact on students' self-efficacy beliefs, and that these beliefs had in turn a direct impact on students' levels of anxiety in a complex manner. When facilitating anxiety was considered, it was impacted positively by self-efficacy, but in the case of debilitating anxiety the impact was negative. This negative influence was complemented by self-efficacy directly impacting students' motivated learning behavior, a path missing from the model describing facilitating anxiety. These results are particularly important for the present study, as the complexity of the relationship between self-efficacy and anxiety, one specific emotion, provided motivation to investigate the relationship of self-efficacy and a range of different emotions.

3.6 The Interrelationship of Motivation, Emotions, Autonomy and Self-Efficacy

It has been repeatedly argued that ID variables need to be investigated in concert in order to reflect the complexity of the learning process (Ryan, 2019) but that the selection of the ID variables should be contextually informed. We have already argued for the importance of the above-reviewed ID variables in the Hungarian context, but the interrelationships of these variables need to be overviewed as well.

One of the first studies that attempted to link various emotions to language learning motivation was conducted by MacIntyre and Vincze (2017) among Italian learners of German. In their questionnaire study involving 10 positive and nine negative emotions and several core variables linked to three important models of language learning motivation – Gardner's integrative motive, Clément's social–contextual model and Dörnyei's L2 self system – they found especially strong positive correlations between positive emotions and confidence, the ideal L2 self, L2 effort and contact quality. Correlations between negative emotions and the motivation scales were negative but tended to be somewhat weaker; nevertheless, the strongest correlations were reported between positivity ratios (the ratio of positive and negative emotions; Fredrickson, 2013) and motivation. When attempting to predict scores on the various motivation scales, a range of emotions, both positive and negative, had significant contributions; however, among the 19 emotions measured, amusement, anger and peacefulness appeared the most frequently as predictors.

Although the study conducted by Saito et al. (2018) reduced the number of emotions examined and in terms of motivation considered only components of the L2 motivational self system, it added a further dimension by exploring an aspect of students' language performance: the comprehensibility of their speech. In their study involving Japanese high school learners, Saito et al. found that students' past learning experiences were mostly related to their ideal and ought-to L2 selves, while their current learning experience mostly depended on their enjoyment of their English classes. Moreover, at the beginning of the language course they were participating in during the study, learners' comprehensibility was negatively affected by their anxiety and their less developed ideal L2 self. In contrast, bigger gains in comprehensibility on the learners' part over the three-month program were associated with enjoyment and a stronger ideal L2 self. These results suggested that besides playing a role in influencing learners' motivation, the emotions experienced by them might be directly linked to learners' language achievements.

Support for the existence of an association between emotions and language achievement has already been found in connection with distinct emotions: in meta-analyses, language anxiety has been linked to lower language achievement (Teimouri *et al.*, 2019) while enjoyment has been associated with higher language achievement (Botes *et al.*, 2022). The relationship between emotions and language achievement was also the focus of investigation in a study by Shao *et al.* (2020) involving Chinese learners of English. Although this piece of research did not consider motivational constructs, it investigated a wider range of emotions than Saito *et al.* (2018). Shao *et al.* reported that perceived control was a significant predictor for all eight investigated achievement emotions (enjoyment, hope, pride, anger, anxiety, shame, hopelessness and boredom), and that the relationship was positive in the case of the three positive emotions but negative in the case of the five negative emotions. Moreover, these relationships were found to be stronger in the case of higher attributed values; thus, the identified interaction effects between control and value appraisals lend support to their multiplicative impact on achievement emotions. Likewise, perceived control was also found to predict language achievement measured as a test score, and this relationship was similarly found to be subject to the interaction effect between control and value: control had a stronger effect when the value was high. Finally, enjoyment, pride, hope and hopelessness were found to be mediators of the relationship between control and value appraisals and performance, while no such mediating effects were identified in the case of anxiety, shame, boredom or anger.

Another study, conducted by Li and Li (2023) among junior secondary learners in rural China, used structural equation modeling to find evidence for the predictive effects of enjoyment, anxiety and boredom on language achievement over time. Based on their results, they were able to find support for the long-term significant effect of language learning enjoyment on achievement, both when measured in isolation and together with anxiety and boredom, while the predictive power of anxiety was much more limited, and boredom had hardly any at all. Both these studies (Li & Li, 2023; Shao *et al.*, 2020) hint that experiencing positive emotions might have a more decisive role than experiencing negative ones when it comes to determining language learning achievements.

Tsang and Dewaele (2023) reached very similar conclusions when investigating the role of boredom, enjoyment and anxiety in predicting engagement and language proficiency among primary school learners of English in Hong Kong. They found that learners' enjoyment was negatively correlated with both boredom and anxiety, while boredom and anxiety were positively correlated with each other. Regression analyses showed that, out of these three emotions, enjoyment was the only significant predictor of both engagement and English proficiency. Interestingly, in their path analysis the authors also found no significant links between engagement, which might be thought of as a manifestation of actual motivated behavior on the spot, and proficiency (i.e. language achievement), a finding that necessitates further exploration of this topic.

In a fairly complex study, Dewaele et al. (2022) set out to examine how teachers' L2 use in the classroom, as well as their predictability, affected learners' enjoyment, anxiety and boredom, how these emotions influenced learners' attitudes towards the L2, and how all these variables could be linked to learners' L2 achievement. The study was conducted online, and it involved learners from various backgrounds learning a variety of L2s. While the authors used scales to measure the three emotions, the rest of the constructs were represented by one item each, language achievement corresponding to the last L2 grade that the learners received.

Many of the hypothesized relationships of the model did not prove to be statistically significant; nevertheless, the three emotions were found to be correlated in the expected manner: enjoyment had negative correlations with both boredom and anxiety and anxiety and boredom were correlated positively, just as in Tsang and Dewaele's (2023) and Shao et al.'s (2020) studies. Teachers' L2 use was only related to learners' enjoyment, while their predictability was related to both enjoyment and boredom. As regards the relationships of emotions with attitudes and achievement, L2 enjoyment and boredom were linked to attitudes positively and negatively respectively, while only anxiety had a direct link with achievement, which was negative. Language achievement was also influenced by attitudes; thus, enjoyment and boredom might have exerted their influence through this construct. However, the direct positive link between enjoyment and achievement that was demonstrated in several other studies (Li & Li, 2023; Shao et al., 2020; Tsang & Dewaele, 2023) is clearly missing here and seems to have been replaced by the negative influence of anxiety. This negative relationship between anxiety and L2 achievement is well known and has been documented earlier, typically in studies examining the effects of anxiety only (Botes et al., 2020a; MacIntyre & Gardner, 1994).

As regards the Hungarian context, outside the present research program there are few studies that have investigated the interrelationships of motivation, emotion, self-efficacy and autonomy in a systematic way. One of the first such investigations focused on how motivation shaped students' autonomy, and as we have already described above, Csizér and Kormos (2012, 2014) not only proved that there is a strong correlation between these two concepts but they also showed that there is a direction to this relationship, and that students' motivated learning behavior shapes autonomous learning behavior as well as autonomous use of technology.

Another possible way to investigate the concerted role of ID variables is to explore correlational relationships by partialing out influences of variables. Albert *et al.* (2018c) found that the investigation of processes between positive/negative emotions and autonomous learning behavior yielded complex results. On the surface, it seemed that negative emotions (anxiety, boredom and apathy) had a negative link with autonomy, but this negative relationship was canceled if the strong association of enjoyment was partialed out of the correlation of negative emotions and autonomy, resulting in some of the negative emotions having a positive relationship with autonomy.

4 Methods

4.1 Brief Overview of the Research Program

Before detailing methods-related information, we would like to provide an overview of the full research program in order to inform the reader of the full picture as well as to show where related information can be found. This project was initially designed in late 2017 and it was rewritten and fine-tuned twice before we managed to win the grant of the National Research, Development and Innovation Office in Hungary to complete the project in 2019, the last full pre-pandemic year. Our initial motivation in designing the project was that, despite modernization of L2 education since the turn of the century in Hungary (Einhorn, 2007; Kapitánffy, 2001; Medgyes & Öveges, 2004; Vágó, 1999) and despite continuous efforts to improve the quality of L2 teaching in both primary and secondary schools (Öveges, 2013; Világ-Nyelv, 2003), European statistics still show that the Hungarian population is generally lagging behind the rest of Europe regarding competence in L2s (see Chapter 2 on our research context). This, by definition, necessitates in-depth investigations into those individual aspects of learning and teaching that, according to international research, are the best predictors of success in L2s (Dörnyei & Ryan, 2015). Despite the fact that a small number of individual difference (ID) variables had been studied in isolation earlier in Hungary (e.g. Dörnyei *et al.*, 2006; Kormos & Csizér, 2008, 2014; Nikolov, 2003), we saw a strong need for exploratory studies that:

(a) could lead to the identification of specific problems that can be linked to the low levels of L2 competence of the population;
(b) investigate related learner variables in concert;
(c) take a multi-perspective approach by also including teachers and the teaching process in the research framework; and
(d) are contextualized and include classroom observations.

Table 4.1 provides the relevant details including the sources of the data, the data-collection instruments, the main aims and the relevant publications.

Table 4.1 Overview of the full research program

Source of data/instrument	Main aim(s)	Relevant publication(s)
Pilot study/Cross-sectional questionnaire	To design a questionnaire that can reliably measure students' L2 motivation, emotions, autonomy and self-efficacy.	Albert et al. (2019) Albert et al. (2021) Csizér & Öveges (2019) Csizér & Öveges (2020) Csizér et al. (2021)
	To discover what emotional experiences characterize the sample.	
	To map the possible relationships between students' motivational and exam-related dispositions.	
	To map students' attitudes towards L2 learning autonomy and its relation to other important IDs.	
	To map the description of language policy regulations pertaining to L2 learning autonomy.	
Students/Cross-sectional questionnaire	To explore students' dispositions towards various ID variables: the role of autonomy.	Albert et al. (2022) Csizér & Albert (2024a, 2024b)
	The interrelationships of ID variables.	
Students/Longitudinal questionnaire 2019–2020	To map changes in students' IDs over two school years.	Albert & Piniel (2021) Albert (2022) Piniel & Albert (in press)
Students/ Tasks and short questionnaire	To investigate the relationships between task-related and ID variables.	Albert (2022)
Students and teachers/ Classroom observation schedule	To provide insight into what is happening in the English classrooms in Hungary.	Dóczi & Csizér (2021)
Interview guide	To explore teachers' beliefs about learning English.	Smid & Zólyomi (2021) Zólyomi (2022) Albert (2022)
	To explore teachers' perceptions about differentiated instruction and related practices.	
	To explore teachers' beliefs about language tasks.	
	To explore teachers' beliefs about individual differences.	

It is beyond the scope of this volume to present and discuss the results of the full research program. Accordingly, in this volume we set out to answer a number of overarching research questions to understand students' and teachers' perspectives:

(1) What characterizes Hungarian secondary school students' L2 motivation, emotions, autonomy and self-efficacy?
(2) What profiles can be established pertaining to Hungarian secondary school students' L2 motivation, emotions, autonomy and self-efficacy?
(3) What views do teachers express in connection with Hungarian secondary school students' L2 motivation, emotions, autonomy and self-efficacy?
(4) What characterizes differences between students' dispositions and teachers' views?

In order to achieve this, we employed a mixed-methods design that will be detailed in the following section.

4.2 Overview of the Research Design

In this study, we implemented a mixed-methods design (Creswell & Clark, 2018), a concurrent combination of collecting quantitative and qualitative data, mainly because our aim was to integrate the results from both datasets so that we could see the overall picture from multiple perspectives (Dörnyei, 2007). This included analysis of cross-sectional and longitudinal student questionnaires, teacher interviews, tasks and classroom observations. The various parts of the study were affected differently by the pandemic. While the cross-sectional student questionnaire and teacher interviews could have been completed by switching the empirical work to an online platform, both the longitudinal and task-based phases proved to be more difficult to complete; as for the lesson observation part of the research program, we had to abandon it altogether. This mixed-methods perspective is additionally retained in this volume because we are analyzing data coming from the large-scale cross-sectional student questionnaires and the interviews conducted with the students' teachers.

4.3 The Participants

The population of this study was secondary school teachers and their students. We used quota sampling (Dörnyei, 2007) and made sure that schools were sampled from each region of the country: the capital city and the western and eastern parts of Hungary. We included data from 11 schools from seven cities all over the country; the final sample included 1152 secondary school students (467 males, 682 females, 3 missing) and 32 English language teachers (3 male, 29 female). The ratio of the latter faithfully depicts the usual gender distribution in the language teaching profession. The students' ages ranged between 14 and 20 ($M = 16$, $SD = 1.22$; 3 missing); for all of them their first language was Hungarian. They had all been learning English as a first or second L2 at the time of the data collection, and their level of English ranged between A1 and C1 with an average starting age of 9.2 years ($SD = 3.1$) of learning the English language. As for our teacher participants, the youngest teacher in the study was 27 years old at the time of the data collection, and the oldest teacher was 64 ($M = 47.47$, $SD = 7.74$). Detailed background information for the teacher participants is displayed in Table 4.2

Methods 41

Table 4.2 Summary of the participating teachers' background information

Pseudonym	Location	Age	Gender	Years teaching English	Highest level of education	Another subject taught
Abigél	W	42	F	17	University	Spanish
Alexandra	E	50	F	28	University	–
Amália	W	53	F	35	University	–
Anasztázia	E	43	F	20	University	–
Anett	C	35	F	12	University (PhD)	Spanish in the past
Anikó	W	56	F	22	University	Russian in the past
Anna	C	47	F	17	University	–
Aranka	W	47	F	15	University	–
Bettina	W	45	F	22	University	Hungarian literature
Borbála	E	50	F	26	University	Russian
Botond	C	50	M	32	University	–
Brigitta	C	50	F	25	University	–
Daniella	C	27	F	5	University	–
Edina	W	51	F	27	University	–
Edit	C	49	F	17	University	–
Emese	W	53	F	29	University	–
Emma	W	56	F	34	University	Russian in the past
Enikő	C	37	F	11	University	Media
Imre	W	51	M	27	University	History
Janka	E	51	F	21	University	–
Jázmin	E	53	F	28	University	–
Jolán	W	39	F	23	University	–
Júlia	E	58	F	27	University	History
Klára	E	50	F	27	University	History
Levente	C	31	M	5	University	Hungarian as an FL
Magdolna	E	46	F	18	University	–
Margit	C	64	F	24	University	–
Marianna	C	54	F	28	University	–
Mária	W	44	F	12	University	PE
Márta	W	46	F	22	University (PhD)	–
Réka	W	43	F	8	University	German
Zsóka	W	48	F	22	University	–

Note: W = Western Hungary, E = Eastern Hungary, C = Capital city, F = female, M = male, FL = foreign language and PE = physical education.

4.4 The Instruments

In the following subsections, we present the data-collection instruments, including the theoretical background to their development, their design, their validation and the piloting processes. As for the sequencing of our instruments, first we developed our questionnaire (see Appendix A and in the IRIS database: https://www.iris-database.org/) and, following its pilot, we determined the content of the interview guide (see Appendix B).

4.4.1 The questionnaire

We designed a cross-sectional questionnaire, and the initial item pool ready for piloting contained 118 statements with a 5-point Likert-type scale indicating the extent to which students agreed with the statements (1 = not at all true; 2 = not really true; 3 = partly true, partly not; 4 = mostly true; 5 = completely true). The finalized questionnaire included four main IDs: namely, motivation, autonomy, emotions and self-efficacy. Specifically, these involved 5 motivation-related scales, 2 autonomy-related scales, 9 emotion scales (4 positive emotions, 5 negative emotions) and 1 self-efficacy scale. Besides these scales, the questionnaire subsumed questions regarding the participants' language learning background, including their age, gender and language learning history (age of onset, etc.). The questionnaire was in Hungarian, the first language of the participants.

In the following subsections, we introduce the scales along with their sources, definitions, the number of items they contain, the internal consistency measured by Cronbach's alpha (α), and a translated sample item is provided for each scale.

4.4.1.1 Motivation

Our instrument included 5 motivation-related scales, closely drawing on Dörnyei (2005, 2009), Kormos and Csizér (2008) and Csizér and Kormos (2012). These were the following:

(1) *Motivated learning behavior* (5 items, α = .82): measures the extent to which learners are ready to invest energy in their L2 learning. Example: *I can honestly say that I do everything I can to master the English language.*
(2) *Ideal L2 self* (5 items, α = .86): explores participants' vision about their future language use. Example: *When I think of my future life, I imagine myself using English regularly.*
(3) *Ought-to L2 self* (6 items, α = .74): reflects what participants perceive as expectations in terms of their own language learning. Example: *For all the people around me, English proficiency is an important part of general knowledge.*

(4) *Language learning experiences* (4 items, α = .90): signals participants' positive experiences concerning learning English. Examples: *I like the activities that we do in English lessons. I have a good time during English classes.*
(5) *Perceived importance of contact* (5 items, α = .76): reflects the extent to which learners find it important to use English with native or non-native speakers outside the language classroom. Example: *I believe it is good to speak to foreigners because I can get to know their ways of speaking, accents and vocabulary.*

4.4.1.2 Autonomy

Two scales, based on Csizér and Kormos (2012), tapped into the autonomy of language learners:

(6) *Autonomous language learning behavior* (6 items, α = .82): reflects the extent to which participants are able to learn and practice English on their own. Example: *I spend more time practicing elements in English that I find difficult to understand.*
(7) *Autonomous use of technology* (5 items, α = .83): signals learners' abilities to utilize internet-based and computer-based opportunities in order to improve their English knowledge. Example: *I often use the internet to improve my English.*

4.4.1.3 Emotions

The instrument employed in our study also measured a wide range of positive and negative emotions (Pekrun, 2014; Pekrun et al., 2011) relevant in the EFL classroom context. We adopted these scales from Albert et al. (2018a, 2018b, 2019, 2020). We start by introducing positive emotions (numbers 8–11), which are then followed by negative emotions (numbers 12–16).

(8) *Enjoyment* (6 items, α = .78): refers to learners' feelings of enjoyment while taking part in the activities and topics during language lessons. Example: *I enjoy the topics that we discuss in English lessons.*
(9) *Hope* (6 items, α = .78): measures how hopeful learners feel about achieving success in learning English at school. Example: *I feel hopeful about overcoming challenges in the process of learning English.*
(10) *Pride* (5 items, α = .88): taps into the extent to which learners feel proud of their achievements in language learning. Example: *I am proud of my achievements in language learning.*
(11) *Curiosity* (6 items, α = .83): measures how curious and interested learners feel about learning English and the topics and activities they encounter during the English lessons. Example: *In English lessons, we deal with topics that arouse my curiosity.*

(12) *Anxiety* (5 items, α = .69): taps into learners' feelings of inhibition experienced in connection with English language activities in school lessons. Example: *I get frustrated if I can't understand an English-language text.*
(13) *Boredom* (5 items, α = .79): measures the extent to which learners feel bored during the activities and topics in the English language lessons. Example: *I get bored by the activities in English lessons.*
(14) *Apathy* (4 items, α = .77): refers to learners' feeling of hopelessness related to success in English language learning in school. Example: *I feel hopeless about ever mastering English in the school.*
(15) *Confusion* (5 items, α = .78): measures the extent to which learners feel confused about language learning in class. Example: *Sometimes I feel confused because I don't understand what is happening in the English lessons.*
(16) *Shame* (5 items, α = .80): taps into learners' feelings of shame about their achievements and actions during English lessons. Example*: I feel ashamed if I can't answer a question during our English lessons.*

4.4.1.4 Self-efficacy

We measured students' self-efficacy beliefs with one scale, which was based on Piniel and Csizér (2013) and Albert *et al.* (2018a, 2018b):

(17) *Self-efficacy beliefs* (6 items, α = .93): investigates learners' beliefs about their abilities to successfully learn a L2. Example: *I believe that I can do the speaking tasks we are given during English lessons.*

4.4.2 The interview guide

The questions of the interview guide were pooled based on the results of the pilot study of the questionnaire employed in the research program as well as upon the theoretical and empirical background presented above, i.e. several recent studies investigating various IDs. We implemented this approach to be able to include multiple perspectives of IDs. These comprised the following topics:

- language teaching background and experience (Csizér & Kálmán, 2019; You et al., 2016);
- ways to maintain and develop the knowledge of the target language and the teaching methods (Celce-Murcia & Olshtain, 2000; Illés, 2020; Omaggio Hadley, 1993);
- future plans on the language teacher profession (Kubanyiova, 2015, 2020);
- planning and preparing the classroom work (Csizér, 2019; Hiver, 2016);

- tasks, materials and assessment applied in language classes (Albert et al., 2018a, 2018b; Long, 2014);
- perceptions about language learners' language-learning-related emotions (positive and negative), motivation, confidence, autonomy, etc. (Pawlak et al., 2020a);
- the role of language learning outside the classroom (Ellis, 2015);
- perceptions about own role as a language teacher (Csizér, 2020).

We opted for a semi-structured interview guide so that teachers have a certain freedom to bring up aspects that they find important or relevant regarding the topic (Galletta & Cross, 2013; Wallace, 1998). The interview guide was compiled in Hungarian, and all the interviews were carried out in Hungarian, the mother tongue of the participants (and the researchers, for that matter). For the sake of this book, the interview guide was translated by the researchers, and an EFL teacher back-translated the instrument, which enabled us to check the appropriateness of our translation. The final, English version of the interview guide can be found in Appendix B.

4.5 Data Collection

A defining characteristic of our data collection is that it was marred by the COVID-19 pandemic, as we started collecting data in the autumn term of 2019 and completed the process in the spring term of 2021. The instruments were extensively piloted in the first year of our project (Albert et al., 2019; Csizér & Öveges, 2019, 2020) and the main data collection began in the autumn term of 2019 after the required permissions and consent were obtained for data collection. In the first phase of the data collection, data were obtained in the presence of one of the researchers using a paper-based questionnaire during the participants' respective English lessons. This was switched to online data collection after March 2020, when schools were temporarily closed and education moved to online spaces. In this case, the online version of the instrument was sent out to students by their English teacher but the recorded data were received by the research team. Generating teacher-interview data followed a similar pattern: we started with face-to-face interviews and moved to online data collection using a platform preferred by the individual interviewee. Participation in the study was voluntary, and both the teachers and the students were assured of the anonymity of their responses. The length of the interviews ranged between 28 and 90 minutes ($M = 49.69$, $SD = 14.57$). Altogether, we have a fairly large audio database (1590 minutes, i.e. 26.5 hours). We transcribed the interview recordings verbatim, which yielded a rich transcript of around 189,000 words.

4.6 Data Analysis

Data analysis was carried out sequentially, and then results were compared and contrasted when possible. All through the quantitative analysis we worked with a significance level of 5%. As for the actual steps of data analysis, first, quantitative data were analyzed by summarizing descriptive statistical results. In terms of multivariate statistical procedures, we have used the following:

(1) Group-related statistics: several rounds of paired-samples *t*-tests were run to see whether there were significant differences between the means of the scales.
(2) Cluster analysis (Crowther *et al.*, 2021; Csizér & Jamieson, 2013): profiling students along their dispositions and creating comparable subgroups in our sample. Cluster analysis was done in several steps in order to establish the number of clusters within the sample and then finalizing the cluster solutions.
(3) Relationship-related statistics: we looked at cross-tabulations (contingency tables) to analyze the interrelationships between the different learner profiles created by cluster analysis. We also computed multiple linear regression analyses for exploratory purposes.

For the *t*-tests, we used Cohen's *d* as an indicator of effect size with the following cut-off points: 0.20 indicating a small difference, 0.50 a medium difference and 0.80 a large difference (Cohen *et al.*, 2018). In the case of the analysis of variance (ANOVA) tests, the eta-squared (η^2) value was calculated for effect size (Dörnyei, 2007), with 0.01 referring to a small effect, 0.06 to a medium effect and 0.14 to a large effect (Cohen *et al.*, 2018). We used multiple linear regression models (stepwise method) to determine which independent variables contributed meaningfully to the variance in our dependent variable. In the regression analyses, we selected the appropriate models based on the effect-size values the individual scales represented (Cohen's f^2; Cohen, 1988). Based on Cohen's guidelines, we excluded from the analysis those scales with too small a contribution ($f^2 < 0.02$). In cross-tabulations, we calculated Cramer's V, an effect size measuring the strength of relationship between two nominal variables, with the following cutoffs: 0.00–0.10 negligible association, 0.10–0.20 weak association, 0.20–0.40 moderate association, 0.40–0.60 relatively strong association, 0.60–0.80 strong association and 0.80–1.00 very strong association (Cohen, 1988; Rea & Parker, 2014).

Naturally, these advanced procedures were preceded by rigorous reliability analyses. As the Cronbach's alpha internal consistency measure does not imply one-dimensionality (Hoekstra *et al.*, 2018), we ran principal components analysis (principal components extraction method, no rotation) to check whether the items load to one

Table 4.3 The final round of the reliability analysis

IDs	Scales	k	α	PCA (%)	KMO	χ²(df)
Motivation	Motivated learning behavior	5	.82	1 (59)	0.84	1924.27* (10)
	Ideal L2 self	5	.86	1 (64)	0.84	2473.61* (10)
	Ought-to L2 self	6	.74	1 (45)	0.80	1380.23* (15)
	Language learning experiences	5	.90	1 (71)	0.89	3332.19* (10)
	Perceived importance of contact	5	.76	1 (52)	0.75	1431.67* (10)
Autonomy	Autonomous learning behavior	6	.82	1 (52)	0.84	2078.88* (15)
	Autonomous use of technology	5	.83	1 (62)	0.85	2254.04* (10)
Positive emotions	Enjoyment	6	.78	1 (48)	0.80	1706.21* (15)
	Hope	6	.78	1 (48)	0.84	1652.84* (15)
	Pride	5	.88	1 (68)	0.84	3107.80* (10)
	Curiosity	6	.83	1 (55)	0.85	2535.84* (15)
Negative emotions	Anxiety	5	.69	1 (45)	0.75	894.71* (10)
	Boredom	5	.79	1 (56)	0.80	1871.01* (10)
	Apathy	4	.77	1 (60)	0.74	1371.72* (6)
	Confusion	5	.78	1 (54)	0.82	1402.86* (10)
	Shame	5	.80	1 (57)	0.79	1993.47* (10)
Self-efficacy	Self-efficacy beliefs	6	.93	1 (75)	0.91	5528.53* (15)

Note: k = number of items in the scale; α = Cronbach's alpha; PCA = the number of dimensions yielded by principal components analysis without rotation; % = the cumulative percent; KMO = Kaiser–Meyer–Olkin measure of sampling adequacy; χ^2 = Bartlett's test of sphericity; df = degrees of freedom.
* $p < .05$.

dimension. We checked the Kaiser–Meyer–Olkin (KMO) measure of sampling adequacy and Bartlett's test of sphericity and concluded that this set of items is appropriate for factorability. After further rounds of reliability analysis, which involved deleting items based on the low extraction values in the communalities and low factor loadings, we arrived at 90 items. Table 4.3 contains the final round of the reliability analysis.

Qualitative interview data were analyzed with the help of qualitative content analysis (Dörnyei, 2007; Elo *et al.*, 2014), adopting an inductive approach (Charmaz, 2006). This means that after becoming familiar with the transcripts, open coding was applied first, in an attempt to use the interview texts as the starting point of analysis instead of pre-defined categories. Different coding procedures were used in light of our aims (e.g. process coding, emotion coding, values coding; Saldaña, 2013) along with the constant-comparative method (Maykut & Morehouse, 1994) in order to ensure that, throughout the inductive coding process, the coded units were simultaneously compared to all units of coding obtained so far.

As a first step, all four authors of this book read the transcripts to familiarize themselves with the texts. Then one of the authors coded all the interviews in Atlas.ti, arriving at an initial list of 566 coded segments in the categories of emotion, motivation, autonomy and self-confidence/self-efficacy. Another author checked these initial codes and indicated any disagreements, which were later resolved through discussions between all four authors. Once agreement had been reached, the two coders worked together to condense the initial codes into larger categories, pinpoint re-occurring common patterns in the dataset, and identify emerging themes. Once the preliminary data analysis was ready, the other two researchers were contacted, and the results of data analysis were presented to them. They were asked to reflect on the codes, categories and themes in light of the interviews.

This method of data analysis ensured that recommended quality-control steps aiming to increase the trustworthiness of the research (Albert & Csizér, 2022) had been observed. Peer debriefing (Guba, 1981) helped increase the credibility of data analysis and interpretations, and feedback from members of the research team corroborated the findings (Mirhosseini, 2020). Additionally, providing a thick description through a detailed introduction of the research context in Chapter 2 and the interview data with the help of quotes offers readers a chance to form their own interpretations of the data presented (Guba, 1981; Howitt, 2016; Patton, 2015). Finally, data collected from students with the help of questionnaires have also been used to triangulate these findings (Howitt, 2016; Mirhosseini, 2020; Tracy, 2020). The final categories, codes and number of coded segments identified based on the interview data are summarized in Table 4.4, with definitions and sample quotes.

4.7 Ethical Considerations and Quality Control

Throughout the research project, we paid attention to aspects of ethical considerations. Permission to conduct research at the participating schools was obtained from the school principals, the English teachers and the parents. Participation in every phase of the project was completely voluntary; the participants were assured that they had the right to opt out at any point during data collection. Data collected from students contained no sensitive information and were completely anonymous. During the interview phase of the study, we kept the data confidential. We did so by using pseudonyms to ensure that the identity of the participants was not traceable and we removed any markers based on which teachers could be identified during data transcription. Hence, full anonymity was maintained both during data analysis and when presenting the findings of the qualitative analysis. We recorded the interviews with the participants' informed consent that included information about the project and the

Table 4.4 Categories, codes and the number of coded segments in the qualitative data

Categories	Codes	Number of coded segments
IDs (36)	Individual differences taken into consideration by teachers	36
Motivation (102)	General comments about motivation	20
	Specific comments about what student motivation entails	56
	Teachers' role in increasing and maintaining students' motivation	26
Emotions (255)	General comments about emotions in the classroom	59
	Specific positive and negative emotions	73
	The role of emotions in the classroom	36
	Teachers' role in connection with emotions	44
	Students' emotions influence teachers	20
	Teachers' emotions influence students	23
Self-confidence/ self-efficacy (73)	General comments about self-confidence/self-efficacy	10
	Specific comments about what self-confidence/self-efficacy entails	45
	Teachers' role in increasing and maintaining students' self-confidence/self-efficacy	18
Autonomy (100)	General comments about autonomy	16
	Specific comments about what student autonomy entails	46
	Teachers' role in developing student autonomy, including instruction on strategy use, customizing the learning material, awareness-raising of life-long learning and the omnipresence of English, time management and positive feedback	38

storage of the data as well. After describing and inputting the data, the original recordings and the questionnaires were destroyed.

In terms of quality control, each step of our research was carried out giving appropriate consideration to the relevant and important quality control issues. In order to have a high level of construct validity, we synthesized all relevant pieces of research in a contextual manner after a careful and critical evaluation of the published studies. Specifying our population, our sampling procedures, and arriving at an acceptable volume of samples resulted in having an appropriate possibility to generalize our quantitative results as well as offer easily transferable findings concerning the interview study phase. With respect to providing high-quality instruments, we focused on rigorous piloting processes, designs and validations. As detailed in Table 4.1, the pilot studies, as well as earlier smaller-scale investigations of parts of this dataset, have also been published elsewhere. We believe that publishing the pilot results is an important step in ensuring the transparency of our investigation.

5 Results and Discussion: Dispositions and Views of Participants

In this first of the four chapters discussing our results we concentrate on describing the dispositions and views of our participants. We outline the descriptive statistics of the questionnaire study and analyze the students' dispositions towards the various measures of motivation, autonomy, self-efficacy and emotions.

5.1 Students' Individual Difference Characteristics

To summarize what the collected data indicated about the sample members, we conducted a descriptive statistical analysis (Table 5.1). Additionally, in order to see whether the differences between the values obtained on the different scales were statistically significant, we ran several rounds of paired samples t-tests (see Appendix C). We present the results according to the four themes that the 17 targeted scales represent.

As to the L2 learning motivation-related measures presented in Table 5.1, the data show that our participants were fairly motivated on average, since they tended to score around 4 (on a 5-points scale) on the motivated learning behavior scale, as well as on the scales of the ought-to L2 self, L2 learning experience and perceived importance of contact. This means that they were not only likely to invest considerable effort into L2 learning but had a rather developed image of what is expected of them in terms of language learning, had fairly positive L2 classroom experiences and had favorable attitudes toward contact experiences with speakers of the L2. The results of the paired samples t-test ($t = 29.224$, $df = 1151$, $p < .001$) demonstrate that the students had more salient ideal L2 selves ($M = 4.51$, $SD = 0.66$) than ought-to L2 selves ($M = 3.93$, $SD = 0.73$), which suggests that high school English learners in Hungary are likely to have stronger internalized motives (e.g. hopes and wishes) than externalized ones (e.g. obligations, responsibilities) when it comes to L2 learning (Dörnyei, 2009). The magnitude of this

Table 5.1 Results of the descriptive statistical analysis

Scales	M	SD
L2 motivation		
Ideal L2 self	4.51	0.66
Perceived importance of contact	4.10	0.76
L2 learning experience	4.01	0.82
Motivated learning behavior	3.94	0.75
Ought-to L2 self	3.93	0.73
L2 autonomy		
Autonomous use of technology	4.05	0.91
Autonomous learning behavior	3.58	0.79
L2 self-efficacy		
Self-efficacy	4.04	0.83
L2 emotions		
Hope	4.32	0.60
Enjoyment	4.02	0.66
Pride	3.84	0.93
Curiosity	3.50	0.78
Shame	2.72	0.98
Anxiety	2.64	0.82
Confusion	2.56	0.87
Boredom	2.05	0.77
Apathy	1.90	0.87

difference was large (Cohen's $d = 0.84$) for the population of Hungarian secondary school EFL learners. In fact, the difference between the mean value of the ideal L2 self and all other motivation-related scales is statistically significant, which makes it likely that the ideal L2 self is the main driving force fueling high school language learners' motivation.

The data concerning the L2 learner autonomy-related measures suggest that the examined students were more inclined to take charge of their L2 learning when it came to internet-based and computer-based opportunities, but they were less inclined in connection with their tasks related to their in-class English learning (see Table 5.1). The paired samples *t*-test ($t = 19.87$, $df = 1151$, $p < .001$) confirmed that the informants' autonomous behavior was more intense with respect to the use of technology in L2 learning ($M = 4.05$, $SD = 0.91$) than in the case of general in-class L2 learning ($M = 3.58$, $SD = 0.79$) and that such a difference was rather meaningful, as indicated by the large effect size (Cohen's $d = 0.55$). These results are quite similar to those presented above on the motivational variables, which might indicate a link between motivation and autonomy that was also found by earlier studies (e.g. Csizér & Kormos, 2012, 2014). Our results regarding the difference between the obtained measures on the two autonomy scales that show a lower level of autonomy in connection with classroom-related issues seem to lend support to previous studies that reported the prevalence of teacher-centered approaches and frontal teaching in L2 classrooms in Hungary (Öveges & Csizér, 2018), as the strict control exercised by teachers in such settings is probably not conducive to learner autonomy.

Our participants' responses on the scale of L2 self-efficacy show that, overall, they were likely to believe that they would be able to solve English learning related tasks successfully (see Table 5.1). It must be emphasized, though, that we used a broad measure of L2 self-efficacy covering all the skills, so students' beliefs might be somewhat different when it comes to one particular domain of L2 competence given the domain specificity of the construct (Mills, 2014). The fairly high mean value of self-efficacy beliefs is judged favorable since strong self-efficacy beliefs have been shown to contribute to higher motivation and language achievements (Clément *et al.*, 1994; Kormos & Dörnyei, 2004).

The final construct covers the various emotions that our study sought to measure. The data regarding the four targeted positive emotions – namely, enjoyment, hope, pride and curiosity – show that our sample members were rather likely to experience these emotions in general, since all the scale means are above the theoretical mean of the 5-point Likert scale (see Table 5.1). By contrast, when it comes to the measured negative emotions of shame, anxiety, confusion, boredom and apathy, the participants were less prone to experience them during L2 learning, since all the scale means are less than 3.

In order to tell whether the differences between the values obtained for the different positive and negative emotions were statistically significant or random, we conducted multiple rounds of paired samples *t*-tests comparing the scales with the means closest to each other (see Appendix C). This way we managed to establish that there is a statistically significant difference between the mean values of all the scales, which means that all nine emotions measured by us can be characterized by different levels and that there is a clear rank order among them. This rank order is slightly different from what we found in our pilot studies, but the trend that positive emotions are followed by negative ones was the same there (Csizér *et al.*, 2021).

The order of the positive emotion scales shows that learners tend to experience hope most strongly, followed by enjoyment, pride and curiosity. Perhaps the high level of hope reported by the students should not be surprising since their ideal L2 self also proved to be very well developed, which indicates clear future images of themselves with high expectancy of success: a link that has been confirmed by Ross and Rivers (2018). The fairly high level of enjoyment, which is likely to reflect a balance between the skills the learners possess and the challenges they face in the English classroom (Csíkszentmihályi, 1990), is also encouraging, since Jin and Zhang (2021) were able to prove the existence of a positive link between enjoyment and language achievement. The relatively high level of pride is also encouraging, since it has been associated with high levels of achievement in various educational contexts (Pekrun et al., 2002), although the investigation of this important achievement emotion has only begun fairly recently within our field (Ross & Stracke, 2016). What is somewhat discouraging is that curiosity ranked at the lowest level among the positive emotions explored in this study and in our pilot study too. This is surprising since in an educational context this epistemic emotion might be expected to feature more prominently; moreover, interest – which is intimately linked with curiosity – is considered a driving force in theories of motivation (Noels et al., 2003).

As regards the order of negative emotions, we found that shame was the emotion most intensively perceived by the students in our study, followed by anxiety, confusion, boredom and apathy. The fact that apathy occupies the last position in the rank order is quite encouraging, since the feeling of apathy typically arises in situations that are characterized by low levels of skills and challenges (Csíkszentmihályi, 1975), and this emotion has been associated with low levels of achievement by Shao et al. (2020). The level of the other negative deactivating emotion – boredom – was also low, which is another positive finding as well, since boredom has been linked with low levels of success and achievement in earlier studies (Pawlak et al., 2020b; Shao et al., 2020). The remaining negative emotions are negative activating emotions, whose effects on motivation are complex according to Pekrun (2006). For example, while anxiety might impair interest and reduce intrinsic motivation, at the same time it might increase extrinsic motivation in an attempt to avoid failure. Nevertheless, in the language-learning context, anxiety has been associated mostly with negative achievements (MacIntyre & Gardner, 1994; Teimouri et al., 2019), similarly to shame (Teimouri, 2017).

5.1.1 Gender differences

To check whether there were any significant differences between students based on their gender, we ran independent samples t-tests. The results pointed to differences in 11 scales (see Table 5.2). It is notable that the students showed significant differences regarding the motivation-related constructs in 2 scales: girls tended to be more motivated in their learning behavior, and they also showed higher means on the perceived importance of contact scale. This means that girls seemed to invest more effort into their language learning processes; additionally, they attributed

Table 5.2 Gender differences

Scales	Boys (n = 467)		Girls (n = 682)		t	p	Cohen's d
	M	SD	M	SD			
L2 motivation							
Motivated learning behavior	3.86	0.73	4.00	0.76	−3.045	.002	0.19
Ideal L2 self	4.51	0.62	4.51	0.69	−0.008	.993	
Ought-to L2 self	3.89	0.76	3.95	0.70	−1.262	.207	
L2 learning experience	4.02	0.77	4.00	0.86	0.440	.660	
Perceived importance of contact	3.96	0.77	4.19	0.73	−5.107	.001	0.31
L2 autonomy							
Autonomous use of technology	4.17	0.87	3.97	0.93	3.579	.001	0.22
Autonomous learning behavior	3.47	0.75	3.65	0.81	−3.714	.001	0.23
L2 emotions							
Enjoyment	3.98	0.66	4.06	0.66	−2.115	.035	0.12
Hope	4.34	0.53	4.30	0.64	1.291	.197	
Pride	3.89	0.86	3.80	0.98	1.538	.124	
Curiosity	3.43	0.79	3.55	0.77	−2.635	.009	0.15
Anxiety	2.41	0.75	2.79	0.84	−7.995	.001	0.48
Boredom	2.16	0.80	1.98	0.75	3.868	.001	0.23
Apathy	1.84	0.83	1.93	0.89	−1.805	.071	
Confusion	2.41	0.81	2.65	0.89	−4.793	.001	0.28
Shame	2.50	0.91	2.87	1.00	−6.388	.001	0.39
L2 self-efficacy							
Self-efficacy	4.20	0.72	3.93	0.88	5.662	.001	0.34

Note: The responses of those participants who did not reveal their gender are excluded from the analysis.

a great role to communicating with foreigners. Boys, however, had higher self-efficacy beliefs. Interestingly, as per the 2 scales of autonomy, boys appeared to be more autonomous when it came to technology, while girls were more autonomous with respect to classroom L2 learning. It is perhaps not surprising that girls were susceptible to reporting higher degrees of emotions, be they positive (enjoyment and curiosity) or negative (anxiety, confusion, shame). Boys seemed to experience the emotion of boredom in a more intensive way as compared to girls.

The effect sizes of these results indicated that anxiety ($d = 0.48$) has the largest practical significance, but it is still around medium based on Cohen *et al.*'s (2018) cut-off point. Our result – namely, that girls tend to be more anxious than boys – is in line with a number of previous studies (e.g. Dewaele *et al.*, 2016; Donovan & MacIntyre, 2004). However, it must be noted that previous research endeavors showed great variance in their results regarding the relationship of gender and L2 classroom anxiety. Some other studies, for example, showed that there are no significant differences in the L2 anxiety of males and females (e.g. Aida, 1994; Dewaele *et al.*, 2008). There were also studies that showed that males are more anxious when it comes to L2 learning (e.g. Kitano, 2001; Zhang, 2001). Based on a recent meta-analysis summarizing the results of 48 studies, females and males do not show a significant difference in their L2 anxiety (Piniel & Zólyomi, 2022). However, the meta-analysis used articles employing one specific instrument – the Foreign Language Classroom Anxiety Scale – (Horwitz *et al.*, 1986) and thus it does not exclude the possibility of identifying gender differences with the help of other instruments.

The effect sizes in the case of motivated learning behavior ($d = 0.19$), enjoyment ($d = 0.12$), and curiosity ($d = 0.15$) are small, but in the case of motivated learning behavior and that of enjoyment, they show trends that have been reported in earlier studies: females usually tend to be more motivated than males (Albert *et al.*, 2018a, 2018b; Dörnyei *et al.*, 2006; Iwaniec, 2019; Kissau *et al.*, 2010; Williams *et al.*, 2002), and they appear to enjoy language learning more (Dewaele *et al.*, 2016; Dewaele & MacIntyre, 2014).

Regarding other medium-sized effects besides anxiety, the higher level of boredom ($d = 0.23$) reported by male students reinforces similar results found in the same context in earlier studies (Albert *et al.*, 2018a, 2018b), where higher levels of boredom were identified among boys in grade 7 and grade 11. These findings appear to be in line with Vodanovich *et al.*'s (2011) claim that boredom-proneness is more characteristic of males in general, a prediction whose validity in L2 learning should be further explored.

The fact that girls turned out to be more autonomous regarding classroom-related aspects of autonomy as reflected by their autonomous learning behavior ($d = 0.23$) is not surprising, since females have been found to be more autonomous than males in several contexts (Şakrak-Ekin & Balçıkanlı, 2019; Zhao & Chen, 2014) and in an earlier Hungarian study as well (Albert *et al.*, 2018a, 2018b). It is the higher autonomous use of technology ($d = 0.22$) of males that requires an explanation. Such an explanation might be related to the fact that there are many different facets of autonomy (Benson, 2013), and it is possible that earlier studies failed to measure autonomous use of technology. However, earlier studies have established that male learners tend to use computer games for language learning more (Jensen, 2017; Muñoz, 2020), and it can be hypothesized that this familiarity with computer games might carry over to other technology-related activities, making boys more autonomous in this respect. The higher self-efficacy beliefs ($d = 0.34$) reported by male students can also be considered a unique finding in the sense that Kissau *et al.* (2010) found no gender differences regarding self-efficacy, and Mills *et al.* (2007) reported higher self-efficacy for females. However, an earlier nationwide representative study in Hungary already identified the same patterns of higher self-efficacy for boys among 11th graders (Albert et al., 2018a, 2018b), which is in line with Iwaniec's (2019) hypothesis that male learners are likely to overestimate their abilities, while female students are more prone to underestimate them.

5.1.2 Differences regarding attendance of extracurricular English classes

We also computed independent samples *t*-tests to see the differences in the means regarding extracurricular English classes, and we found significant differences in 9 scales altogether (see Table 5.3). We find it important to note that those students who were not attending extracurricular English classes at the time of the data collection seemed

Table 5.3 Differences regarding attendance of extracurricular English classes

Scales	Participation in extracurricular class				t	p	Cohen's d
	Yes (n = 313)		No (n = 838)				
	M	SD	M	SD			
L2 motivation							
Motivated learning behavior	4.18	0.60	3.86	0.78	−7.384	.001	0.46
Ideal L2 self	4.60	0.56	4.48	0.69	−2.979	.003	0.19
Ought-to L2 self	4.01	0.68	3.90	0.74	−2.320	.021	0.15
L2 learning experience	4.00	0.78	4.01	0.84	0.249	.803	
Perceived importance of contact	4.14	0.67	4.08	0.78	−1.436	.152	
L2 autonomy							
Autonomous use of technology	4.07	0.83	4.04	0.94	−0.594	.553	
Autonomous learning behavior	3.79	0.68	3.50	0.82	−6.093	.001	0.38
L2 emotions							
Enjoyment	4.07	0.60	4.01	0.68	−1.372	.171	
Hope	4.39	0.51	4.29	0.62	−2.869	.004	0.18
Pride	3.93	0.83	3.80	0.97	−2.225	.026	0.14
Curiosity	3.52	0.73	3.50	0.80	−0.480	.631	
Anxiety	2.67	0.77	2.63	0.84	−0.820	.413	
Boredom	2.09	0.76	2.04	0.78	−0.941	.347	
Apathy	2.01	0.86	1.85	0.87	−2.821	.005	0.18
Confusion	2.56	0.83	2.56	0.88	−0.056	.955	
Shame	2.82	0.96	2.68	0.99	−2.169	.030	0.14
L2 self-efficacy							
Self-efficacy	4.14	0.73	4.00	0.86	−2.776	.006	0.18

Note: The responses of those participants who did not reveal whether they attended extracurricular classes are excluded from the analysis.

to be more passive in general. What is meant by this is that these students displayed lower means on all the 9 scales where significant differences were apparent. It is logical that students who did attend extracurricular classes were generally more motivated, as they showed higher means in motivated learning behavior, ideal L2 self and ought-to L2 self. They also showed higher self-efficacy beliefs, and they were more autonomous regarding general L2 learning. These students also experienced two positive emotions (hope and pride) and two negative emotions (apathy and shame) in a more intensive way than those who did not attend extracurricular classes. The presence of stronger negative emotions in the case of those learners who attended extracurricular language classes is perhaps more understandable in light of the fact that learners were asked to report emotions they experienced in connection with the English classes they took in their high schools. Experiencing shame and hopelessness during their regular English classes might encourage learners to pay for private English lessons, but the problem with this solution is that, since it requires considerable financial resources, it is not a viable option for all high school students.

5.1.3 Differences regarding the order of L2 learning for English

We also checked whether there were any differences between students according to the order of L2 acquisition for English. In Table 5.4, the results of the independent samples *t*-tests show that there were significant differences with regard to six scales, i.e. students whose first L2 was English were more autonomous and possessed a higher level of L2 self-efficacy than students for whom English was a second L2. Seeing that the majority of the students started English first is considered a positive sign in and of itself given the findings of an earlier study in Hungary (Csizér & Lukács, 2010), in which students' preference was clear concerning the fact that they wanted to learn English first.

The difference on the L2 self-efficacy scale seems understandable given that the group that started learning English first had a longer L2 learning history and that a L2 learner's level of L2 self-efficacy hinges on one's past L2 learning experiences (Mills, 2014). Similarly, as L2 learning autonomy is conceived of as a capacity (Benson, 2011; Illés, 2012), we can attribute the difference on the two autonomy-related scales to learners' having had more experiences with the learning of the language.

As to the measured emotions, it was found that having English as the second L2 meant experiencing the positive emotion, enjoyment, to a larger extent, while having English as the first L2 indicated experiencing the negative emotions, boredom and shame, to a greater degree during L2 learning. These results imply that the activities and topics featured in high school English classes are possibly too repetitive for those having learned English in an instructed setting for a longer period. Fortunately, as no

Table 5.4 Differences regarding the order of L2 acquisition for English

Scales	Order of L2 acquisition for English				t	p	Cohen's d
	1st (n = 918)		2nd (n = 232)				
	M	SD	M	SD			
L2 motivation							
Motivated learning behavior	3.96	0.76	3.89	0.70	1.148	.251	
Ideal L2 self	4.51	0.67	4.51	0.64	−0.005	.996	
Ought-to L2 self	3.93	0.72	3.92	0.74	0.110	.913	
L2 learning experience	3.99	0.81	4.10	0.87	−1.842	.066	
Perceived importance of contact	4.09	0.76	4.14	0.74	−0.907	.365	
L2 autonomy							
Autonomous use of technology	4.11	0.90	3.83	0.92	4.202	.001	0.31
Autonomous learning behavior	3.61	0.79	3.45	0.78	2.640	.008	0.20
L2 emotions							
Enjoyment	4.00	0.66	4.12	0.66	−2.457	.014	0.18
Hope	4.30	0.60	4.37	0.58	−1.662	.097	
Pride	3.84	0.93	3.81	0.94	0.496	.620	
Curiosity	3.49	0.79	3.58	0.75	−1.635	.102	
Anxiety	2.65	0.83	2.56	0.80	1.036	.300	
Boredom	2.08	0.77	1.94	0.77	2.488	.013	0.18
Apathy	1.89	0.84	1.90	0.95	−0.048	.962	
Confusion	2.53	0.88	2.64	0.80	−1.706	.088	
Shame	2.75	0.99	2.59	0.93	2.252	.024	0.17
L2 self-efficacy							
Self-efficacy	4.06	0.82	3.94	0.85	1.998	.046	0.14

Note: The responses of those participants who did not reveal the order of L2 acquisition for English are excluded from the analysis.

difference was detected between the two groups in terms of motivation, it seems that their experiences of boredom were not as defining in their L2 learning process as to have a negative effect on their motivation and performance (Pawlak et al., 2020b; Shao et al., 2020). The same can be assumed in relation to our result on the measure of shame given the potential detrimental effect of shame on motivation (Teimouri, 2017). However, the small effect sizes should make us cautious when interpreting these findings (i.e. Cohen's d < 0.20; Cohen et al., 2018).

5.1.4 Differences regarding weekly number of English lessons

Our ANOVA test results presented in Table 5.5 show that there were also significant differences between students in terms of their weekly number of English lessons. Upon closer scrutiny, it can be inferred from

Table 5.5 Differences with respect to students' weekly number of English lessons

Scales	Weekly number of English classes				F	p	η^2	Post-hoc comparison[1]
	A (n = 352)	B (n = 370)	C (n = 271)	D (n = 61)				
	M (SD)							
L2 motivation								
Motivated learning behavior	4.00 (0.74)	3.94 (0.71)	3.82 (0.80)	4.23 (0.76)	5.984	.001	0.017	C < A < D; B < D
Ideal L2 self	4.59 (0.61)	4.47 (0.67)	4.45 (0.74)	4.50 (0.66)	3.000	.030		ns
Ought-to L2 self	3.94 (0.70)	3.97 (0.72)	3.86 (0.75)	3.70 (0.75)	3.044	.028	0.009	D < C, A, B
L2 learning experience	4.06 (0.82)	3.93 (0.87)	3.94 (0.84)	4.40 (0.64)	6.658	.001	0.019	B, C, A < D
Perceived importance of contact	4.16 (0.72)	4.05 (0.77)	4.06 (0.81)	4.25 (0.63)	2.391	.067		ns
L2 autonomy								
Autonomous use of technology	4.15 (0.85)	3.98 (0.95)	3.90 (0.95)	4.30 (0.74)	6.257	.001	0.018	C < A; B < D
Autonomous learning behavior	3.73 (0.77)	3.56 (0.77)	3.37 (0.81)	3.91 (0.69)	14.818	.001	0.041	C < B < A < D
L2 emotions								
Enjoyment	4.10 (0.63)	3.96 (0.70)	3.95 (0.66)	4.39 (0.51)	9.976	.001	0.028	C, B, A < D
Hope	4.34 (0.61)	4.30 (0.61)	4.27 (0.60)	4.41 (0.47)	1.295	.275		ns
Pride	3.89 (0.98)	3.79 (0.92)	3.71 (0.96)	4.08 (0.77)	3.466	.016	0.010	C, B < D
Curiosity	3.54 (0.79)	3.46 (0.79)	3.42 (0.77)	4.01 (0.64)	10.384	.001	0.029	C, B, A < D
Anxiety	2.63 (0.81)	2.69 (0.81)	2.62 (0.86)	2.56 (0.77)	0.710	.546		ns
Boredom	2.00 (0.78)	2.12 (0.81)	2.10 (0.77)	1.57 (0.50)	9.980	.001	0.028	D < A, C, B
Apathy	1.92 (0.84)	1.96 (0.91)	1.94 (0.91)	1.36 (0.49)	8.815	.001	0.004	D < A, C, B
Confusion	2.51 (0.86)	2.63 (0.90)	2.56 (0.83)	2.56 (0.92)	1.195	.310		ns
Shame	2.74 (0.99)	2.79 (0.92)	2.64 (1.04)	2.68 (0.99)	1.198	.309		ns
L2 self-efficacy								
Self-efficacy	4.07 (0.81)	4.02 (0.82)	3.92 (0.92)	4.24 (0.74)	2.986	.030	0.008	C, B < D

Note: [1]Post-hoc test used: Duncan. Number of lessons: A = 2–3, B = 4, C = 5, D = 6–7. ns = no significant difference.
The responses of those participants who did not reveal the weekly number of their English lessons are excluded from the analysis.

the post-hoc comparison column that students with the highest number of weekly lessons (i.e. 6–7) scored significantly more favorably on almost all the observed variables than students with a lower number of lessons (i.e. 2–5), although the magnitude of effect sizes warrants caution when interpreting these findings (Cohen et al., 2018). The group of learners with the highest number of classes seemed to be the least susceptible to outside pressures, reflected by the ought-to L2 self, and they reported the highest levels of enjoyment, pride and curiosity, together with the lowest levels of boredom and apathy. They displayed the highest levels of both autonomy measures and were the most self-efficacious. It is intriguing to see that in their case the high exposure to English classes, i.e. 6–7 lessons a week, did not affect their motivation negatively, which is a trend we observed in the case of those learners who learnt English as a first L2 (see Table 5.4). This suggests that those students with the largest number of weekly English lessons were not only likely to have chosen to have that many lessons of their own free will, because of being intrinsically motivated (Ryan & Deci, 2020), but they were also exposed to a classroom environment that was conducive to their L2 learning (Ryan & Deci, 2020), which can mean activities and topics matching the students' interests and competence levels.

5.1.5 Differences according to school year

Table 5.6 exhibits the results of the ANOVA test that featured school year as the independent scale. We found significant differences in the case of all constructs except L2 autonomy. Where there was a significant difference, students in the lower grades (i.e. 9 and/or 10) tended to score more favorably than those in the upper grades (i.e. 11 and/or 12). This suggests that in the lower years of high schools, Hungarian L2 learners of English are likely to be more motivated and experience positive emotions to a greater degree and negative emotions (with the exception of confusion) to a lesser degree than in the upper grades. Nevertheless, based on the effect sizes, the magnitudes of these differences appeared to be negligible (i.e. close to 0.01; Cohen et al., 2018). Despite the small effect sizes, these findings reinforce the results of an earlier study conducted among 7th and 11th graders in Hungary, where 11th graders were consistently found to report lower motivation, autonomy and enjoyment and higher boredom and apathy (Albert et al., 2018b). We can probably attribute the differences found on the various emotion-related scales to the instructed L2 learning context given the context-dependent nature of emotions (Shao et al., 2019); that is, it seems that as students advance in their studies in Hungarian high schools, the activities and topics presented to them during English classes are increasingly less likely to suit their interests and competence levels. As such, these

Table 5.6 Differences according to school year

Scales	School year				F	p	η^2	Post-hoc comparison[a]
	9 (n = 410)	10 (n = 341)	11 (n = 283)	12 (n = 94)				
	M (SD)							
L2 motivation								
Motivated learning behavior	4.04 (0.70)	4.00 (0.72)	3.81 (0.79)	3.77 (0.77)	7.630	.001	0.020	12, 11 < 10, 9
Ideal L2 self	4.53 (0.60)	4.55 (0.63)	4.48 (0.74)	4.39 (0.76)	1.750	.155		
Ought-to L2 self	3.92 (0.66)	3.96 (0.77)	3.91 (0.75)	3.83 (0.73)	0.843	.470		
L2 learning experience	4.07 (0.80)	4.03 (0.86)	3.93 (0.80)	3.91 (0.88)	2.171	.090		
Perceived importance of contact	4.09 (0.75)	4.19 (0.73)	4.02 (0.77)	4.02 (0.79)	3.278	.020	0.009	12, 11 < 10
L2 autonomy								
Autonomous use of technology	4.00 (0.95)	4.09 (0.88)	4.06 (0.91)	4.20 (0.83)	1.501	.213		
Autonomous learning behavior	3.61 (0.77)	3.60 (0.77)	3.53 (0.83)	3.55 (0.84)	0.777	.507		
L2 emotions								
Enjoyment	4.08 (0.65)	4.06 (0.71)	3.93 (0.61)	3.93 (0.67)	3.840	.009	0.010	12, 11 < 10, 9
Hope	4.32 (0.60)	4.38 (0.54)	4.24 (0.63)	4.29 (0.63)	2.633	.049	0.007	11 < 10
Pride	3.83 (0.94)	3.91 (0.92)	3.77 (0.98)	3.85 (0.80)	1.265	.285		
Curiosity	3.62 (0.74)	3.53 (0.83)	3.34 (0.75)	3.41 (0.81)	8.130	.001	0.021	11 < 10 < 9; 12 < 9
Anxiety	2.66 (0.85)	2.54 (0.76)	2.74 (0.83)	2.59 (0.87)	3.233	.022	0.009	10 < 11
Boredom	1.87 (0.68)	2.02 (0.82)	2.30 (0.78)	2.25 (0.76)	19.995	.001	0.051	9 < 10 < 12, 11
Apathy	1.80 (0.84)	1.83 (0.84)	2.08 (0.89)	1.98 (0.95)	7.192	.001	0.019	9 < 12 < 11; 10 < 11
Confusion	2.63 (0.88)	2.49 (0.81)	2.61 (0.88)	2.28 (0.89)	5.374	.001	0.014	12 < 10, 11, 9
Shame	2.78 (0.99)	2.69 (0.94)	2.73 (1.04)	2.64 (0.96)	0.786	.502		
L2 self-efficacy								
Self-efficacy	3.96 (0.85)	4.14 (0.78)	3.97 (0.84)	4.21 (0.81)	4.774	.003	.012	9, 11 < 10, 12

Note: [a]Post-hoc test used: Duncan.
The responses of those participants who did not reveal their school year are excluded from the analysis.

results correspond to what we have found in relation to the order of L2 acquisition for English, in which case the length of time spent in an instructed L2 setting also had a negative effect on students' emotional experiences. As to the differences observed on the L2 motivation-related scales, we can put forward a similar argument, since L2 motivation is also known for its context-dependence (Dörnyei & Ushioda, 2011). More specifically, the decline in L2 learners' motivation across the high school years might be explained by contextual features, such as the quality of the classroom environment and the exam-centeredness of the Hungarian public education system (Öveges & Csizér, 2018), a result of which is that students in the upper years are under growing pressure to obtain a language exam and pass the school-leaving L2 exam successfully so as to be able to continue their studies at a desired tertiary-level institution. The two scales where 12th graders fared more favorably might also be in connection with approaching the school leaving exam, since higher levels of self-efficacy beliefs and a lower sense of confusion are probably much needed for successful exam completion.

5.1.6 Differences according to region

We ran another ANOVA test to see if there were any differences in Hungarian high school EFL learners' profiles regarding the geographical region in which they were attending high school. As can be seen in Table 5.7, we detected significant differences in all constructs except L2 self-efficacy. The post-hoc comparison column of Table 5.7 tells us that whenever there was a significant difference, students from Central Hungary scored less favorably than those from the western or eastern part of the country (except on L2 anxiety, in which case there was no difference between Central and Eastern Hungarian students). This implies that high school EFL learners living in Budapest were less motivated, less autonomous, and experienced positive emotions to a lesser extent and negative emotions to a larger extent compared to students in Western and Eastern Hungary. It needs to be mentioned though that, according to the effect sizes, the observed differences were either unimportant or moderately meaningful (Cohen et al., 2018). These results are rather unexpected in light of previous research (Dörnyei et al., 2006) and the fact that Central Hungary is the most developed part of the country and ranks ahead of Western and Eastern Hungary in various measures of well-being, including education (OECD, 2020). One possible explanation for these findings might be that students from Central Hungary who participated in the study might be more critical towards the English language instruction they receive in public education, and their lack of satisfaction might account for the less favorable results reported by them. However, further research is needed to determine the validity

Table 5.7 Differences according to region

Scales	Region			F	p	η²	Post-hoc comparison[a]
	C (n = 337)	W (n = 442)	E (n = 373)				
	M (SD)						
L2 motivation							
Motivated learning behavior	3.83 (0.73)	3.98 (0.75)	4.00 (0.74)	5.800	.003	0.010	C < W, E
Ideal L2 self	4.54 (0.59)	4.49 (0.72)	4.51 (0.66)	0.688	.503		
Ought-to L2 self	4.02 (0.69)	3.88 (0.74)	3.89 (0.73)	4.313	.014	0.007	W, E < C
L2 learning experience	3.68 (0.89)	4.19 (0.74)	4.10 (0.77)	42.365	.001	0.069	C < E, W
Perceived importance of contact	4.03 (0.75)	4.13 (0.77)	4.12 (0.74)	1.869	.155		
L2 autonomy							
Autonomous use of technology	3.97 (0.97)	4.07 (0.88)	4.10 (0.89)	2.032	.132		
Autonomous learning behavior	3.43 (0.80)	3.61 (0.78)	3.66 (0.79)	8.167	.001	0.014	C < W, E
L2 emotions							
Enjoyment	3.87 (0.61)	4.10 (0.67)	4.07 (0.67)	14.046	.001	0.024	C < E, W
Hope	4.29 (0.57)	4.35 (0.59)	4.29 (0.63)	1.299	.273		
Pride	3.67 (0.98)	3.90 (0.90)	3.91 (0.91)	8.134	.001	0.014	C < W, E
Curiosity	3.23 (0.71)	3.61 (0.78)	3.63 (0.79)	29.609	.001	0.049	C < W, E
Anxiety	2.69 (0.81)	2.54 (0.81)	2.70 (0.85)	4.971	.007	0.009	W < C, E
Boredom	2.36 (0.77)	1.89 (0.75)	1.97 (0.73)	40.976	.001	0.067	W, E < C
Apathy	2.21 (0.88)	1.70 (0.80)	1.84 (0.86)	35.938	.001	0.059	W < E < C
Confusion	2.57 (0.80)	2.49 (0.86)	2.62 (0.93)	2.346	.096		
Shame	2.70 (0.99)	2.71 (0.97)	2.75 (0.99)	0.301	.740		
L2 self-efficacy							
Self-efficacy	3.99 (0.85)	4.08 (0.79)	4.02 (0.86)	1.030	.357		

Note: [a]Post-hoc test used: Duncan. C = Central Hungary, W = Western Hungary, E = Eastern Hungary.

of such a hypothesis and to gain a deeper understanding of this issue: in particular, of the ways in which English classroom practices might differ across the three geographical regions in Hungary.

5.1.7 Differences regarding the time of data collection

Because of the COVID-19 pandemic a fairly large proportion of our sample members ($n = 499$ students) was attending classes remotely and online during the data collection. Thus, we were curious to see if there were any differences on the obtained measures regarding the time of data collection, i.e. prior to and during the pandemic. As Table 5.8 shows, we found a significant difference between students on the overwhelming majority of the measures. While in eight cases the effect sizes indicated small importance, there were six measures for which we detected an effect size

Table 5.8 Differences regarding the time of data collection

Scales	Time of Data Collection		t	p	Cohen's d
	Pre-COVID-19 (n = 653)	COVID-19 (n = 499)			
	M (SD)				
L2 motivation					
Motivated learning behavior	3.90 (0.73)	4.01 (0.77)	−2.503	.012	0.15
Ideal L2 self	4.51 (0.63)	4.52 (0.70)	−0.197	.844	ns
Ought-to L2 self	3.96 (0.71)	3.89 (0.75)	1.542	.123	ns
L2 learning experience	3.83 (0.85)	4.25 (0.71)	−9.253	.001	0.54
Perceived importance of contact	4.02 (0.74)	4.19 (0.76)	−3.867	.001	0.23
L2 autonomy					
Autonomous use of technology	3.96 (0.95)	4.17 (0.85)	−4.033	.001	0.23
Autonomous learning behavior	3.49 (0.78)	3.68 (0.80)	−4.058	.001	0.24
L2 emotions					
Enjoyment	3.92 (0.63)	4.17 (0.66)	−6.449	.001	0.39
Hope	4.26 (0.58)	4.39 (0.60)	−3.840	.001	0.22
Pride	3.70 (0.98)	4.02 (0.84)	−5.915	.001	0.35
Curiosity	3.34 (0.73)	3.71 (0.80)	−8.212	.001	0.48
Anxiety	2.69 (0.81)	2.57 (0.83)	2.417	.016	0.15
Boredom	2.18 (0.77)	1.89 (0.75)	6.302	.001	0.38
Apathy	2.05 (0.87)	1.70 (0.82)	6.964	.001	0.41
Confusion	2.62 (0.85)	2.47 (0.87)	2.842	.005	0.17
Shame	2.74 (0.98)	2.70 (0.99)	0.543	.587	ns
L2 self-efficacy					
Self-efficacy	3.96 (0.84)	4.14 (0.80)	−3.675	.001	0.22

Note: ns = no significant difference.

value nearing or even reaching the cut-off point indicative of medium importance ($d = 0.5$; Cohen et al., 2018).

Interestingly, the more meaningful differences were identified in relation to students' L2 learning experience – one global measure and some specific emotions. These results confirm the context-dependent nature of both the L2 learning experience (Csizér & Galántai, 2012; Csizér & Kálmán, 2019; Piniel & Csizér, 2015) and emotions (Keltner et al., 2014; Piniel & Albert, 2018; Shao et al., 2019). In all these instances, students were found to score more favorably during the COVID-19 pandemic. In other words, Hungarian high school English learners were likely to have a more positive learning experience during remote online teaching and more likely to experience feelings of enjoyment, pride and curiosity more intensively and those of boredom and apathy less intensively than prior to the COVID-19 pandemic. In light of the definitions of these emotions, our results imply that students were more satisfied with the class content and pacing, were more likely to be able to sustain their attention (Pawlak et al., 2020a), received tasks that suited their competences and interests better (Dewaele & MacIntyre, 2014), had a stronger desire to learn new content (Litman & Spielberger, 2003), were less likely to have negative anticipations toward their future achievements (Liu, 2021) and felt more proud of their achievements (Pekrun, 2006) than prior to the COVID-19 era. Perhaps these changes are not independent of the small but significant increase found in both aspects of autonomy: a possibility that is definitely worth investigating in the future. It is likely that having greater control over various aspects of the learning process, and getting rid of the close surveillance characteristic of frontal teaching, might lead to more favorable affective experiences.

While several non-representative studies highlighted the difficulties teachers faced (e.g. lack of information and communications technology (ICT] competence, overburden, exhaustion) during the emergency remote teaching period in Hungary (e.g. Fekete, 2020; Kóródi et al., 2020) and internationally alike (e.g. MacIntyre et al., 2020), our results seem to paint a brighter picture than usual. As such, they correspond to Fekete and Porkoláb's (2020) survey results that showed favorable attitudes toward the implementation of remote teaching in the Hungarian research context both from students and teachers. This positive outlook might be attributed to the fact that data were collected during the early stages of the COVID-19 pandemic, when the novelty of online education provided a positive impetus for both teachers and students. These initial favorable dispositions have been consistently documented, with studies indicating that students were enthusiastic about discovering new platforms and online resources (e.g. Fekete, 2023). However, as the novelty wears off, so do the positive attitudes.

6 Results and Discussion: Teachers' Views of the Individual Difference Variables Measured in the Study

This chapter contains data from the teacher interviews that were related to the ID variables investigated with the help of our questionnaire among the student population. On the one hand, we attempted to shed light on which individual difference variables teachers spontaneously bring up as ones they consider important in their own teaching practice; on the other, we asked teachers their views on the significance of those ID variables we targeted in the student questionnaire and their own role in connection with them in the classroom.

6.1 Individual Differences Taken into Consideration by Teachers

Before exploring teachers' views about specific ID variables that our project focused on, we aimed to shed light on those ID variables that teachers judged significant when making pedagogical choices about personalized instruction in their English classroom. Teachers' responses revealed that what they were most concerned about was whether they had special needs students in their classes, whose needs required catering for. Besides this most frequently mentioned concern, teachers also talked about considering students' personalities, in particular their communicative abilities and general willingness to talk in the classroom; some teachers labeled this as bravery versus shyness/anxiety. They also mentioned students' abilities (referring to cognitive abilities), which were claimed to be a reason for concern both in case they were higher than average but also if they were lower. Some teachers were probably referring to a very similar concept when they talked about students who were either faster or slower than average when completing language tasks. The fourth most frequent category covered students' interests, which according to our respondents is also something the teachers consider when teaching. Finally, there were a number of issues that were raised by either one, or at maximum two, respondents. These included the socioeconomic status (SES) of students (especially low SES seemed to be a reason for concern), personal problems, the specialized track that students attended in the high school, the other language that students were learning, their personal goals, and even ad hoc issues like whether students were ill or absent in previous lessons. What this list of unprompted IDs suggests is that there seems to be relatively little overlap between what researchers consider important and devote serious efforts to researching (see Dörnyei & Ryan, 2015, for example) and what classroom teachers judge significant based on their own practice. Interestingly, as teachers' answers given in response to specific prompts described in the following paragraphs will demonstrate, they do hold firm views about such classic IDs as motivation and even newer ones like autonomy. Still, bridging this gap between researchers and teachers, and establishing a common ground regarding the most significant determinants of language learning, would be highly desirable.

6.2 Motivation

When asked about motivation, it was revealed that it is a concept well known to teachers, together with its indispensable role in the learning process. Even so, a couple of our participants said that it was not their responsibility to motivate students: the students should motivate themselves. There were others who expressed the view that even if they wanted to have a positive influence on their students' motivation, it was not within their reach: they cannot influence it.

In considering how to motivate students, more participants mentioned interest as a central component of motivation and the need to set interesting tasks/games for students. Interest is seen as important by researchers as well: Dörnyei and Ushioda (2011) treat interest as a motivational conglomerate (2011: 93), which was also used by Gardner (1985) when conceptualizing integrative motivation, as well as by other psychologists linking it to enjoyment (Eccles, 2009) and cognitive processes (Renninger, 2009). These ideas are in line with what our participants said:

> It is very important that we have different specializations [in high schools]. These specializations define students' interest and their plans for university studies. And these influence how we plan the 4 years [high school education]. (Alexandra)

Students' interests being woven into other subjects is not a novel idea: this is basically what Content and Language Integrated Learning is built upon (de Zaróba & Catalán, 2009), as well as the characteristics of out-of-school learning experiences when students can use English for whatever purposes they want to, based on their interests. These interests could and should be harnessed for classroom learning as well by establishing links between the two contexts of learning (for some examples, see Henry *et al.*, 2019).

The importance of the role of interest also means that it is vital to maintain student interest, and indeed this was expressed by one of our participants:

> I think that a foreign language, especially English, is indispensable. No matter what, everyone has to speak English to a certain level. If students start hating the language from a young age because of me, because learning English only about vocabulary and tests, then it is the end. I kill their interests and I can ruin their whole lives. I cannot do that. I cannot do that. (Emese)

Some teachers presented the other side of the coin when they found it difficult to understand what students were interested in, and this posed difficulty in teaching. As one teacher put it:

> There is no one-size-fits-all when it comes to English teaching. There are students who collect information [about the English language] and learn English [outside the classroom]. It is always surprising that there are students, albeit not many, who do not. Who do not watch films, who have no interest that they can engage with in English, or who would read [in English outside the classroom] or listen [to English outside the classroom], they only learn English in the English classroom. It is more difficult for them. You can learn a language easier if you are receiving it from multiple sources. (Edina)

It is not a novel idea in L2 motivation research that teachers should use specific strategies to motivate their students (Csizér, 2020; Dörnyei & Ushioda, 2021), but there are fewer research results to establish how teachers can motivate students by creating a bridge between classroom instruction and out-of-class language-use activities initiated by students in their own time and on their own terms.

6.3 Emotions

When asked about the emotions they witnessed in their English classes, our interviewees expressed various views and raised different issues. Teachers identified a number of different emotions, both positive and negative, that they may see in their students. Positive emotions mentioned included love, liking, enjoyment, joy, admiration, enthusiasm, cheerfulness, happiness and good mood, which all seem to signal positive attitudes and overall enjoyment of whatever is happening in the English classroom. Besides these, relatively similar sentiments – a sense of liberation, calmness, interest, hope and pride – were recalled as well.

The list of negative emotions was equally long, and it included boredom, anger, annoyance, apathy, disappointment, suffering, frustration, hate, uneasiness, doubt, fear, stress, lack of interest and anxiety.

Despite the relatively wide range of emotions reported by our 32 participants, our respondents differed in whether they talked about distinct emotions like the ones listed or just referred to students as having positive or negative feelings during their English classes. Interestingly, teachers used a much more limited range of labels when describing their own emotions: they mostly claimed that they enjoyed teaching and had a good time in their classroom, with occasional mentions of negative states like tiredness, sadness or grumpiness.

Regarding the topic of the importance of emotions, there was a general consensus that emotions had a significant role in language learning, in particular emphasizing the importance of positive emotions. Most teachers agreed that there was a need to create positive emotions/a positive atmosphere in the classroom in order to help students progress in learning English. Quite a few teachers emphasized explicitly the motivating effects of positive emotions:

> So it is very important that they feel good in the class, more comfortable, because then they will be motivated and willing to use the language, the foreign language. They will not be frustrated. (Alexandra)

In addition to the motivating effects of positive emotions, others also claimed that monitoring emotions provides teachers with valuable feedback about their English class:

> Well, it's important, it's important for me to get feedback. It's important for them to enjoy what they're doing, so they don't just sit there, doing a boring thing where they fall asleep, so it's important for motivation. But as I'm telling you, for me it's feedback. (Brigitta)

Instead of emphasizing the need for positive emotions, some teachers stressed that avoiding negative emotions might be even more important in language learning:

> But these emotions I think, so very positive emotions… obviously there should not be a terrible atmosphere in the language lesson. But I think ambition or motivation can replace or substitute them [positive emotions] quite well, I don't know. Even if it [the language lesson] doesn't feel like, I don't know, it's not a wonderful, exciting thing… But it's very important

that it's not depressing or scary, because then they won't learn anything. It's like, if there's anxiety in it, it will block them, and I don't think there will be any results. I'm hoping, I'm trying very hard not to make them afraid, not to make students fear language lessons. (Aranka)

These results are in line with current research in positive psychology (Fredrickson, 2003, 2008, 2013) concerning the importance of positive emotions throughout the learning process, and of course they also echo earlier research emphasizing the detrimental effects of anxiety (Horwitz *et al.*, 1986, 1991; MacIntyre & Gardner, 1989, 1994).

Besides detecting the emotional atmosphere of their classrooms, many teachers voiced their conviction that they actively shape the emotions that arise in their classes. Apart from acknowledging their role in setting a positive emotional tone, they also took responsibility for reducing negative emotions, even if those have been created by the students themselves:

So, it's the teacher who controls, who defines these emotions. So that most of the time the teacher sets the tone. So, in a given case... so the teacher's behavior should be so that students are not afraid of her, not afraid to ask questions. And it's also the teacher's job to limit or eliminate peers... peers, I don't know, negative fears or negative emotions generated by peers. That is the teacher's job. (Edina)

Another teacher also expressed the need to act with intention upon the emotions witnessed in a problem-oriented manner, which simultaneously reflects the teacher's high level of awareness and the crucial significance he ascribed to emotions:

Obviously, I have to constantly react to these emotions during the lesson to keep the lesson dynamic. So, I'm always looking for an emotion in the lesson that might be hindering learning, which can be positive or negative. So, there might be a negative emotion, which is an experience of failure, and how can we overcome it now so that we can move on. Or it could be an overly positive emotion, which, let's say, can get completely out of control, and that's why we can't move forward. So, I deal with them in such a problem-oriented manner, and I immediately react, divert, channel their energies in a different direction. (Levente)

It is probably obvious, based on the quotes above, that teachers feel they can and should influence their learners' emotions in their classes. Clearly, the intended effect is always the creation of a positive learning environment and enjoyable lessons:

I think it's the teacher's job to make sure the child enjoys the lesson and the task. I think it's definitely her job, it would be difficult to get through... 8 classes a day, 7–8 classes a day if the student is not interested in any of the lessons, if he's not having fun in any of the lessons. I think that's terrible. (Edit)

Of course, teachers are human beings too, who can have bad days when their mood is rather negative. Besides acknowledging that students are sensitive to their teachers' negative emotions and often act in an empathic and supporting manner when sensing these, quite a few teachers appeared to make an effort to leave their negative emotions outside their classrooms:

So it's like the actors, I think, that they go on stage and forget... but I think we're like that too, that I have a sore throat, I didn't sleep well, I don't know why I slept badly, but you go there, close the door, and then you don't think about it until you come out and sit down, and you go, 'Wow!... My throat hurts'. (Margit)

Based on the interviews, the issue of emotional effects is definitely not a one-way street: teachers are also affected by the emotions they sense coming from their learners, as this description of a high school entrance exam situation recalled by one of the teachers so nicely demonstrates:

When we were examining little ones, eighth-grade students, eighth graders, and at the end of the day, I, for one, would be terribly drained because I would take on their anxiety. So, they would come up, and there would be a panel of three examiners, strangers, before them, and they would have to speak like that for the first time in their life. I take on their anxiety. So being empathetic... I shouldn't be... but I'm not... so we're trying to release the tension, but I'm getting much more tired than I should be because of work. (Edina)

Besides being emotionally draining, sensing students' emotions can occasionally also influence the actual learning process, i.e. the content of the lesson:

What they transmit to me always determines whether the lesson I planned can go as I originally intended. So, I don't at all costs put through them what I've decided. So, if I see that it's not going to work, because the sentiments of the class or the group can be picked up instantly, then I have to adapt immediately. (Klára)

Based on our interview data, the influence of emotions is active in both directions. Thus, the emotions of teachers and students can probably be more precisely described as being in a circular relationship, which is how the majority of our respondents saw it as well:

I think it goes back and forth [between students and teachers]. I cannot imagine a lesson where the students are enjoying themselves but the teacher is bored out of their mind. And vice versa, if students feel terrible in a class and they are bored but the teacher is doing great. This does not exist. (Edit)

As for this circular relationship between teachers' and students' emotions, there is a dearth of research, probably because circular relationships are notoriously difficult to measure. Csizér (2020a) reported very similar results between teachers' and researchers' definitions of L2 motivation: the role of the teacher and interplay between teacher and student motivation was mentioned by almost all teachers, while the conceptualization of L2 motivation among researchers rarely goes beyond the level of students.

In sum, we can see that the fact that students reported more positive emotions in the classroom than negative ones coincides with teachers' views as well. It does not mean that we are seeing an overall rosy picture, as teachers are not only well aware of the possible detrimental effects of negative emotions but also of the fact that they cannot be avoided: they are a natural part of the tapestry of the lesson.

6.4 Self-Efficacy and Self-Confidence

When asked about issues related to self-efficacy, teachers expressed various ideas in connection with students' beliefs that they can learn and use English. One idea that stands out in terms of how many teachers mentioned it, is WTC as a source of both self-confidence and self-efficacy, in the sense that they are linking WTC to both general self-confidence:

> [WTC] is clearly very important. Many students are too scared to speak. But what if they hardly speak in their mother tongue either? (Imre)

Or to specific situations or tasks:

> I have students who speak English beautifully, but they are afraid to take the language exam and they are too anxious to speak. (Aranka)

Self-confidence is most often linked to speaking skills, but there was one participant who mentioned that self-confidence might differ across skills, with a marked difference between receptive and productive skills:

> Our [teachers'] most important experience is that students are too scared of speaking. They rather read, students' listening skills are really good nowadays. But writing... and speaking are difficult. For some reason it is ingrained in them that they should not speak until they can do it without mistakes. (Márta)

This last idea is echoed by many teachers, and they say that they try to encourage students to speak even if students make mistakes.

Teachers are confident that self-confidence/self-efficacy can be developed through learning. As one participant aptly said:

> I think this [self-confidence/WTC] is very important. And this is the reason that I think it is very important to develop strategic competence from very early on in order for students to feel that they can speak, and it is not a problem if they do not know a word or use the wrong tenses, they are not important. What is important is to speak even if you do not know something, still try to say it. At the beginning of the school year, students often say that, 'No, I cannot say this in English,' and I encourage them, 'Yes, you can, say it the way you can' and then they realize that they can speak. And this makes their self-confidence develop well, which is very important, especially when it comes to speaking. (Anett)

Another way to develop students' self-confidence is to provide them with positive feedback, or even more: 'I create situations [for students] in which I know that they will be able to develop their self-confidence' (Edina). Some teachers also mentioned the opposite:

> I say this based on my sister's experiences, who was really, really scared of her own English teachers and felt really stupid in the lessons. She was a good student, still this negative feeling stayed with her for a long time. It was a nightmare... I think if the teacher does not believe in the student, does not think that they are good, this takes a lot out of students' self-confidence. (Aranka)

Developing students' self-confidence is also important, because it is easier to teach those students who are willing to speak in the classroom:

> It is really challenging to work with groups in which the majority of students lack self-confidence. We had one student who passed the C1 language exam with flying colors but never uttered a word. Not one word. He had the vocabulary knowledge but still refused to speak. It was really, really difficult. (Imre)

One possible explanation concerning the lack of students' self-confidence when it comes to speaking is that the Hungarian educational system is very exam-oriented, whereby success in language learning is measured by the language exams that students pass (Öveges & Csizér, 2018). Some teachers told us that self-confidence/self-efficacy is needed for the language exams as well: 'they must be self-confident to a certain extent because it is important for the language exam, especially for the spoken part it is indispensable for success' (Anett).

This is problematic because in language exams error-free language use is expected and appreciated, which is in contrast with everyday language use when reaching the communication goals is more important than the impeccable use of the language. This makes it difficult to have students understand that making mistakes is a general part of language learning: 'if they are afraid of making mistakes, they will not be able to speak' (Daniella). Teachers seem to be aware of this anomaly, but they cannot disregard system-level expectations in which, for example, schools' rank-order is affected by the number of language exams their students take.

6.5 Autonomy

In the opinion of almost all our participants, it was important to use English independently outside the classroom, and there is a need to do so. An illustrative quote is as follows:

> It [autonomy] is really important because when you only have three lessons a week you cannot learn the language. It is not enough to do the homework and learn the words. English is all around us, it is impossible to avoid it. (Edit)

When it comes to using English outside the classroom, one participant explained the role of the family:

> All depends on students' homes. It is on the family, not on the school. The school can contribute to or shape it [using English] a bit, but it is the responsibility of the parents [to help students]. (Margit)

Emphasizing the role of the family does not mean that teachers shy away from the responsibility of helping students develop their autonomous learning behavior, and a number of ways to do this were mentioned. When it comes to this support, one teacher said:

> It is important. In my view, this is the most important role of the teacher. It is obvious that you have to know the different methods or at least some of them. You have to show students how to learn the language, you have to show them different methods and you have to motivate them to use these methods. For example, I teach younger learners how to draw mind-maps, and I let them use them during spoken tests. These help students to learn how to organize their thoughts. Some students find this method useful, and some do not find it useful. It is also important for students to know about themselves, whether they are visual or auditory learners. Or maybe kinesthetic style suits them. It is important to know these things. (Jolán)

Based on these quotes, teachers' views are that learner autonomy does not develop on its own. Students need to know how they learn the L2, and they need to be able to reflect on the learning processes. If teachers have the theoretical knowledge, they can share that with students, which could help the students to learn and use the language in an autonomous way.

Teachers mentioned several ideas regarding how to help students develop autonomous learning behavior. One, as already mentioned, was showing students methods, techniques and strategies about how to learn: 'Each skill has its own strategy. Each type of task has its own strategy. Telling these to students is the responsibility of the teacher' (Imre). In other words, teaching the language and teaching students how to learn the language are equally important teacher tasks. We would like to argue here that it is important that teachers do not only share their own personal journey of learning a language but that they also use their experience of teaching:

> I share a lot of tricks and tips that I have learnt throughout the years, seeing what the usual shortcomings are, to help them to overcome those classic difficulties that I have experienced in my teaching. (Klára)

It is interesting how this teacher continued her argument:

> I teach them these basic things that could work and could be effective. I have to teach them because no one taught me this; I had to learn them during my teaching. (Klára)

What is telling here is that this teacher does not talk about her pre-service teacher education, and she does not refer to ideas that she *was* taught.

Another emerging idea in connection with increasing learner autonomy was the customization or individualization of learning. Some of our respondents mentioned that English is used in various ways for various purposes by students outside the classroom; therefore, students come with a wide variety of experiences in terms of using English, based on their hobbies, preferences and interests. It seems that customization of the learning process should be the rule not the exception, not only outside the classroom but also even when it comes to classroom learning. As one teacher described his practice:

> Students can gain points by completing individual and independent projects that are built on the classroom materials. One example is when we cover the vocabulary of 'house and home', students can complete a short video introducing their own homes. (Levente)

Making learners realize that their language learning experiences can, and should be, customized to their own interests and needs is also expected to raise learner autonomy.

The next idea mentioned by teachers that might enhance learner autonomy concerns raising awareness to lifelong learning. The following coded segment includes a number of issues:

> We always talk about it that students should pay attention to the fact that, when formal language teaching finishes at school, they should not lose their knowledge. Students should be helped to grow in the habit of using English. They should watch movies in English, they should read articles in English, they should try reading books in English, first graded readers then full books. Students have to be shown what to do in order not to lose English. It is another question to what extent they take these pieces of advice seriously. (Edit)

Perhaps it is just our viewpoint as researchers, but what we are sensing here is that this particular teacher differentiated between English inside and outside the classroom. This seems to be drawing attention to the fact that lifelong learning should not be considered as a habit developed after formal education but, rather, that habitual use of English outside the classroom should already be part of formal education (Dörnyei & Henry, 2022).

Autonomous learning behavior cannot be imagined without students being able to manage their own time (Kormos & Csizér, 2014). Interestingly, time-management issues emerged in this context as students managing their own preparation for various tests in various subjects. In the Hungarian system, tests have different weights in the grading system and, therefore, in one teacher's opinion, students always have to set aside time to prepare for tests with a higher weighting. Although time management is considered in a broader sense in autonomy research, since it concerns the extent to which students can manage their time when completing school assignments as well as seeking out opportunities to use English (Kormos & Csizér, 2014), setting time aside for test preparation certainly constitutes a part of it.

Although it is an oft-repeated comment that English is all around us, or that it is difficult to avoid English outside the classroom, some teachers still claimed that, in order to help students develop their autonomous learning behavior, the students need to be helped by showing them how to surround themselves with English outside the classroom:

> I have to show students the possibilities [outside the classroom] from which they can select. What are those safe websites where they can learn English independently? What are the steps that produce continuous development? I tell them my own experiences and what works for me. Maybe personal examples will have an impact on them. (Anasztázia)

This teacher thought that showing students these opportunities might make them more likely to avail themselves of these in the future and exercise their autonomy.

Finally, positive feedback is a theme that repeatedly emerged in connection with a number of topics in the interviews, including learner autonomy. In the case of autonomy, positive feedback was mentioned in relation to language use outside the classroom, and teachers emphasized the need for providing positive feedback when and if a student uses the language outside the classroom. Therefore, our interviewees believed that positive feedback can lead to the reinforcement of autonomous actions and thus eventually to increasing learner autonomy.

In conclusion, it appears that teachers' views fleshed out students' answers in the sense that the teachers put autonomy in perspective and provided ways to incorporate awareness-raising discussions and tasks that can help students learn and use the language on their own. It is interesting to see how teachers reflected on the fact that one size indeed does not fit all. Therefore, it is not only teachers' responsibility to help students but, since students know themselves best, it is their responsibility to learn and understand how they best learn language.

7 Results and Discussion: Student Profiles

In this chapter, we deal with the students' profiles and how, within different groups of students, the interrelationships of ID variables show different patterns. To better understand Hungarian high school EFL learners' L2 learning profiles, we conducted a series of cluster analyses. This resulted in the emergence of multiple, distinct groups of students in terms of four salient aspects of the L2 learning process: L2 learning motivation, L2 learner autonomy, positive emotions and negative emotions. In what follows, we present and discuss the results theme by theme.

7.1 L2 Learning Motivation-Based Student Profiles

L2 learning motivation has been known as one of the most reliable predictors of L2 learning achievement in the field of applied linguistics (Dörnyei & Ryan, 2015; Dörnyei & Ushioda, 2011). There have been numerous studies in Hungary establishing correlational and cause–effect relationships between L2 learners' motivation and other variables (e.g. Csizér & Kormos, 2014; Csizér & Lukács, 2010; Kormos & Csizér, 2014); however, few studies have explored the motivational profiles of different L2 learner populations (see Csizér & Dörnyei, 2005, for such an inquiry involving Hungarian elementary schoolers). This is unfortunate given that understanding different subgroups of learners can form the basis of pedagogical intervention. Inspired by this gap, we set out to identify and to describe potential subgroups of Hungarian secondary school EFL learners according to their L2 learning motivation.

To fulfill our aims, we conducted a cluster analysis. For the construction of the clusters, we chose the following 4 scales: ideal L2 self, ought-to L2 self, L2 learning experience and perceived importance of contact. All of these have been linked to L2 learning motivation by previous research. The first three variables can be associated with Dörnyei's (2009) L2 motivational self system, while the role of contact experiences in L2 learning motivation has been postulated by several social psychologists, most notably Clément (1980). Having completed the steps we described earlier in Chapter 4, we arrived at a four-cluster solution.

Table 7.1 presents the mean values for the four grouping variables across the four clusters, while Table 7.2 demonstrates the percentage of the clusters within our sample. Of the four groups, Group 1 (overall high motivation) and Group 4 (overall lower motivation) exhibit fairly straightforward patterns in that the former consists of students who scored highly on all four variables, while the latter includes individuals with much lower scores – hence the labels: overall high motivation and overall lower motivation, respectively. In contrast, the other clusters portray more complex profiles. The members of Group 2 (high motivation with negative L2 learning experience), despite being rather motivated, appear to have the most ambivalent L2 learning experiences, hence the label. Finally, the students subsumed by Group 3 (internal motivation with positive L2 learning experience) seem, rather, to be motivated internally but not externally, given the high score on the scale

Table 7.1 Results of the ANOVA in L2 learning motivation-based student profiles: The scales used for the construction of the clusters

	Groups				F*	Post-hoc comparison[a]
	Overall high motivation (Group 1)	High motivation with negative L2 learning experience (Group 2)	Internal motivation with positive L2 learning experience (Group 3)	Overall lower motivation (Group 4)		
Ideal L2 self	4.85	4.69	4.47	3.20	523.732	4 < 3 < 2 < 1
Ought-to L2 self	4.37	4.22	3.48	3.04	322.165	4 < 3 < 2 < 1
L2 learning experience	4.56	3.02	4.36	3.47	603.401	2 < 4 < 3 < 1
Perceived importance of contact	4.59	4.13	3.87	3.03	277.042	4 < 3 < 2 < 1

[a] Post-hoc test used: Duncan.
* $p < .001$

Table 7.2 The number and percentage of the participants belonging to each cluster in L2 learning motivation-based student profiles

Groups and their labels	n	%
Overall high motivation (Group 1)	419	36
High motivation with negative L2 learning experience (Group 2)	276	24
Internal motivation with positive L2 learning experience (Group 3)	321	28
Overall lower motivation (Group 4)	136	12
Total	1152	100

of ideal L2 self and the lower ones on the ought-to L2 self and perceived importance of contact measures. In addition, they have fairly good L2 learning experiences; therefore, we decided that the label 'internal motivation with positive L2 learning experience' would best describe this group. It must be stressed that, fortunately, the most frequently occurring motivational profile within our sample belongs to the group with overall high motivation, and the least common one is associated with students who have lower motivation overall. Nevertheless, these results cannot be generalized to our whole target population – a shortcoming of cluster analysis (Cohen *et al*., 2018).

The results presented thus far are intriguing in two respects.

First, the variable, L2 learning experience, seems to occupy a central role in Hungarian secondary school EFL learners' L2 learning motivation in that its quality can significantly alter one's motivational profile. This result points to the interdependence of motivation and the L2 classroom context, thereby lending support to prior research in Hungary (Csizér & Galántai, 2012; Kormos & Csizér, 2008; Piniel & Csizér, 2015). More specifically, the group with high motivation and negative L2 learning experience is proof that, even if a student has salient future L2 self-guides, they may not be so motivated when it comes to the L2 classroom. We can assume that the ambivalent L2 learning experience of the members of this group stems from such contextual variables as student grouping and L2 teaching methods, with which previous inquiries in our research context have highlighted issues (Albert *et al*., 2018a, 2018b; Illés & Csizér, 2018; Kálmán & Tiboldi, 2018; Öveges, 2018; Tartsayné Németh *et al*., 2018); and it might also be closely linked to the emotional experiences of the learners, a possibility we will explore below. This result also contradicts some of our participant teachers' views presented earlier: namely, that influencing students' motivation was out of their reach; and it potentially supports those views on the important role of setting interesting tasks in the classroom learning process. It is important to highlight that the group with high motivation and negative L2 learning experience is different from the group with overall high motivation with reference to their L2 learning experience only. Thus, by improving issues pertaining to L2 learning experiences, the members of Group 2 might become as motivated as those in the group of overall high motivation (Group 1). While previous empirical research adopting a longitudinal design has indeed proved the susceptibility of the L2 learning experience to change, even during the course of a semester (Piniel & Csizér, 2015), our assumptions should be verified by further investigations involving high schoolers.

Second, the data show a somewhat fascinating pattern regarding students' ought-to L2 self in that it was represented to the same extent as the ideal L2 self in all but one student profile. The significance of the ought-to L2 self in high school student profiles could be expected given that they have to meet many social demands in the form of school exams and language exams, which has been well documented by previous studies conducted in Hungary (Albert et al., 2018b; Tartsayné Németh et al., 2018). It remains to be seen to what extent this pattern will be influenced by Act no. 59/2022, abolishing the language exam requirement for university graduates in Hungary.

For a better understanding of the four emerging motivational profiles, we examined how the members of the different groups scored on the rest of the scales. The results of the ANOVA tests are presented in Table 7.3. As can be seen, the four-cluster solution was justified in six instances: more specifically, L2 self-efficacy, most of the positive emotions and two negative emotions. As to L2 self-efficacy, what can be seen is that the group with overall high motivation (Group 1) and the group with overall lower motivation (Group 4) emerged as the two extreme ends of the same continuum and, interestingly, students associated with the profile of internal motivation with positive L2

Table 7.3 Results of the ANOVA: Group performance on the rest of the measures in L2 learning motivation-based student profiles

	Groups				F (3,1148)	Post-hoc comparison[a]
	Overall high motivation (Group 1)	High motivation with negative L2 learning experience (Group 2)	Internal motivation with positive L2 learning experience (Group 3)	Overall lower motivation (Group 4)		
Motivated learning behavior	4.36	3.90	3.87	2.93	190.480	4 < 2, 3 < 1
Autonomous use of technology	4.34	4.01	4.03	3.28	53.439	4 < 2, 3 < 1
Autonomous learning behavior	3.98	3.47	3.50	2.70	125.829	4 < 2, 3 < 1
L2 self-efficacy	4.39	3.81	4.05	3.37	73.259	4 < 2 < 3 < 1
Enjoyment	4.45	3.57	4.17	3.30	217.979	4 < 2 < 3 < 1
Hope	4.65	4.13	4.32	3.64	158.215	4 < 2 < 3 < 1
Pride	4.27	3.51	3.91	2.99	101.330	4 < 2 < 3 < 1
Curiosity	3.99	2.92	3.64	2.85	220.479	4, 2 < 3 < 1
Anxiety	2.53	2.94	2.48	2.73	20.155	1, 3 < 4 < 2
Boredom	1.67	2.68	1.83	2.48	170.052	1 < 3 < 4 < 2
Apathy	1.51	2.55	1.66	2.31	131.445	1 < 3 < 4 < 2
Confusion	2.42	2.80	2.42	2.82	18.345	1, 3 < 2, 4
Shame	2.76	3.01	2.47	2.62	15.871	3 < 1 < 2, 4 < 2

[a] Post-hoc test used: Duncan.
* $p < .001$

learning experience (Group 3) proved to have the second highest sense of confidence in their L2 ability, preceding those who have high motivation with negative L2 learning experience (Group 2). This is probably not surprising in light of the fact that favorable L2 learning experience can act as the source of L2 self-efficacy beliefs by providing mastery and vicarious experiences (Mills, 2014). The same ranking of the motivational profiles can be discerned from Table 7.3 as to the positive emotions-related measures: enjoyment, hope and pride. Finally, when it comes to the negative emotions-related measures, the 4-cluster solution was confirmed in the case of boredom and apathy, with the members of the group having high motivation with negative L2 learning experience (Group 2) emerging as the most likely to experience these emotions most intensively. The relatively low levels of positive emotions and the high levels of negative ones paint a grim picture of the affective state of those learners who report unfavorable L2 learning experience.

Our results have multiple implications.

First, they suggest that the valence of the L2 learning experience in the students' motivational profiles matters when it comes to their L2 self-efficacy and emotional experiences. The former link lends support to Bandura's (1995) assumption that L2 self-efficacy is largely formed based on a person's mastery, vicarious and affective experiences, with which the L2 classroom is replete. In light of the affective dimension of the L2 learning experience highlighted by previous research (e.g. Csizér, 2018; Csizér & Kálmán, 2019) as well as the motivation-promoting effect of positive emotions (Fredrickson, 2003, 2008), the group having internal motivation with positive L2 learning experience (Group 3) outscoring the group having high motivation with negative L2 learning experience (Group 2) on the positive emotions-related measures also makes sense, because students in the former group scored higher on the positive emotion scales and lower on the negative ones.

Second, the fact that it was not the group with the overall lower motivation (Group 4) but the one labeled high motivation with negative L2 learning experience (Group 2) that scored lowest on the two negative emotions-related measures further points to the significance of the L2 learning experiences for the latter group. As experiences of boredom and apathy signal unfavorable environmental factors – such as monotony and repetitiveness of class content and tasks, and lack of challenges (Csíkszentmihályi, 1975; Pawlak *et al.*, 2020b) – these results further underscore the need for pedagogical intervention in the case of Group 2. The rationale behind such an intervention also makes sense based on our teacher interviewees, who claimed that they have an active role in the shaping of the emotions that arise in the classroom as well as a responsibility for diminishing negative emotions.

Next, in order to see the causal relationships between students' motivated learning behavior and emotions, we computed stepwise multiple linear regression analyses to find out whether the nine emotions shape motivated learning behavior differently in the four motivational clusters (see Table 7.4). In the regression analyses, we selected the appropriate models based on the effect size values that the individual scales represented (Cohen's f^2; Cohen, 1988). Based on Cohen's guidelines, we excluded from the analysis scales with too small a contribution ($f^2 < 0.02$). With this, we intended to make sure that the remaining scales did indeed form a meaningful part of the model (see Table 7.4 for the final models). From this, we can see that for those who have overall high motivation, the emotions of hope, curiosity and pride contributed to a high motivated learning behavior. Pride and

Table 7.4 Stepwise multiple linear regression controlling for motivated learning behavior in L2 learning motivation-based student profiles

	B	SE	β	t	f^2
MLB[a] in the overall high motivation (Group 1)					
Hope	0.38	0.08	0.27	4.95*	0.05
Curiosity	0.34	0.05	0.32	7.01*	0.09
Pride	0.22	0.05	0.26	4.76*	0.04
R^2			0.41		
F			73.77*		
MLB in the high motivation with negative L2 learning experience (Group 2)					
Pride	0.29	0.05	0.44	5.81*	0.14
Enjoyment	0.28	0.07	0.31	4.07*	0.07
R^2			0.43		
F			51.09*		
MLB in the internally motivated with positive L2 learning experience (Group 3)					
Pride	0.19	0.04	0.26	5.21*	0.04
Curiosity	0.22	0.04	0.26	6.05*	0.06
Hope	0.29	0.07	0.20	4.04*	0.03
R^2			0.31		
F			62.85*		
MLB in the overall lower motivation (Group 4)					
Hope	0.41	0.06	0.39	7.06*	0.13
Enjoyment	0.30	0.07	0.25	4.47*	0.05
R^2			0.28		
F			52.64*		

[a] MLB = Motivated learning behavior.
* $p < .05$

enjoyment seemed to be important in predicting motivated learning behavior in students who have high motivation with negative L2 learning experiences. For those who are internally motivated and have positive L2 learning experiences, besides pride and hope, curiosity also contributed to high motivated learning behavior. Students with overall lower motivation showed that hope and enjoyment seem to have a role in their motivated learning behavior.

From this, we can conclude that mainly achievement emotions relating to success (Pekrun *et al.*, 2007) seemed to contribute to students' investing effort into language learning, with hope and pride being the most important constructs. This means that those students who experience hopefulness in contrast to hopelessness – which can be highly detrimental (MacIntyre & Gardner, 1994; Shao *et al.*, 2020) – and are proud of their own achievements (as compared to experiencing the emotion of shame, which has a harmful influence on motivation; Teimouri, 2017) are generally displaying higher degrees of motivated learning behavior. Interestingly, these results are not in line with MacIntyre and Vincze's (2017) results whereby the researchers showed that scales related to motivation are best explained by scales related to both positive and negative emotions. From our results, positive emotions seemed to be important in predicting students' motivated learning behavior.

7.2 L2 Learner Autonomy-Based Student Profiles

We were also interested in identifying and describing underlying subgroups in our sample with respect to L2 learner autonomy. While we do not know of any empirical research in the Hungarian context that has profiled L2 learners according to their autonomy, such an investigation is likely to inform the work of L2 teachers and policymakers. This is because of the importance attributed to L2 learner autonomy in the L2 learning process (Benson, 2011; Csizér & Kormos, 2012; Illés, 2012; Little *et al.*, 2017). Again, cluster analysis was carried out to achieve our research aims. We included both the L2 learner autonomy-related measures targeted by our study in the cluster construction process: namely, autonomous use of technology and autonomous learning behavior. Based on the outcomes of our analysis, we opted for a three-cluster solution.

We present the mean values of the two clustering variables across the three groups in Table 7.5, while the percentage of the clusters in our sample is shown in Table 7.6. As is observable, the members of Group 1 performed highly on both the given measures, while those of Group 3 did poorly: hence, the labels 'more autonomous overall' and 'less autonomous overall', respectively. In addition, the students belonging to Group 2 exhibited fairly high autonomous use of technology but

Table 7.5 Results of the ANOVA in L2 learner autonomy-based student profiles: The scales used for the construction of the clusters

	Groups			F*	Post-hoc comparison[a]
	More autonomous overall (Group 1)	Technologically autonomous (Group 2)	Less autonomous overall (Group 3)		
Autonomous use of technology	4.67	4.13	2.59	1400.468	3 < 2 < 1
Autonomous learning behavior	4.27	3.23	2.76	905.074	3 < 2 < 1

[a] Post-hoc test used: Duncan.
*$p < .001$

Table 7.6 The number and percentage of participants belonging to each cluster in L2 learner autonomy-based student profiles

Groups and their labels	n	%
More autonomous overall (Group 1)	485	42
Technologically autonomous (Group 2)	437	38
Less autonomous overall (Group 3)	230	20
Total	1152	100

ambivalent autonomous learning behavior; therefore, we labeled them 'technologically autonomous'. The composition of the sample proved to be as favorable as earlier in connection with L2 learning motivation, with members of Group 1 and Group 2 making up the overwhelming majority of the sample, while students demonstrating the profile of less autonomous overall (Group 3) made up only one-fifth of our database (Table 7.6).

To see how the three emerging groups performed on the rest of the scales, we conducted ANOVA analyses. As is evident from Table 7.7, the three-cluster solution was further corroborated in all but two instances. More precisely, the student profiles created on the basis of the two autonomy scales follow the same ranking when it comes to the L2 learning motivation-related measures, positive emotions-related measures and L2 self-efficacy, as in the case of the variables used for cluster construction. This means that the students labeled as more autonomous overall exhibited the highest level of motivation, were the most likely to experience positive emotions and had the highest sense of confidence in their L2 ability, followed by the technologically autonomous students and by the students who are less autonomous overall. With regard to the negative emotions-related measures, as might be expected the ranking of the three clusters followed a reversed pattern: i.e. the individuals who were less autonomous overall tended to

Table 7.7 Results of ANOVA analyses for L2 learner autonomy-based student profiles: Group performance on the rest of the measures

	Groups			F*	Post-hoc comparison[a]
	More autonomous overall (Group 1)	Technologically autonomous (Group 2)	Less autonomous overall (Group 3)		
Motivated learning behavior	4.41	3.75	3.33	272.536	3 < 2 < 1
Ideal L2 self	4.78	4.49	3.98	143.106	3 < 2 < 1
Ought-to L2 self	4.09	3.85	3.71	26.317	3 < 2 < 1
L2 learning experience	4.23	3.94	3.68	41.095	3 < 2 < 1
Perceived importance of contact	4.44	3.94	3.68	112.585	3 < 2 < 1
L2 self-efficacy	4.51	3.92	3.25	267.988	3 < 2 < 1
Enjoyment	4.36	3.86	3.63	145.624	3 < 2 < 1
Hope	4.63	4.22	3.84	200.334	3 < 2 < 1
Pride	4.34	3.68	3.07	213.059	3 < 2 < 1
Curiosity	3.79	3.35	3.19	65.557	3 < 2 < 1
Anxiety	2.44	2.66	3.01	39.265	1 < 2 < 3
Boredom	1.89	2.14	2.22	19.056	1 < 2, 3
Apathy	1.68	1.92	2.30	42.680	1 < 2 < 3
Confusion	2.22	2.63	3.13	104.574	1 < 2 < 3
Shame	2.67	2.61	3.04	16.234	1, 2 < 3

[a] Post-hoc test used: Duncan.
*$p < .001$

experience anxiety, apathy and confusion the most intensively, followed by the students who were technologically autonomous and by the more autonomous overall.

Our results have important implications. The more autonomous overall group is proof that being highly autonomous both in the classroom and in out-of-school contexts is associated with a more favorable L2 learning profile. This outcome seems to support the existence of the positive feedback loop between the two types of learning contexts posited by Sayer and Ban (2014). The emergence of the technologically autonomous group indicates that being more autonomous outside the classroom is not enough for overall success in L2 learning, as it means a lower level of motivated learning behavior, L2 self-efficacy and less favorable L2 learning experiences, among others, compared to the more autonomous overall group. This, again, confirms the interrelationship between formal and informal L2 learning contexts (Henry et al., 2019).

At the same time, these results also point to the need for pedagogical intervention for the technologically autonomous group, which could potentially lead to a similar learning profile to the more autonomous overall group. As highlighted in our literature review, students' learner autonomy can indeed be developed through training and classroom activities related to, for example, problem-solving, use of literature and translation (Illés, 2012). Nevertheless, as our interview data showed, this issue is more complex, as it is not only about the need to be aware of and foster students' learner autonomy but also about how to differentiate between students, especially in heterogeneous groups, since students use English outside the classroom in various ways.

Finally, the results on the less autonomous overall group also call for pedagogical intervention, not only in relation to the classroom context but outside as well given the low scores its members exhibited on both autonomy-related measures. Luckily, our interviewees seemed to be cognizant of the need to develop students' autonomous use of technology as well, of which raising awareness of the importance of lifelong learning was the most conspicuous example. We think that an intervention of such a kind would be highly relevant in the case of Group 3, as it aligns well with Dörnyei and Henry's (2022) argument that fostering the habitual, out-of-school use of English should be a key aspect of instructed L2 learning.

We also used stepwise multiple linear regression analyses to map which constructs shape the two autonomy constructs in the three different autonomy clusters. In accordance with our previous analysis, we used Cohen's f^2 to exclude scales that may not have a meaningful contribution to our models. First, we looked at the scales shaping autonomous learning behavior in the three autonomy clusters (for the final models, see Table 7.8). Motivated learning behavior seemed to shape classroom-related autonomy independently in the group where there are students who are more autonomous overall (Group 1). Besides motivated learning behavior, enjoyment contributed positively and learning experience negatively to high autonomous learning behavior in those students who are technologically autonomous (Group 2). Interestingly, in the case of those students who are less autonomous overall (Group 3), motivated learning behavior, enjoyment and apathy contributed to high autonomous learning behavior.

When we checked what has an influence on students' high autonomous use of technology, it was revealed that self-efficacy beliefs and boredom both have an impact on this construct in the case of students who are more autonomous overall (Group 1). Besides self-efficacy beliefs, curiosity and motivated learning behavior seemed to contribute negatively to students' high autonomous use of technology in students who are more technologically autonomous. However, in the case of students who are less autonomous overall, self-efficacy seemed to contribute to high autonomous use of technology besides the perceived importance of contact and boredom.

Table 7.8 Stepwise multiple linear regression controlling for the two autonomy constructs in the L2 learner autonomy-based student profiles

	B	SE	β	t	r^2
Autonomous learning behavior in the more autonomous overall group (Group 1)					
MLB[a]	0.43	0.03	0.54	14.08	0.29
R^2			0.29		
F			198.09*		
Autonomous learning behavior in the technologically autonomous group (Group 2)					
MLB	0.29	0.03	0.40	9.11	0.13
Enjoyment	0.30	0.05	0.39	6.60	0.07
Learning experience	−0.13	0.03	−0.22	−3.90	0.02
R^2			0.33		
F			71.38*		
Autonomous learning behavior in the less autonomous overall group (Group 3)					
MLB	0.56	0.05	0.63	12.29	0.27
Enjoyment	0.25	0.05	0.28	4.89	0.04
Apathy	0.12	0.04	0.17	3.48	0.02
R^2			0.59		
$F_{(3, 226)}$			108.94*		
Autonomous use of technology in the more autonomous overall group (Group 1)					
Self-efficacy	0.19	0.03	0.26	5.99	0.07
Boredom	0.08	0.02	0.15	3.34	0.02
R^2			0.09		
F			23.82*		
Autonomous use of technology in the technologically autonomous group (Group 2)					
Curiosity	−0.20	0.03	−0.27	−5.94	0.06
Self-efficacy	0.24	0.03	0.33	7.71	0.11
MLB	−0.13	0.04	−0.17	−3.58	0.02
R^2			0.22		
F			39.89*		
Autonomous use of technology in the less autonomous overall group (Group 3)					
Contact	0.22	0.24	0.31	4.97	0.09
Self-efficacy	0.21	0.04	0.30	4.82	0.08
Boredom	0.14	0.04	0.18	2.93	0.03
R^2			0.22		
F			20.64		

[a] MLB = Motivated learning behavior.
* $p < .05$.

From this, we can conclude that motivation and autonomy are strongly linked, which is in accordance with previous studies (e.g. Csizér & Kormos, 2012, 2014). This is true especially in the case of autonomous learning behavior, as motivated learning behavior seemed to contribute to it highly in all three cluster groups. Another interesting finding is that the lower the level of autonomy characterizing the cluster, the larger the number of predictors needed in the models, which may reflect longitudinal processes involved in the development of autonomy, which we were unable to trace with cross-sectional means. In the overall less autonomous group, besides being motivated, enjoyment and boredom experienced in connection with the English classes were needed to predict autonomy, while in the case of the technologically autonomous group, enjoyment of the English classes and bad learning experiences were necessary. Without having more background information about the specific learning contexts, it is difficult to say precisely how boredom and negative learning experiences might actually contribute to autonomous learning behavior, yet it cannot be denied that negative affectivity seems to be present in both cases and might possibly be held at least partially responsible for the lower autonomy levels found in these groups.

Interestingly, self-efficacy beliefs seemed to contribute to autonomous use of technology in all three cluster groups; however, its degree of impact seemed to be different in these groups. The claim made above about higher levels of autonomy requiring fewer predictors out of the ones measured in our study seems to hold true in connection with autonomous use of technology as well, although more predictors mean better models as reflected by the variance explained, just like in the previous case. Only 9% of the variance in the autonomous use of technology score of the overall more autonomous group could be predicted by their self-efficacy beliefs and the level of boredom they reported in connection with their English classes, whereas the variance explained is 22% in the case of the other two groups. However, additional factors seemed to be at play, since in the technologically more autonomous group the negative effect of curiosity and motivated learning behavior played a role, while in the overall less autonomous group it was the positive contribution of in-class boredom and contact with the English language outside the classroom that mattered besides self-efficacy beliefs. Thus, negative affectivity seems to have a role shaping this aspect of autonomy as well, but clarifying their precise role should be attempted in further investigations. Moreover, although based on the three models, self-efficacy beliefs clearly do seem to have a role in shaping technology-related autonomy, their contribution seems to be somewhat less important than the contribution of motivated learning to autonomous learning behavior.

7.3 Positive Emotions Profiles

We created clusters based on the four scales related to positive emotions (i.e. enjoyment, hope, pride, curiosity). We accepted a four-cluster solution encompassing

(a) students who are less likely to experience positive emotions,
(b) students who are hopeful and enjoy learning,
(c) students who are more likely to experience positive emotions, and
(d) students who are hopeful and proud.

The results of the ANOVA for the clustering scales are displayed in Table 7.9. Based on the Duncan post-hoc test, we were able to establish that these four groups indeed show significant differences concerning positive emotions. The distribution of the participants in each group is presented in Table 7.10 beside the labels we assigned for these specific groups. Fortunately, only 19% of this sample of Hungarian secondary school students is less likely to experience positive emotions, which is in accordance with our qualitative findings of the perceptions of students' emotions by teachers, who mostly claimed that learners appear to enjoy their English classes.

Table 7.9 The ANOVA of each cluster on the clustering scales in the positive emotions profiles

Scales	Groups				F	Post-hoc comparison[a]
	Less likely to experience positive emotions (Group 1)	Hopeful and enjoy learning (Group 2)	More likely to experience positive emotions (Group 3)	Hopeful and proud (Group 4)		
Enjoyment	3.19	4.10	4.65	3.78	623.128*	1 < 4 < 2 < 3
Hope	3.54	4.17	4.77	4.50	458.469*	1 < 2 < 4 < 3
Pride	2.44	3.49	4.61	4.35	1108.138*	1 < 2 < 4 < 3
Curiosity	2.71	3.65	4.28	2.91	697.095*	1 < 4 < 2 < 3

[a] Post-hoc test used: Duncan.
*$p < .001$

Table 7.10 The number and percentage of the participants belonging to each cluster in the positive emotions profiles (N = 1152)

Groups and their labels	n	%
Less likely to experience positive emotions (Group 1)	219	19
Hopeful and enjoy learning (Group 2)	312	27
More likely to experience positive emotions (Group 3)	360	31
Hopeful and proud (Group 4)	261	23
Total	1152	100

Having checked the cluster solution, seeing that all four groups show significant differences in their positive emotions, and having examined the distribution of participants in these groups, it is vital to compare the results of the clusters in light of the other scales (see Table 7.11). In motivation-related scales, the patterns are inconsistent: there are significant differences in motivated learning behavior, ideal L2 self, and L2 learning experience, whereas the ought-to L2 self and perceived importance of contact do not show significant differences in each cluster. In the two autonomy-related scales, the order of the clusters remained the same, but the statistically significant differences are at different places. L2 self-efficacy, along with most negative emotions, shows clear differences except for confusion and shame. L2 self-efficacy shows the same patterns as motivated learning behavior and the ideal L2 self, while boredom and apathy show identical patterns as well, just like anxiety and confusion.

Table 7.11 The ANOVA of each cluster on the remaining scales in the positive emotions profiles

Scales	Groups				F	Post-hoc comparison[a]
	Less likely to experience positive emotions (Group 1)	Hopeful and enjoy learning (Group 2)	More likely to experience positive emotions (Group 3)	Hopeful and proud (Group 4)		
Motivated learning behavior	3.17	3.83	4.50	3.97	234.648*	1 < 2 < 4 < 3
Ideal L2 self	3.98	4.45	4.79	4.66	88.869*	1 < 2 < 4 < 3
Ought-to L2 self	3.74	3.88	4.06	3.96	10.003*	1 < 2, 4, 3
L2 learning experience	3.25	4.11	4.67	3.63	270.752*	1 < 4 < 2 < 3
Perceived importance of contact	3.49	4.11	4.45	4.09	92.704*	1 < 4, 2 < 3
Autonomous use of technology	3.36	3.85	4.40	4.39	95.195*	1 < 2 < 4, 3
Autonomous learning behavior	2.81	3.48	4.13	3.57	195.287*	1 < 2, 4 < 3
L2 self-efficacy	3.12	3.82	4.54	4.37	254.499*	1 < 2 < 4 < 3
Anxiety	3.09	2.78	2.37	2.45	46.307*	3, 4 < 2 < 1
Boredom	2.66	1.84	1.52	2.54	228.277*	3 < 2 < 4 < 1
Apathy	2.72	1.78	1.36	2.07	169.444*	3 < 2 < 4 < 1
Confusion	3.12	2.79	2.21	2.28	81.174*	3, 4 < 2 < 1
Shame	2.99	2.82	2.64	2.50	11.839*	4, 3 < 2 < 1

[a] Post-hoc test used: Duncan.
* $p < .001$

The students who are less likely to experience positive emotions seemed to be the least motivated, least autonomous and the least self-efficacious, and they showed the most intensive experiences of negative emotions. The negative characteristics displayed by this group again highlight the importance of experiencing positive emotions, as also indicated by our teacher participants. This is especially striking if we compare the group of students who are less likely to experience positive emotions with the members of the group who are generally more likely to experience positive emotions. Members of the latter group display diametrically opposite tendencies to the less likely to experience positive emotions group, meaning that they are the most motivated, the most autonomous and the most self-efficacious, and they report the lowest levels of negative emotion. These findings lend additional support to Fredrickson's (2003, 2008) broaden-and-build theory stating that positive emotions contribute to an individual's psychological resources.

Besides these two extremes, it is also interesting to examine the tendencies of the two other groups: Group 2, labeled as 'Hopeful and enjoy learning', with hopeful students who claim to enjoy the learning process, and Group 4, labeled as 'Hopeful and proud', who are also hopeful but are also proud of their achievements. These groups occupy the middle positions between the students who are less likely to experience positive emotions (Group 1) and the students who are more likely to experience positive emotions (Group 3). Overall, it seems that having a higher level of pride might be more advantageous, since members of the hopeful and proud group (Group 4) appear to exhibit higher levels of motivated learning behavior and stronger ideal L2 self than the group labeled as hopeful and enjoy learning (Group 2); and their autonomous use of technology and self-efficacy beliefs are also higher. They also experience less anxiety, confusion and shame than those students who enjoy language learning more. There are scales where students in the hopeful and enjoys learning group performed better than students in the hopeful and proud group, which means that enjoyment appears to be more favorable considering L2 learning experience, apathy and boredom.

Regarding which emotion should be the target of pedagogical intervention, hope appears an obvious choice, since its level is relatively high in three out of the four clusters identified (hopeful and enjoy learning, more likely to experience positive emotions, hopeful and proud), so it seems as if the presence of hope was a precondition of experiencing positive emotions in connection with language learning. The significance of the emotion of hope, which is a future-oriented emotion, is also theoretically plausible, since the ideal L2 self, which represents the positive future self-image of language learners, has been found consistently to be an important motivator (Boo *et al.*, 2015), and its links with hope appear to be quite obvious. Apart from hope, there is of course reason to argue for the importance of all the remaining positive emotions. The more likely to experience positive emotions group whose members display very favorable characteristics on all the remaining scales exhibit high levels of curiosity, whereas the distinctive emotion of pride in the hopeful and proud group appears to be associated with high levels of motivation, autonomy and self-efficacy. Finally, high levels of enjoyment displayed by the hopeful and enjoy learning group seem to be linked to positive learning experiences.

7.4 Negative Emotions Profiles

We opted for a three-cluster solution in negative emotions (i.e. anxiety, boredom, apathy, confusion, shame) including (a) students who are more likely to experience negative emotions, (b) students who are less likely to experience negative emotions and (c) students who have higher activating (anxiety, shame and confusion) and lower deactivating (boredom and apathy) negative emotions. The Duncan post-hoc test of the ANOVA on the clustering scales indicates that there are significant differences in the negative emotions experienced by these three groups (see Table 7.12). The number and percentage of the participants is displayed in Table 7.13 next to the assigned names of the groups: we can

Table 7.12 The ANOVA of each cluster on the clustering scales in the negative emotions profiles

Scales	Groups			F	Post-hoc comparison[a]
	More likely to experience negative emotions (Group 1)	Less likely to experience negative emotions Group 2)	Higher activating and lower deactivating negative emotions (Group 3)		
Anxiety	3.35	1.99	2.95	569.028*	2 < 3 < 1
Boredom	2.68	2.00	1.65	193.221*	3 < 2 < 1
Apathy	2.96	1.63	1.44	588.237*	3 < 2 < 1
Confusion	3.27	2.00	2.75	319.813*	2 < 3 < 1
Shame	3.43	1.89	3.27	656.982*	2 < 3 < 1

[a] Post-hoc test used: Duncan.
*$p < .001$

Table 7.13 The number and percentage of the participants belonging to each cluster in the negative emotions profiles ($N = 1152$)

Groups and their labels	n	%
More likely to experience negative emotions (Group 1)	285	25
Less likely to experience negative emotions (Group 2)	492	43
Higher activating and lower deactivating negative emotions (Group 3)	375	32
Total	1152	100

see that 43% of this sample is less likely to experience negative emotions; the mean value of negative emotions is around or below 2 in this group. However, it is also apparent from the results shown in Table 7.12 that those students who are less likely to experience negative emotions overall (Group 2) still experience higher levels of the deactivating emotions of boredom and apathy (Pekrun et al., 2007) when compared to the cluster group with higher negative activating emotions (Group 3).

Next, we checked the results of each cluster with regard to the other scales (Table 7.14). Except for the ideal L2 self and the ought-to L2 self, all motivation-related scales show significant differences. It is noteworthy that autonomy-related scales show different patterns, and students grouped based on their negative emotional profiles tend to differ significantly in their autonomous use of technology only. Interestingly, L2 self-efficacy, hope and pride show significant differences with the same patterns, while enjoyment and curiosity display a different order as compared to the other emotion-related scales. These results may possibly be explained by the specificity of response patterns linked to negative emotions (Fredrickson, 2003, 2008).

Table 7.14 The ANOVA of each cluster on the remaining scales in the negative emotions profiles

Scales	Groups			F	Post-hoc comparison[a]
	More likely to experience negative emotions (Group 1)	Less likely to experience negative emotions (Group 2)	Higher activating and lower deactivating negative emotions (Group 3)		
Motivated learning behavior	3.59	4.01	4.12	48.188*	1 < 2 < 3
Ideal L2 self	4.34	4.59	4.55	13.944*	1 < 3, 2
Ought-to L2 self	4.02	3.79	4.04	16.211*	2 < 1, 3
L2 learning experience	3.33	4.16	4.34	176.579*	1 < 2 < 3
Perceived importance of contact	3.94	4.08	4.23	12.242*	1 < 2 < 3
Autonomous use of technology	3.64	4.34	3.98	61.436*	1 < 3 < 2
Autonomous learning behavior	3.21	3.68	3.71	43.049*	1 < 2, 3
L2 self-efficacy	3.41	4.41	4.02	165.620*	1 < 3 < 2
Enjoyment	3.56	4.11	4.27	122.415*	1 < 2 < 3
Hope	3.88	4.50	4.40	127.576*	1 < 3 < 2
Pride	3.15	4.13	3.98	127.249*	1 < 3 < 2
Curiosity	2.99	3.52	3.87	123.694*	1 < 2 < 3

[a] Post hoc test used: Duncan.
*p < .001

On the whole, those students who are more likely to experience negative emotions seemed to show the lowest levels of motivation, autonomy and positive emotions. This is in line with the results of earlier studies that associated anxiety (MacIntyre & Gardner, 1994; Saito et al., 2018), shame (Teimouri, 2017) and boredom (Shao et al., 2020) with negative outcomes. An exception to this is the ought-to L2 self scale, where those students who seemed to be less likely to experience negative emotions had the lowest mean. Perhaps this points to an association between sensitivity to external pressures and experiencing the intensity of negative emotions in the sense that those learners who were less likely to experience negative emotions displayed the lowest level of the ought-to L2 self, embodying social pressures deriving from the milieu.

Despite the tendency of Group 1, whose members were more likely to experience negative emotions, to be associated with low levels of motivation, autonomy, motivation, self-efficacy and positive emotions, the opposite cannot be said for Group 2, whose members were less likely to experience negative emotions. As regards motivation, belonging to Group 3, the group whose members were characterized by higher levels of activating and lower levels of deactivating emotions appears to be more favorable, since reporting higher levels of the negative activating emotions of anxiety, shame and confusion was associated with higher levels of motivated behavior, better learning experiences and higher perceived importance of contact. These findings seem to contradict earlier studies that associated anxiety (MacIntyre & Gardner, 1994; Saito et al., 2018) with lower performance and shame (Teimouri, 2017) with lower levels of motivation.

A different picture emerges regarding the autonomous use of technology and L2 self-efficacy beliefs, in their case belonging to Group 2, that is, being less likely to experience negative emotions seemed to be liked to higher levels on these constructs. The same is true for hope and pride, meaning that those less likely to experience negative emotions were more hopeful and prouder, while higher levels of enjoyment and curiosity were reported by those experiencing higher levels of activating and lower levels of deactivating negative emotions.

When attempting to identify points of pedagogical intervention, one possible route to follow could be trying to reduce negative emotions, since their lower levels seem to be associated with higher levels of autonomy and self-efficacy and stronger positive emotions of hope and pride. However, the results of the motivation scales clearly show that the presence of negative activating emotions is linked to higher scores on the majority of the motivation scales, which is a finding that seems to contradict the results of previous studies about the harmful effects of anxiety and shame (MacIntyre & Gardner, 1994; Teimouri, 2017). Still, it is questionable what benefits increasing motivation through negative emotions might bear in the long run, since it is the group of learners who are less likely to experience negative emotions (Group 2) that was found to be more autonomous and more self-efficacious, as stated earlier.

7.5 Results of the Cross-Tabulations: Analyzing the Interrelationships of the Different Learner Profiles

In order to be able to make sense of the complexity of the relationships within the 14 clusters, we tried to simplify the picture by creating and analyzing contingency tables (cross-tabulations). In these cross-tabulations, we included information regarding the counts (distribution of participants or cases) and their percentages regarding all the clusters belonging to one construct (motivation, autonomy, positive emotions and negative emotions). These cross-tabulations also display the result of the chi-square test related to the specific scales and Cramer's V value. The adjusted standardized residuals represent whether the counts in the cells of the contingency tables are significantly different from the expected value (>2.0 and < −2.0 are considered to be significant; Field, 2018).

To recap the assigned labels for each cluster: altogether, there are four motivational groups:

(a) overall higher motivation,
(b) high motivation with negative learning experience,
(c) internally motivated with positive classroom experience, and
(d) overall lower motivation.

As regards autonomy, there are three groups:

(a) more autonomous overall,
(b) technologically autonomous, and
(c) less autonomous overall.

Finally, there are four positive emotions groups:

(a) less likely to experience positive emotions,
(b) hopeful and enjoy learning,
(c) more likely to experience positive emotions, and
(d) hopeful and proud;

and three negative emotions groups:

(a) more likely to experience negative emotions,
(b) less likely to experience negative emotions, and
(c) higher activating/lower deactivating negative emotions.

Table 7.15 Cross-tabulation of the motivational clusters and the autonomy clusters (N = 1152)

Motivational groups	Autonomy groups (%)			Total	$\chi^2(df)$	Cramer's V
	More autonomous overall	Technologically autonomous	Less autonomous overall			
Overall higher motivation	277 (57)	108 (25)	34 (15)	419		
Adjusted residuals	12.5	–6.4	–7.6			
High motivation with negative learning experience	96 (20)	118 (27)	62 (27)	276		
Adjusted residuals	–2.8	1.9	1.2		237.039(6)*	0.321*
Internally motivated with positive classroom experience	102 (21)	156 (36)	63 (27)	321		
Adjusted residuals	–4.4	4.6	–.2			
Overall lower motivation	10 (2)	55 (12)	71 (31)	136		
Adjusted residuals	–8.7	.6	10.0			
Total	485 (100)	437 (100)	230 (100)	1152		

*p < .001

In the following subsections, we will analyze the relationship between these pairs of groups: motivation and autonomy, motivation and positive emotions, motivation and negative emotions, autonomy and positive emotions, autonomy and negative emotions and finally, positive emotions and negative emotions.

To start with, Table 7.15 presents the relationship between the motivational groups and the autonomy groups where Cramer's V signaled an association of medium strength, indicating an uneven distribution within the table (Cohen, 1988; Rea & Parker, 2014). Because we decided to include column percentages in our table, we analyze the distribution in the cells by selecting a column first and then reading the percentages in the different rows in order to detect uneven distributions indicated by the adjusted standardized residuals (>2.0 or <–2.0) according to Field (2018). Based on the distributional frequencies, it is apparent that students who are overall more autonomous are more likely to display overall high motivation and quite unlikely to show overall low motivation, providing further support to the hypothesized link between motivation and autonomy (Csizér & Kormos, 2012, 2014). The same association is confirmed by looking at the cells in the third column of the autonomy groups, where the majority of those in the less autonomous cluster can be found in the overall low motivation cell, and only 15% of students belonging to this cluster can be characterized by overall high motivation.

The distribution of the technologically autonomous group in the second column of the autonomy groups also shows interesting tendencies: A relatively high percentage (36%) of the learners belonging to this group tend to be internally motivated with positive learning experience, but their number in the overall higher motivation cell is lower than expected. Therefore, students' autonomous use of technology seems to be linked to a distinct motivation profile where external pressures and the expectations of the social context do not seem to matter that much.

In the following analysis, we looked at motivational groups and positive emotions groups, and, as can be seen in Table 7.16, Cramer's

Table 7.16 Cross-tabulation of the motivational clusters and the positive emotions clusters (N = 1152)

Motivational groups	Positive emotions groups (%)				Total	$\chi^2(df)$	Cramer's V
	Less likely to experience positive emotions	Hopeful and enjoy learning	More likely to experience positive emotions	Hopeful and proud			
Overall high motivation	14 (6)	104 (33)	243 (68)	58 (22)	419		
Adjusted residuals	−10.2	−1.3	14.8	−5.4			
High motivation with negative learning experience	87 (40)	67 (22)	12 (3)	110 (42)	276		
Adjusted residuals	6.1	−1.2	−11.1	7.8		489.180(9)*	0.376*
Internally motivated with positive classroom experience	33 (15)	116 (37)	102 (28)	70 (27)	321		
Adjusted residuals	−4.7	4.3	.2	−.4			
Overall lower motivation	85 (39)	25 (8)	3 (1)	23 (9)	136		
Adjusted residuals	13.8	−2.4	−7.8	−1.7			
Total	219 (100)	312 (100)	360 (100)	261 (100)	1152		

*p < .001

V displays a moderate association between the motivational and positive emotions clusters (Cohen, 1988; Rea & Parker, 2014). Students in the less likely to experience positive emotions group tended to be either less motivated overall or to have high motivation with negative learning experience. However, they were unlikely to display high levels of motivation overall or to show internal motivation with positive classroom experience. Learners in the hopeful and enjoys learning cluster were more likely to be internally motivated with positive classroom experience and less likely to show overall lower motivation. As regards students who were more likely to experience positive emotions, 68% of them were likely to display positive emotions overall but only 1% of them belonged in the cell with overall low motivation and 3% in the cell with high motivation with negative learning experience, so they can be said to be the mirror image of the less likely to experience negative emotions group. Finally, the hopeful and proud cluster tended to display high motivation with negative learning experience but, overall, high motivation characterized them less than might be expected. What these trends imply is that there is a meaningful link between motivation and positive emotions, since it was only the group of learners less likely to experience positive emotions who had a sizeable percentage of their members in the low motivation group. It seems that having even a few positive emotions is likely to lead to motivation, although the resulting motivation profiles tend to be different: hope and enjoyment seemed to be associated with positive learning experiences while hope and pride seemed to be associated with negative ones. The link identified here between positive emotions and motivation is in line with our findings from the interview data, where teachers confidently argued for a link between positive emotions and motivation.

Table 7.17 displays the overlaps between the clusters created based on the motivation scales and those created on the basis of negative emotions, with Cramer's V suggesting a moderately strong relationship between these two groups of clusters (Cohen, 1988; Rea & Parker, 2014). While 50% of the students belonging to the more likely to experience negative emotions cluster also belonged to the cluster containing students with high motivation and negative learning experience, the rest of the members of this cluster were spread more or less evenly among the remaining three motivation clusters, although they were more likely to be found in the overall low motivation cluster and less likely to be part of the internally motivated with positive learning experience and the overall more motivated clusters than expected.

When examining the less likely to experience negative emotions cluster, they were more likely to appear in the internally motivated with positive classroom experience cell than expected, and they were considerably less likely to belong to the high motivation with negative learning experience cluster. Finally, 49% of the members of the higher

Table 7.17 Cross-tabulation of the motivational clusters and the negative emotions clusters (N = 1152)

Motivational groups	Negative emotions groups (%)			Total	$\chi^2(df)$	Cramer's V
	More likely to experience negative emotions	Less likely to experience negative emotions	Higher activating/ lower deactivating negative emotions			
Overall higher motivation	45 (16)	190 (39)	184 (49)	419		
Adjusted residuals	−8.3	1.4	6.2			
High motivation with negative learning experience	143 (50)	84 (17)	49 (13)	276		
Adjusted residuals	12.0	−4.7	−6.0		204.215(6)*	0.298*
Internally motivated with positive classroom experience	42 (15)	168 (34)	111 (30)	321		
Adjusted residuals	−5.7	4.1	.9			
Overall lower motivation	55 (19)	50 (10)	31 (8)	136		
Adjusted residuals	4.5	−1.5	−2.6			
Total	285 (100)	492 (100)	375 (100)	1152		

*$p < .001$

activating and lower deactivating negative emotions cluster occupied the overall higher motivation cluster, but they were less likely to belong to the overall lower motivation or the high motivation with negative learning experience clusters. What these results seem to indicate is that the reverse of the positive relationship we observed between positive emotions and motivation in connection with the previous clusters (see Table 7.16) does not seem to hold for the negative emotions measures here, as they do not seem to coincide with a lack of motivation. In other words, it seems perfectly possible to be motivated and experience negative emotions at the same time, and this holds especially true for negative activating emotions. This finding lends support to MacIntyre and Vincze's (2017) results, who in their questionnaire study also identified the negative activating emotion of anger as an important predictor for a number of their motivation scales. However, this result seems to be at odds with the findings of the teacher interviews, where teachers expressed reservation about negative emotions, fearing that they might destroy students' motivation. Of course, questions can be raised about the quality and long-term effects of motivation resulting from

Table 7.18 Cross-tabulation of the autonomy clusters and the positive emotions clusters (N = 1152)

Autonomy groups	Positive emotions groups (%)				Total	$\chi^2(df)$	Cramer's V
	Less likely to experience positive emotions	Hopeful and enjoy learning	More likely to experience positive emotions	Hopeful and proud			
More autonomous overall	19 (9)	87 (28)	260 (72)	119 (45)	485		
Adjusted residuals	−11.1	−6.0	14.0	1.3			
Technologically autonomous	91 (41)	153 (49)	79 (22)	114 (44)	437	334.993(6)*	0.381*
Adjusted residuals	1.2	4.7	−7.5	2.2			
Less autonomous overall	109 (50)	72 (23)	21 (6)	28 (11)	230		
Adjusted residuals	12.3	1.6	−8.1	−4.2			
Total	219 (100)	312 (100)	360 (100)	261 (100)	1152		

* $p < .001$

negative emotions, which is definitely a topic that should be explored further in future studies.

In order to analyze the relationship between autonomy groups and positive emotions groups, another contingency table was created (see Table 7.18), where the magnitude of association between autonomy and positive emotions clusters shows that there is a relationship of medium strength between the two (Cohen, 1988; Rea & Parker, 2014). In the first column of the table, the distribution of the less likely to experience positive emotions cluster can be seen across the three autonomy clusters. What is apparent is that 50% of the members of this emotion cluster can be found in the overall less autonomous cluster, while only 9% belongs to the overall more autonomous group. Those in the cluster more likely to experience positive emotions, displayed in the third column, show the opposite trend: 72% of them belong to the overall more autonomous cluster, with only 6% of them in the overall less autonomous one.

As regards the cluster whose members are hopeful and enjoy learning English, 49% of them are technologically more autonomous, while from the cluster of hopeful and proud learners 44% belong to this group. At the same time, hopeful and proud learners are less likely to be less autonomous overall. The pattern displayed here seems to be similar to what we detected in connection with motivation: positive emotions appeared to be linked with a certain degree of autonomy. As regards the details, hope and enjoyment characterized technologically autonomous learners more, as did hope and pride, but, while enjoyment

Table 7.19 Cross-tabulation of the autonomy clusters and the negative emotions clusters ($N = 1152$)

Autonomy groups	Negative emotions groups (%)			Total	$\chi^2(df)$	Cramer's V
	More likely to experience negative emotions	Less likely to experience negative emotions	Higher activating/ lower deactivating negative emotions			
More autonomous overall	64 (23)	254 (51)	167 (44)	485		
Adjusted residuals	–7.7	5.7	1.2		112.405(4)*	0.221*
Technologically autonomous	112 (39)	191 (39)	134 (36)	437		
Adjusted residuals	.5	.5	–1.1			
Less autonomous overall	109 (38)	47 (10)	74 (20)	230		
Adjusted residuals	8.9	–7.6	–.1			
Total	285	492	375	1152		

*$p < .001$

was associated with a lower probability of being more autonomous, pride was associated with a lower probability of being less autonomous overall.

Table 7.19 displays the association between the clusters created based on the autonomy scales and those based on negative emotions, and Cramer's V suggests a moderate relationship between these two types of clusters (Cohen, 1988; Rea & Parker, 2014). Students who were more likely to experience negative emotions displayed a higher probability to be less autonomous overall and a lower probability to be more autonomous overall. At the same time, the less likely to experience negative emotions cluster showed the opposite trend, its members being more likely to be more autonomous overall and less likely to be less autonomous overall. The cluster characterized by higher activating and lower deactivating negative emotions showed a distribution across the autonomy clusters that was in line with expected frequencies, so the high activating and low deactivating cluster did not seem to be associated with any specific autonomy pattern. Thus, our conclusion based on the negative emotions clusters might be that, unlike in the case of motivation, there seems to be a link between a lower level of negative emotions and higher levels of autonomy.

The most interesting part of the cross-tabulations might be the analysis of the relationship of positive and negative emotions groups, displayed in Table 7.20. In this particular case, Cramer's V shows a relationship of medium strength between the clusters (Cohen, 1988; Rea

Table 7.20 Cross-tabulation of the positive emotions clusters and the negative emotions clusters (N = 1152)

Positive emotions groups	Negative emotions groups (%)			Total	$\chi^2(df)$	Cramer's V
	More likely to experience negative emotions	Less likely to experience negative emotions	Higher activating/ lower deactivating negative emotions			
Less likely to experience positive emotions	137 (48)	55 (11)	27 (7)	219		
Adjusted residuals	14.4	−5.8	−7.1			
Hopeful and enjoy learning	67 (24)	107 (22)	138 (37)	312	282.368(6)*	0.350*
Adjusted residuals	−1.6	−3.5	5.2			
More likely to experience positive emotions	18 (6)	189 (38)	153 (41)	360		
Adjusted residuals	−10.5	4.5	4.9			
Hopeful and proud	63 (22)	141 (29)	57 (15)	261		
Adjusted residuals	−.3	4.2	−4.2			
Total	285 (100)	492 (100)	375 (100)	1152		

*$p < .001$

& Parker, 2014). When looking at the column showing the distribution of the more likely to experience negative emotions cluster across the positive emotion clusters, we can see that these learners ended up with higher probability in the less likely to experience positive emotions cluster and with lower probability in the more likely to experience positive emotions cluster. The less likely to experience negative emotions cluster in the second column displays the opposite tendencies, meaning that its members have higher chances to be part of the more likely to experience positive emotions cluster and also of the hopeful and proud group, and lower chances to be not only in the less likely to experience positive emotions group but also in the hopeful and enjoy learning group.

The trends displayed by the higher activating and lower deactivating negative emotions group are slightly different: there is a greater likelihood that they belong to the more likely to experience positive emotions group and the hopeful and enjoy learning group, while their chances of being included in the less likely to experience positive emotions and in the hopeful and proud group are lower. These findings show that the relationships between positive and negative emotions are intricate, and the presence of negative emotions does not necessarily mean the absence of positive ones and vice versa. Although there is a trend where the higher likelihood of negative emotions seems to coincide with a lower likelihood of positive ones, the lower likelihood of negative emotions might be associated with higher likelihood of positive emotions in general or particular positive emotions, like hope and pride. Experiencing negative activating emotions can also happen in parallel with more positive emotions in general, or hope and enjoyment in particular, which means that positive and negative emotions are often present in the same learner at the same time, as claimed by Dewaele and MacIntyre (2014) with reference to enjoyment and anxiety. Although shedding light on the dynamic relationship characterizing emotions is impossible based on data in contingency tables contrasting different learner profiles, this is definitely a topic worthy of further investigation in the future.

8 Results and Discussion: The Comparative Analysis of Student and Teacher Perspectives

In this chapter, we are going to summarize the conclusions that can be drawn regarding the main ID variables examined in our study based on the student and teacher data combined. First, we are going to offer an overview of student motivation through the lens of the L2 motivational self system scales we used for collecting data from the students and from the teacher interview data. Second, the views of teachers on learner autonomy will be compared and contrasted with our findings from the two autonomy scales measuring autonomous learning behavior and autonomous use of technology. Next, questionnaire and interview findings will be harmonized in connection with self-confidence and self-efficacy. Finally, results of the emotions scales will be complemented by what teachers shared with us regarding the role of emotions in language learning.

8.1 Motivation

The purpose of this section is to summarize all the lessons learned from this study regarding motivation. Our findings are probably novel in the sense that we employed various data sources (student questionnaires and teacher interviews) and different analytical tools (descriptive and inferential statistics and qualitative content analysis) to gain a deep understanding of the issue of English learning motivation in a context we know quite well, and we hope that this will make the section of additional interest to the reader.

As shown by the descriptive statistics, our high school sample was characterized by a high level of motivation. Our learners had especially well-developed ideal L2 selves, while their reported ought-to L2 selves and learning experiences were significantly less pronounced and positive.

Their self-reported motivated learning behavior was also high, and they claimed to deem contact with the English language outside the school setting important, although the level of these constructs was again significantly lower than their ideal L2 selves.

When analyzing our sample along a number of background variables, we found gender differences in our learners' motivated learning behavior and in their views concerning the importance of contact. Girls scored significantly higher on both scales, which are findings that reinforced the results of earlier studies with the same outcome (Albert et al., 2018a, 2018b; Dörnyei et al., 2006; Iwaniec, 2019; Kissau et al., 2010; Williams et al., 2002). Certain aspects of motivation seemed to be influenced by the extracurricular activities of students, namely whether students took private English classes or not. Those students who did were found to exhibit higher levels of motivated learning behavior, stronger ideal L2 selves and stronger ought-to L2 selves. It can be hypothesized that the stronger influence of these future self-guides might, in fact, be responsible for their taking private lessons in the first place, since the ideal L2 self represents a stronger inner drive, while the ought-to L2 self signals social pressures. While students taking private English lessons reported having stronger ought-to L2 selves, students who had six or seven English lessons per week were actually characterized by weaker ought-to L2 selves along with higher levels of motivated learning behavior and more favorable learning experiences. This pattern might suggest that these learners chose to study English intensively of their own accord, and they were probably driven to learn the English language not as a consequence of family pressures but perhaps as a result of their favorable classroom experiences.

Interestingly, we also identified regional differences in students' level of motivation in a way that students from Central Hungary reported higher levels of the ought-to L2 self and lower levels of motivated learning behavior and L2 learning experience, which might suggest that students in Central Hungary feel that their parents attribute great significance to learning L2s, while at the same time the students are dissatisfied with their actual learning experience and thus feel less motivated to take those steps that are needed to learn a L2. This potential disappointment can be hypothesized to be a result of having higher expectations in connection with L2 instruction in public education because of their better economic situation compared to the rest of the country but then these expectations remain unfulfilled. Another possibility is that it is merely the differences between the 11 participating schools that are reflected in these results. Since substantial variation has been identified among the schools in our sample (Csizér & Albert, 2024b), the possibility that we simply happened to recruit schools with less motivated learners in the capital city by chance cannot be ruled out either.

Learners' motivation was also found to decrease over the years, because students studying in lower grades reported stronger motivated learning behavior and attributed greater significance to contact experiences than those closer to graduation. This finding might suggest that learning a L2 over many years might carry the danger of students' losing their motivation as a result of the lengthy learning process (Albert et al., 2018b). Finally, learners also appeared to be more motivated after they switched to online education as a result of the COVID-19 pandemic: data collected after the lockdown showed higher motivated learning behavior, more favorable L2 learning experience and a higher importance of extracurricular contact with the English language outside the classroom. The question that should be explored further in this case is which aspects of this change are responsible for the increase in motivation observable after switching to online education.

This summary of the main findings in relation to the contextual influences associated with the above-described background variables highlights several important issues. One such issue is that of stability and change. It seems that detecting changes in a number of motivation-related constructs – like motivated learning behavior, the learning experience and the importance of contact with the L2 – is quite common, so these constructs appear to be quite susceptible to background effects. The number of significant changes in the self-guides appears to be less frequent, and out of them the ought-to L2 self seems to be the one more easily influenced by contextual changes. In contrast, learners' ideal L2 self appears to be quite stable based on our results, which should probably not be surprising, since the ideal L2 self is hypothesized to represent a future self-image that is probably linked to deep-seated inner drives.

Although the second language acquisition (SLA) literature is replete with motivation theories, these do not seem to play a major role in teachers' conceptualization of motivation in the sense that we did not find any reference to either integrative or instrumental motivation (Gardner, 1985), extrinsic or intrinsic motivation (Ryan & Deci, 2000) or ideal or ought-to L2 selves (Dörnyei, 2005) in our interview data. However, teachers did refer to learners' interests quite frequently, which is present either implicitly or explicitly in all the theories listed. While teachers seemed to agree that interest has an important role in motivating learners, they were divided on the issue of whose responsibility maintaining the learners' level of motivation was. Perhaps, in future investigations it might be worth inquiring about the teachers' role in maintaining learners' interest and the possible ways this can be achieved rather than posing questions about the abstract notion of assuming responsibility for learners' motivation.

Besides interest, teachers also attributed a great role to emotions in enhancing or harming learners' motivation. Based on their comments, the relationship between motivation and emotions is quite simple:

positive emotions increase motivation, while negative ones destroy it. This simplistic view does not seem to be supported by our questionnaire data, which show that despite the fact that higher levels of positive emotions and lower levels of negative ones tend to be associated with higher levels of motivation, and higher levels of negative emotions and lower levels of positive ones are often linked to lower levels of motivation, there are certain negative emotions, especially activating ones like anxiety and shame, that can be quite motivating. This relationship seems to be confirmed by the ANOVAs, regressions and contingency tables presented in the previous sections.

Although teachers did not really comment on links between autonomy and motivation, our findings certainly provide support for the existence of such a relationship, which has already been identified in earlier studies (Csizér & Kormos, 2012, 2014). While our ANOVA results and contingency tables merely display the existence of such an association, our multiple linear regression analyses support the idea that learners' motivated learning behavior contributes to their autonomous learning behavior no matter whether the low, high or technologically autonomous profile is being analyzed. This means that the effort learners claim to put into learning English contributes to their greater autonomy in connection with their school-related English learning activities.

8.2 Autonomy

What appears to be unique in our autonomy-related investigations is that we explored two different facets of autonomy and identified marked differences between them. Although the idea that autonomy has domain-specific facets is certainly not new (Benson, 2001, 2007, 2011), these different facets are rarely investigated within the same study, especially if there are other ID variables that are being investigated besides them. However, the viability of our approach is reinforced by our results: we not only established that different facets of autonomy might characterize learners' groups to different degrees and might also vary according to the context, but we also found evidence that they were linked to other ID variables in different ways.

Our questionnaire results showed that learners in our sample were characterized with higher levels of autonomous use of technology than with autonomous learning behavior, meaning that they tended to display higher levels of autonomy when using technological tools for learning English outside the school context than when managing their tasks in connection with their classroom-related English learning. Gender differences were also identified in connection with these two types of autonomy, and while boys scored significantly higher on the autonomous use of technology scale, girls did likewise on the autonomous language learning scale, which means that male learners exhibited higher levels of autonomy when using technology and girls did the same in connection with classroom-related English learning. These findings offer partial support for previous studies where females were found to be more autonomous (Albert *et al.*, 2018a, 2018b; Şakrak-Ekin & Balçıkanlı, 2019; Zhao & Chen, 2014), but they also indicate the possibility that certain aspects of autonomy may favor males. This might be the case, for example, in situations where technology or computers are involved, which is a preference often associated with males (Jensen, 2017; Muñoz, 2020).

Besides gender, there are various other background variables that we found were associated with significant changes in autonomy. For example, it was found that students who learned English as their first L2 displayed higher levels of both autonomous learning behavior and autonomous use of technology than those studying it as a second L2. Since the development of the quality of autonomy is likely to take time, it should be not surprising that those who studied English for a longer time might possess this quality to a larger extent (Benson, 2011; Illés, 2012). Similarly, students taking the highest number of English lessons a week also displayed higher levels of autonomy on both scales. Since this group of learners was found to be the most motivated, it might be hypothesized that it could have been their high level of motivation that made these learners more autonomous.

Another background variable that was linked to increased levels of both the autonomy constructs was the lockdown of schools and the switch to online education due to the COVID-19 pandemic. It appears plausible that, in a situation where face-to-face teaching is no longer possible, teachers' options for strictly controlling and monitoring their students are very limited, and students need to assume more responsibility for their own learning in all domains. What was especially interesting in this case is that the closing of schools brought about a number of other positive changes in motivation, self-efficacy and emotions, so it is an intriguing question whether these changes only occurred in parallel with the changes in autonomy or if experiencing more autonomy might somehow be in the background of these other changes as a catalyst and root cause. Thus, investigating what benefits increasing the levels of autonomy might bring should definitely be a topic for future investigation.

There were two background variables that were associated with changes in one autonomy construct only: that of autonomous learning behavior. Taking part in extracurricular English classes – which basically means paying for private English lessons – was one of these variables and we found that it was associated with higher levels of autonomous learning behavior. It is an intriguing question as to why attending private lessons is not associated with the autonomous use of technology as well; the reason here might be that many learners might take extra lessons to cope with their school-related tasks better and not for the sake of increasing their level of English *per se*.

The other variable associated with the level of autonomous learning behavior only was the region of Hungary where our respondents attended high school. It was found that learners from Central Hungary reported lower levels of autonomous learning behavior than their peers in the western and eastern parts of the country. Moreover, learners from Central Hungary also reported lower motivated learning behavior, lower L2 learning experience and an unfavorable emotional profile, so in their case this finding might be just a further manifestation of their low level of satisfaction with the English instruction they receive at the particular school where they study (Csizér & Albert, 2024b).

As regards data deriving from the teacher interviews, there was no indication of an awareness of the existence of different facets of learner autonomy on the part of teachers, although they acknowledged the importance of this ID construct on the whole. They saw the biggest role of learner autonomy as ensuring that the learner creates those opportunities that ensure their access to the necessary amount of exposure and practice opportunities needed for acquiring the English language, i.e. autonomy serves as a basis for independent language use outside the classroom. Thus, their efforts seemed mainly concentrated upon the following: equipping learners with appropriate strategies, including strategies for time management; making learners aware of the omnipresence of English in their environment and the possibility of customizing the learning process; and raising awareness about lifelong learning. Some teachers were also convinced that the family should also have an important role in enhancing learner autonomy, although it is not quite clear whether pressures deriving from the social milieu might actually make someone more autonomous despite the fact that such expectations certainly have a motivating role, as the conceptualization of Dörnyei's (2005) L2 ought-to self clearly suggests.

The link between autonomy and motivation is clearly confirmed by our questionnaire data as well. Although regression analyses suggest that the two types of autonomy are linked to different ID variables in a way that motivated learning behavior is an important predictor of autonomous learning behavior, while self-efficacy beliefs contribute to the autonomous use of technology, the investigation of the overlaps of motivation and autonomy profiles clearly suggest that higher levels of autonomy are associated with higher levels of motivation. The existence of a positive relationship between these two constructs has been proposed earlier (Csizér & Kormos, 2012, 2014), and their strong links, which have been identified in this study too, make it quite likely that their relationship might be circular, where motivation reinforces autonomy and vice versa.

As regards autonomy's links with emotions, it seems that higher levels of autonomy are associated with higher levels of positive emotions and lower levels of negative ones, while low levels of autonomy are characterized by a higher level of negative emotions and lower levels of positive ones. This is an interesting finding because the association found between negative activating emotions and higher motivation does not seem to hold true for autonomy, thereby questioning the long-term benefits of motivation associated with, or brought about by, negative emotions.

8.3 Self-Confidence and Self-Efficacy

The greatest discrepancy between our questionnaire results and the teacher interviews can be witnessed in connection with the constructs of self-confidence and self-efficacy. As stated in Chapter 3 (see section 3.5 on self-confidence and self-efficacy), in theory these constructs are clearly distinguishable, since self-confidence refers to socially constructed perceptions about the generalized coping potential of the individual (Csizér, 2020a), while self-efficacy describes a specific set of beliefs that refer to the cognitions of the learner about their ability to perform a specific task (Bandura, 1997; Dörnyei & Kormos, 2000). However, in everyday speech the two are often used interchangeably and are considered synonyms. When designing our study, we were intent on including self-efficacy since it is a construct that has been investigated in our context earlier (Albert et al., 2018b; Piniel & Csizér, 2013). However, when designing our interview guide, we realized that the Hungarian term for self-efficacy will probably sound alien to our participants and thus we opted for using the term that translates to self-confidence in English, which is an often-used and familiar word in Hungarian. As with all everyday words, however, its meaning is less precise. Therefore, in the following section we will use the term self-efficacy when reporting our questionnaire results, since we used Bandura's (1997) conceptualization when designing our scale and use the word self-confidence to report our interview data.

Based on our questionnaire results, our sample can be characterized by relatively high levels of self-efficacy, so on average these high school students were convinced that they are capable of performing the tasks assigned to them in their English lessons. On closer inspection, we found gender differences among our participants, specifically that boys in the sample reported stronger self-efficacy beliefs than girls. This finding is in line with previous results found in the Hungarian context, where, in an earlier study, 11th-grade boys were also found to be more self-efficacious than girls (Albert et al., 2018b). Several background variables were also found to be associated with stronger self-efficacy beliefs: learners who attended private English classes, learners who had 6–7 English classes a week, and learners who learned English as their first L2 were all found to be more self-efficacious for quite obvious reasons. Interestingly, while several affective factors displayed unfavorable trends with the passing of time, 12th graders were actually found to display higher levels of self-efficacy than 11th graders, which is probably a good sign since they are about to take their school leaving exams. While, in contrast with affective scales, no regional differences could be detected in self-efficacy beliefs between learners studying in different regions of Hungary, the switch to online education was accompanied with stronger self-efficacy beliefs that might have enabled learners to cope with the new circumstances more successfully.

Although based on our questionnaire data self-efficacy beliefs appear to change with the circumstances, contextual changes were not addressed by teachers in their interviews. Interview data suggested that teachers saw a strong link between learners' self-confidence and their WTC. Because they were convinced that language learning success is strongly linked to learners' readiness to avail of the opportunities to communicate in English, they attributed great importance to the lack of self-confidence as a major obstacle to language learning success. Low levels of self-confidence were often attributed to fear of speaking in front of others or simply to being afraid to speak. However, what teachers referred to as fear can probably also be labeled as anxiety or shame if a more nuanced approach is taken. This reference to fear might suggest that teachers saw self-confidence as a construct incorporating affective elements besides cognitive ones, although according to Bandura (1997) even the purely cognitive self-efficacy beliefs are hypothesized to be shaped by affective factors.

Based on our questionnaire data, self-efficacy beliefs appear to be important contributors to one specific autonomy construct: the autonomous use of technology. Although teachers did not refer to the existence of a direct link between self-efficacy and autonomy, by claiming that self-confidence is an important ingredient of language learning success, they argued for its indispensability for learning the English language. Even though autonomy is also considered crucial by many, teachers believed that self-confidence exerts its influence via increasing learners' WTC, which is actually in line with MacIntyre et al.'s (1998) pyramid model of WTC. The question of whether WTC directly contributes to autonomy is an issue that was not explored in our study but it might well be a topic for future investigation.

8.4 Emotions

It is probably the investigation of emotions that can be considered the most innovative aspect of our study, since we explored a high number of distinct emotions along with traditional ID constructs like motivation, autonomy and self-efficacy. Our findings suggest that the sample of Hungarian high school students investigated can be characterized by higher levels of positive emotions and lower levels of negative ones. The rank order of the emotions in our sample was the following: hope, enjoyment, pride, curiosity, shame, anxiety, confusion, boredom and apathy. The fact that hope was the most strongly experienced emotion in this sample is surprising in the sense that hope is not a very frequently studied emotion, although its high prevalence in our study would probably justify closer scrutiny of this emotion. However, we also detected very well-developed and strong ideal L2 selves in our sample, which is a self-image with a strong orientation towards the future; thus, the high levels of hope found among learners seem to be justified by it. Despite the relatively high levels of positive emotions, what might be considered unfavorable is that curiosity had the lowest mean value among the positive emotions. On the one hand, in an educational context, higher levels of this important epistemic emotion might be expected; on the other, the crucial role of interest in motivation was also emphasized in the teacher interviews, indicating that teachers attribute great significance to this emotion.

The fact that the means of all negative emotions examined by us were below the theoretical mean of the 5-point Likert scale is encouraging, as this seems to indicate relatively low levels of negative emotions in the English classrooms. Our finding that learners reported higher levels of shame than anxiety might suggest a close association between these emotions as suggested by the literature (Galmiche, 2018), highlighting the strong social aspect of L2 learning. However, it is also possible that it might reflect an educational culture where the shaming of students is an accepted pedagogical tool, although our teachers argued very strongly against invoking negative emotions in their classrooms and seemed determined to avoid them as much as possible. What is encouraging when we look at the order of negative emotions is that we find the negative deactivating emotions of boredom and apathy at the bottom of the list; these emotions are generally believed to be harmful regarding educational achievement (Pekrun et al., 2002, 2007).

When examining associations between these emotions and different background variables, we found gender differences: females tended to report higher levels of most of the emotions explored except for hope, pride and apathy, for which emotions there was no difference between boys and girls. Although several studies have reported higher levels of anxiety and enjoyment for females than for males (Albert *et al.*, 2018a, 2018b; Dewaele *et al.*, 2016; Donovan & MacIntyre, 2004), these results are somewhat inconsistent (Piniel & Zólyomi, 2022). Nevertheless, the fact that a higher emotionality of females has been found in connection with a range of emotions seems to lend support to the claim that either females are more emotional than males in general or at least they tend to report higher emotions than males in questionnaire studies. An intriguing exception to this rule is boredom, which was reported more frequently by males, similar to another large-scale Hungarian study (Albert *et al.*, 2018a, 2018b), a finding in line with the higher boredom-proneness found in males in general (Vodanovich *et al.*, 2011).

As might be expected, contextual differences linked to different background variables were in most cases mirrored by evident changes in emotions. For example, taking private English lessons was accompanied by higher levels of hope and pride but also by more apathy and shame; the former two might be linked to the positive outcomes of these extra lessons, while the latter two might be part of the reason why learners decided to take extra lessons. Also, the most devoted learners in our sample, who had 6–7 English lessons per week, were found to be prouder and more curious and enjoyed their English lessons more, while they were at the same time less bored and experienced less apathy than learners in other groups, which signals very favorable affective experiences on their part. Unfortunately, the lengthy process of language learning seems to take its emotional toll: those learners who learned English as their first L2 experienced more boredom and shame and less enjoyment than those who started English later, because it was the second L2 for the latter. A similar trend could be observed when comparing students in different grades at high school: enjoyment, pride and curiosity seemed to characterize learners in lower grades more, while students in higher grades tended to experience more anxiety, boredom and apathy. The exception here was confusion; 12th graders reported the lowest level of this emotion, which is understandable since, with their final exams approaching, they are expected to be confident rather than confused.

Possible reasons for the differences that have been identified in connection with regional variation are less evident, however. The finding that learners in Central Hungary reported less enjoyment, pride and curiosity and more boredom, apathy and anxiety than their fellow learners in Western and Eastern Hungary is somewhat puzzling, and our hypothesis that students' unmet higher expectations might be in the background of these results will need to be checked in future studies. The need for exercising caution when interpreting regional differences is further highlighted by the fact that we found substantial differences between the high schools themselves irrespective of the region where they were located (Csizér & Albert, 2024b), which might in itself account for these findings. We were also surprised to find that the second half of our sample, who filled in our online questionnaire after the lockdown of schools due to the COVID-19 pandemic, reported higher levels of all positive emotions and lower levels of all negative emotions (except for shame) than did those students who filled in our questionnaire in their school in the pre-COVID era. It is not clear whether these positive affective changes were the result of being released from the obligation to attend school, or whether they can be linked to other changes that were identified by our questionnaire – for example, increased levels of autonomy. It is also intriguing why there was no change in the level of shame when normally it could be expected to decrease in a situation where personal contacts are minimized, i.e. with the introduction of online education. We might hypothesize that, as a result of their experiences in the Hungarian educational system, the feeling of shame might be ingrained in learners to such a degree that the actual learning experience might no longer influence it. Further studies will be needed to clarify these issues as well.

As regards teachers' views on emotions, although they listed quite a few emotions that they are able to recognize in their learners, they tended to refer to the groups of positive and negative emotions rather than specific emotions when discussing the role of emotions in language learning. In this sense, they seemed to have a rather simplified view of emotions, claiming that positive emotions enhance learners' motivation to learn English, while negative emotions erode it. Although our questionnaire data clearly indicate that certain negative activating emotions can be linked to high levels of motivation, this phenomenon was not raised by our teacher participants. What teachers seemed somewhat divided about was whether it is the promotion of positive emotions or the avoidance of negative ones that should be prioritized by them. Besides seeing emotions as important sources of motivation, teachers also claimed that they use the emotions they detect in their classroom as feedback, and they shape and modify the course of their lesson according to them.

Most teachers acknowledged that they themselves have a major role in influencing their learners' emotions, and they attempted to exert their influence in a way that is favorable for the learning process. They also stated that there is an interaction and a close link between the emotions they experience and those of their students. This might be the reason why teachers often feel that they need to hide the negative emotions that are caused by events in their personal lives, although such attempts often fail because of the sensitivity of the students. Many teachers emphasized the interconnectedness of teachers' and students' emotions and highlighted the reciprocal nature of this relationship.

Teachers' views about emotions can actually be confirmed by our analysis of the student questionnaire data: based on the regression analyses, positive emotions – especially hope and pride but enjoyment and curiosity as well – contribute to learners' motivated learning behavior no matter which motivational profile the learners belong to. Despite these synergies in our findings, it is also clear that the teachers raised a number of important issues in connection with emotions that did not appear in the questionnaire data. The most important among these is probably the strong interconnectedness of teacher and student emotions. Embracing the truth inherent in this finding means that ensuring teachers' positive affective states and promoting their overall well-being should be a priority in schools, since teacher well-being seems to be intricately linked to the positive emotions that we would like students to experience.

9 Conclusion

First, we summarize the main results of our study by answering explicitly and succinctly our research questions as well as drawing some conclusions. We then outline the limitations of our study before concluding with future research directions.

9.1 The Main Results of Our Study

Research Question 1: What characterizes Hungarian secondary school students' L2 motivation, emotions, autonomy and self-efficacy?

Based on descriptive statistics, a fairly positive picture emerged when we mapped secondary school students' L2 motivation, emotions, autonomy and self-efficacy. It was reassuring to see that L2 motivation scales as well as positive emotions tended towards the positive end of the Likert-scale and that students scored consistently higher on positive emotions than negative ones. This does not mean, however, that there is no room for improvement. Based on our results, we can see two possible points of intervention/improvement: increasing students' autonomous learning behavior as well as their curiosity. We would like to argue that the relatively lower mean value obtained on these scales relates to the fact that English classes in Hungary are still dominated by teachers in the sense that frontal teaching seems to prevail in many schools (Öveges & Csizér, 2018). The dominance of traditional approaches in English lessons within our own sample is also supported by findings obtained in a sub-project of the current investigation that focused on tasks used by teachers in their language classrooms (Albert, 2022). When asked about their own and their students' preferred tasks along with tasks used in their last lesson, it was revealed that despite their expressed preferences for game-like and communicative tasks, teachers mostly reported using grammar- and vocabulary-focused tasks in their previous lesson.

This leads us to the questions that teachers need to ask themselves: e.g. how to increase students' autonomy in the classroom and how to pique their curiosity. We know that this is easier said than done, and at this point we can only talk about our results. Based on the theoretical overview of the emotion of curiosity, Pekrun (2014) argues that it belongs to the group of epistemic emotions that arise when cognitive challenges are presented to students. There are very few empirical studies in L2 learning on curiosity despite the fact that Mahmoodzadeh and Khajavy (2019) recently developed a language learning curiosity scale measuring both feeling-of-interest (communicative) curiosity and feeling-of-deprivation (linguistic) curiosity. In our study, we developed a different measure of curiosity that relates to classroom learning. For students with a high level of motivation, and also for those internally-motivated students, curiosity seemed to be an important antecedent variable, indicating that what our scale measures might be the feeling-of-interest type of curiosity. Interestingly, curiosity contributed negatively to the autonomous use of technology scale in the case of those students who were profiled as technologically autonomous, indicating a reverse relationship between feeling curious about their English lessons and being autonomous in connection with using technology outside the classroom.

When it comes to autonomy, the two measures employed showed significant differences, with autonomous use of technology having a higher mean value than autonomous learning behavior. We hypothesize at this point that autonomous use of technology might be linked to out-of-classroom language use, while autonomous learning behavior represents students' responses to classroom processes more; it seems that developing student autonomy within the classroom is a worthy enterprise. We think that autonomy does not develop on its own, and it even seems to be decreasing within the Hungarian public education system for older learners (Albert *et al.*, 2018b); thus, it would be important to find points of interventions for teachers.

Research Question 2: What profiles can be established pertaining to Hungarian secondary school students' L2 motivation, emotions, autonomy and self-efficacy?

There are several reasons why profiling students is an important line of research. It is advised to put individuals back into ID research and emphasize what makes students unique instead of what makes them similar. Even so, a balance needs to be established between these two ends of the continuum. By systematically establishing typicality in students' dispositions, pedagogical implications can be fine-tuned. Based on several cluster analyses and subsequent comparative analyses, we have a number of conclusions.

(1) Given the fact that every 10th student seems to have low motivation when it comes to learning English in the classroom and that a further quarter of our participants' motivational profile was shaped by ambivalent learning experiences, it seems that motivation is indeed an issue that teachers should deal with in the classroom. Seeing students' profiles, it seems that ensuring that students experience

positive emotions in their language classes could be the most efficient way to increase students' overall motivation; prompting pride and hope appears especially important in this regard. When looking at the relationship suggested by the overlaps of the motivational profiles of students and their negative emotions profiles, although it is apparent that there are cases when high levels of motivation co-occur with high levels of negative emotions, particularly shame, anxiety and confusion, it is not clear what benefits being motivated while experiencing strong negative emotions might bring. It is not likely to lead to greater autonomy, since despite the strong association between motivation and autonomy, autonomous learners were characterized by the higher likelihood of experiencing positive emotions and a lower likelihood of experiencing negative ones.

(2) We think that there is no successful language learning in the 21st century without autonomous learning processes and hence autonomous learners. Less than half our student participants showed overall autonomous learning behavior; the other half were either less autonomous overall or did not show autonomous learning behavior pertaining to the classroom. Why is this a problem? Less autonomous students are losing learning opportunities outside the school by not engaging in English-speaking activities, and indeed they scored lower on all motivation-related scales in our study, as well as on scales of self-efficacy and positive emotions. Integrating out-of-classroom activities in the classroom and motivating learners to use English outside the classroom as often as possible in ways they are interested in will help the learning process and teachers' work by definition.

(3) Our study confirmed the fact that L2 learning is an emotional business, as only 5% of our participants reported being reserved in the sense that their profiles are lacking both positive and negative emotions when it comes to language learning in the classroom. Comparing students' positive and negative emotional profiles, almost half the participants (43%) can be described as emotional learners, by which we mean that these are the students who are experiencing positive and negative emotions alike. A little more than a third of students (38%) are happy campers, reporting a high level of various positive emotions in the classroom without the influence of negative emotions. About every seventh student in our sample seems to be suffering in the language classroom: they experience many negative emotions without the counterbalancing effect of positive ones. Luckily, their number does not seem to be particularly high, but given class and group sizes in the Hungarian secondary schools (Öveges & Csizér, 2018) each class could have such students. Helping these students could be a difficulty for teachers, although techniques enhancing positive emotions could be helpful, as we saw that there are very few reserved students without emotional dispositions toward language learning.

(4) Regression analyses in the various cluster groups indicate some important theoretical contributions to the field. As models are not uniform in the various groups, teachers' theoretical knowledge needs to be enhanced in a way that takes into account those impacts that are student-profile irrelevant and the constructs that are only relevant for students with certain language learning profiles. In this study, hope seems to contribute to students' motivated learning behavior for both high- and low-motivation students, enjoyment is only crucial for students with low motivation, while curiosity is a high motivator with students of overall high motivation. As for the relationship of autonomous learning behavior to motivated learning behavior, it goes hand in hand with motivated learning behavior, regardless of students' level of autonomy. When it comes to autonomous use of technology, self-efficacy beliefs stand out as defining processes. These results imply that autonomy is a complex notion and that different types of autonomy are influenced by different ID variables. As far as we know, this is not reflected in theories pertaining to autonomy in L2 learning and their impact in classroom and out-of-classroom learning.

Research Question 3: What views do teachers express in connection with Hungarian secondary school students' L2 motivation, emotions, autonomy and self-efficacy?

What is clear from our dataset is that when thinking about ID variables and their roles in language learning, teacher views, dispositions, and possibly classroom behavior, are shaped by their prior experiences and not by their previous education. It is even possible that teachers think that their teacher training education was really a waste of time, and they did not learn anything that could be useful for their work in the classroom. As the Hungarian teacher education system has been reformed several times in recent decades in Hungary (see Chapter 2), without empirical data it is difficult to know the exact content of teacher education our participants might not see relevant, but this issue has emerged in other empirical English-teacher-focused studies in Hungary (Csizér, 2020a). Even so, we think that theoretical knowledge on ID variables would help teachers thinking about students and classroom processes and could inform their teaching practices. We only know our context; therefore, the extent to which our country and educational system is similar to, or different from, other countries and systems is unknown.

Research Question 4: What characterizes differences between students' dispositions and teachers' views?

When attempting to synthesize students' and teachers' views, the biggest obstacle seems to be finding the common ground among different interpretations, which is a difficulty inherently present and directly caused by our research design. In this study, we used a questionnaire to collect data from the students and we interviewed teachers about the same constructs. But is this what really happened? The principles of questionnaire construction call for precisely defined constructs that usually derive from a theory (Dörnyei, 2007). However, when interviewing teachers about the 'same' constructs, their interpretations of the terms we used seemed to be based on their experiential knowledge deriving from their teaching practice and not on the carefully chosen theoretical background applied in the questionnaire. For this reason, the constructs in the questionnaire and interview are never entirely the same. Therefore, the biggest challenge in synthesizing learners' and teachers' views resulted from this mismatch between the theory-based questionnaire data and the experiential-knowledge-based interview data.

Of course, once we come to terms with the fact that our interviewees will probably talk about the theoretical constructs measured by our questionnaire in a less sophisticated and nuanced manner, the results are not so difficult to reconcile. Teachers acknowledge the importance of all the ID variables we set out to investigate (even though they might come up with different ones without our prompting), and they even see many of them linked to each other in the same ways that we identified using statistical procedures. Despite some discrepancies, which were discussed in detail in Chapter 8, where we synthesized our results from the student questionnaires and teacher interviews, our findings from the two datasets can be seen as complementary rather than contrasting, drawing attention to such evident truths like the impossibility of creating a more favorable emotional atmosphere for students without also ensuring the well-being of teachers. Therefore, we call for future research endeavors to adopt a multi-perspective approach, as such studies seem better suited to deal with the complexities that are inherent in our research topic.

9.2 The Limitations of Our Research Project

There is no research without limitations, and ours is no exception. When designing this mixed-methods study, we planned to execute a complex research project in which the strengths and weaknesses are balanced, but we did not foresee the global pandemic. Hence, many limitations of our study are linked to the fact that the COVID-19 pandemic cut across our fieldwork. As this was a funded project, we were not at liberty to stop the project in order to regroup but had to push forward. As a result, we were unable to complete our classroom observation phase and, therefore, in the interviews we could not reflect on observed classes with the interviewees. The reason for this is that, when teaching was transferred to various online platforms, we decided not to follow our teachers in the sample, as they had to deal with a number of unprecedented challenges. Nevertheless, some of our classroom observation data were published in Dóczi and Csizér (2021), but these results represent the pre-COVID classrooms.

As for the cross-sectional student questionnaire data we focused on here, after the switch to online education paper-and-pencil questionnaires were abandoned, the instrument was put online and data collection resumed. Results (as detailed in section 5.1.7 of Chapter 5 pertaining to differences regarding the time of the data collection) show that students were happy with online teaching, but we do not have follow-up data explaining the reasons behind the positive turn regarding this. Luckily, the longitudinal data collection managed to follow some of our students for two years, but those results are to be published elsewhere (Piniel & Albert, in press).

When designing this research project, one novelty of the project was our proposition to carefully match teachers' perspectives with that of their students. At the time of writing the grant application we argued that, since the role of teachers is unquestionable in the process of successful language learning, it is important to gain an insight into how teachers might influence their learners' behavior. Teachers are known to greatly impact on learners' motivation, autonomy and self-regulation by setting an example. Previous research has also revealed that emotions play a central role in the classroom, which implies that teachers need to have an understanding of how to handle them (Pekrun, 2014). Given the Hungarian context, where – as we have seen before – the majority of the Hungarian population lacks usable L2 knowledge, this understanding would be essential in order to encourage and achieve lifelong learning. Naturally, negative emotions, lack of learner autonomy and self-efficacy might reduce accomplishment in the classroom, while positive emotions promote the learning process by leading to higher motivation and enhancing self-regulation and learner autonomy. We think that we were only partially able to fulfill this aim of our project. One limitation is that teacher and student-related data could have been matched better. Our initial plan was to collect enough student data from each teacher to enable us to analyze teacher-related differences. However, despite the fact that calculations regarding teacher–student ratios were carried out based on a nationwide representative study (Öveges & Csizér, 2018), some of the teachers did not have enough volunteering students to create independent subsamples; therefore, this plan had to be abandoned.

A second issue is that, without good quality classroom data, researchers – including us – cannot talk about learning processes in a valid way. In subsequent, hopefully pandemic-free research projects classroom observations need to receive much more emphasis. In the interviews, we were able to shed light on different ways that emotions, motivation, self-confidence and autonomy were conceptualized as important characteristics of learning and teaching by teachers, but we were unable to collect observational data on how teachers' words translate into actions. Moreover, teaching is an emotional profession, and it involves several affective components apart from teaching that a teacher needs to address. This might explain why many teachers leave the profession within the first five years (Schutz & Zemblyas, 2009), while others might lose motivation, which naturally has a demotivating effect on learners. We have data on teachers' views and their perspectives on how they handle the issues of motivation, autonomy, learners' self-efficacy and emotions in the classroom, and how they cope with these in different parts of the teaching process, but we could not gain insights into how teachers use these perspectives in the classroom and how they engage with learners. Therefore, we could not obtain a comprehensive view on learners' language learning processes with regard to their motivation, autonomy and emotions.

9.3 Future Research Directions

When coming to the end of a large research project, it is difficult not to think about what comes next. As this project was conceived almost a decade ago, it is essential to see how the field progresses and what issues stand out as important over time. In what follows, we would like to summarize the most important next steps in our Hungarian context with the caveat that despite the fact that what we present here are context-specific results, we do not think that context-comparative studies are unimportant, as these types of studies can inform us about the large-scale effects of context (see Sulis *et al.*, 2023, for an excellent example of a cross-country study).

However, as we realized when examining the regional distribution of our data, there can be differences even within the context of one country: Hungary. The regional differences we observed were surprising, because they reflected lower motivated language learning behavior, worse learning experiences, lower autonomous learning behavior and higher levels of negative emotions accompanied by lower levels of positive ones in the most developed region of the country: Central Hungary. We hypothesized that such differences might be related to the higher expectations of students in this privileged part of Hungary, but observing what is happening in language classes in different parts of the country might also be illuminating when attempting to shed light on what might account for this unexpected finding.

However, what is missing from the research palette in Hungary (and beyond) are observational studies. It is difficult to investigate classroom-related learning processes without having a clear understanding of what is happening in the classrooms. One excellent example of a classroom-based study comes from Sweden, where Alastair Henry and his colleagues investigated how teachers were motivating their students by integrating extracurricular activities into the classroom (Henry *et al.*, 2019). One difficulty in our context with similar studies is access to schools, teachers and students. It is not only the general European data protection laws that make many school principals wary of welcoming researchers onto the premises but also the fact that the general low level of well-being of Hungarian teachers makes them very often unwilling to burden themselves with yet another task of participating in research studies. Knowing this, we still decided to plan a classroom observation phase within the present research program, but this was cut short due to the COVID-19 pandemic. The focus of our data collection would have been to investigate what tasks were used in the English classroom in Hungary; some of our results were published (Dóczi & Csizér, 2021), but definitely more data would be needed, not just on tasks but other aspects of learning as well. We need to add at this point, however, that classroom observation data cannot do justice to any research purpose without also actually talking to teachers after their observed classes about why they did what they did on that day in that particular classroom. Within Hungary, the interactional nature of ID variables (Csizér, 2020a), the washback effect of language exams on teaching and learning processes (Csizér *et al.*, 2020), and the impact of teacher education on classroom processes should be investigated.

A further important topic to be investigated in Hungary and in other similar contexts as well is the notion of 'success'. The question is not only what is considered successful acquisition of a language in a particular context but also how these ideas are endorsed at various levels, not only in the classrooms and schools but in wider society. Does language learning have an end point that is measured by an exam? What are the expectations of parents? What are the guidelines based on which schools in Hungary are assessed? One hypothesis about Hungarians scoring low on surveys measuring their L2 knowledge is that when they are asked whether they can converse in a L2, the question they think they hear is the following: 'Can you use error-free language in various situations?'. This is due to the fact that the fetish of error-free language use is deeply ingrained in Hungarian learners through a number of language exam preparation classes, a.k.a. language teaching.

Another issue that we have tried to tackle in the present research program is collecting longitudinal data to investigate how ID variables change over time. Results of the longitudinal aspects of our research program will be published elsewhere (Piniel & Albert, in press), but we would like to reiterate how important it is to take time as a variable into consideration in analyses concerning various IDs. The importance of time has been long established, and its conceptualization convincingly argued for (see, for example, Dörnyei *et al.*, 2015). Accordingly, previous studies have used various time frames to investigate changes, and continuing this tradition is highly important. To add complexity to such analyses, it would be important to investigate which aspects of ID variables seem to be more stable over time and which are more malleable to change.

The investigation of ID variables in concert is still an item of the research agenda that should be emphasized. L2 motivation, autonomy, emotions and self-efficacy were selected in this project because of their importance in the local educational context; different variables might be important in other contexts. The reconceptualization of motivation in recent years means that a more complex understanding can be reached when investigating how effort and persistence over time shape learning processes and students' achievement (Csizér et al., 2023). The old and new conceptualization of L2 motivation should be linked to the notion of success mentioned above as well as to various achievement variables. In addition, after seeing student profiles in the sample and the role of negative experience and negative emotions, investigating how to maintain self-motivation in the face of difficulties could be an important research direction in the Hungarian context. In connection with motivation, much work is still needed to investigate the role of autonomy, a concept that has received somewhat less attention in recent years than motivation has. Teaching students how to learn English outside the classroom will not only help teachers and educators in the short run but will provide students with skills for lifelong learning. Theoretical and empirical studies about ID variables need to provide information for teachers, researchers, stakeholders and policymakers alike.

When investigating teachers' views about and dispositions towards teaching, it is important to consider them as a non-homogeneous population and to differentiate between pre-service and in-service teachers as well as teachers at various stages in their career (e.g. Shin et al., 2021; Sulis et al., 2023). Comparative research can shed light not only on how teacher education impacts short- and long-term teaching practices but also what changes can be detected over teachers' careers. Moreover, the changing face of teacher education is another important research topic. We need studies on how the content of English teacher education shapes teachers' work in the classroom. The work of Sulis et al. (2023) provides an excellent example of investigating language teachers' well-being across the career span; similar studies on teaching motivation would yield important new results.

Speaking of teachers, more studies should focus on the influence of teachers' ID variables on students, both directly and indirectly. As Gardner (1985) talked about the direct and indirect roles of the parents in encouraging L2 learning, so the same seems to be valid for teachers. We need to construct and validate circular theories in which a dynamic interplay between teachers and students is accounted for. As one of our participants convincingly argued, teachers' and students' positive/negative emotions go hand in hand, and similar data exist on L2 motivation as well (Csizér, 2020a). Additionally, it would be important to complement data deriving from learners with data from their teachers as in this study, because such an arrangement has resulted in important insights – for example, about the dynamic interplay of emotions. Thus, the above-mentioned concurrent examination of several ID variables should be complemented by this further methodological innovation.

Another issue that needs to be highlighted here is the lingua franca status of the English language. Given that English is not just another language in our globalized world but the language of international communication, or, as Seidlhofer (2011: 7) defined it, the language used 'among speakers of different first languages for whom English is the communicative medium of choice, and often the only option', this has multiple effects on teaching and learning. English as a lingua franca poses a number of communication challenges, such as the varying amount of shared knowledge between speakers of English, the processes through which meaning is negotiated in interactions, and the contextual diversity of users of English (Csizér & Illés, 2020; Illés, 2020). These challenges influence a wide array of ID variables, including the ones investigated in this volume. For example, English as a lingua franca presents a multilingual reality for most of its speakers: therefore, ID variables should be investigated taking into account various languages, identities and their possible interactional impact. In addition, the investigation of self-confidence and self-efficacy seems to be especially important when addressing the above-mentioned challenges (Csizér, 2020a; Csizér & Illés, 2020).

An additional consideration pertaining to English as a lingua franca has been highlighted by Illés (2012) when she reconceptualized the notion of autonomy and called our attention to the importance of considering not only the language learner but also the language user. The fact that language learners are simultaneously language users as well (see, for example, the study of Henry *et al.*, 2019) means that ID variables should be at least partly reconceptualized to reflect this reality. Obviously, this is not a novel idea, and work has been underway (e.g. Illés, 2012; MacIntyre *et al.*, 1998; Noels, 2001a), but a more pronounced investigation of learners as users of L2s seems to be important in the Hungarian context and beyond.

Teaching and learning moved to digital spaces during the months of the pandemic, and it is important to carry out research studies in connection with how the role of ID variables changes in these spaces and what the possible negative and positive effects are that we should consider. For example, the concurrent increases in motivation, autonomy and positive emotions accompanied by a drop in negative ones that have been observed in our study should be investigated further to determine whether causal relationships can be established between these changes. One example of such a study is offered by Henry and Lamb (2019) concerning the role of contact and motivation in digital spaces. It is unclear at this point, however, to what extent ID variables need to be reconceptualized when teaching/learning is happening in a digital space and not in a physical classroom. This also means that both in-service and pre-service teacher education should equip teachers with adequate theoretical knowledge about teaching in digital spaces. In this way their own learning and teaching experience will not only shape their teaching work but also their theoretical knowledge.

Moreover, we should also reflect on the ever-changing field of ID variables, both in terms of their increasing number as well as the reconceptualization of classic variables. For example, there are constant efforts to measure L2 motivation in an increasingly specific way, moving away from the traditional effort-related measurement that was used in the present study. A more detailed and complex conceptualization of what effort in L2 learning actually entails has recently given way to measuring L2 grit (Csizér *et al.*, 2022; Keegan, 2017; Teimouri *et al.*, 2020), persistence (Dörnyei & Henry, 2022), academic buoyancy and resilience (Yun *et al.*, 2018) just to mention a few.

The investigation of emotions also brought interesting insights that seem to justify the approach that involves the concurrent examination of several emotions chosen by us because of the complex effect they can exert on language learning processes. Focusing on anxiety and enjoyment only would have left the important contribution of hope and pride to motivated learning behavior and the significance of curiosity to go unnoticed, as well as the association between the presence of strong negative activating emotions and high levels of motivation. In addition, when it comes to language learning, besides valence the activating and deactivating nature of emotions should also be focused upon.

Finally, we made several suggestions for interventions when discussing our findings, which center around two main themes to improve the learning experiences of learners: by changing the emotional climate of the English lessons and by increasing learner autonomy. Based on our findings, emotion-focused interventions should probably target hope, since creating positive expectation regarding their future English learning and use will likely strengthen learners' ideal L2 selves, which is known to be positively associated with motivated learning behavior and language achievements (Csizér, 2019b). Increasing learners' curiosity by assigning tasks that they find engaging is also worth trying, since this emotion was found to contribute to motivated learning behavior in both highly-motivated and internally-motivated groups of learners. Of course, there will be learners for whom increasing their pride or their enjoyment of learning will bring the greatest benefits, so teachers should try to customize their efforts to fit the needs of their learners.

Besides fostering positive emotions, lowering the negative emotions felt by learners should not be neglected either. Autonomy-focused interventions might try to increase the problem-solving potential of learners, as suggested by Illés (2012), thereby encouraging them to take responsibility for their successes and failures. This process should ideally be accompanied by decreasing the strict control that teachers tend to exercise in frontal teaching arrangements. Since, based on our results, autonomy appears to be somewhat domain-specific, enhancing learner autonomy outside the school context by fostering the out-of-school use of English should be attempted as well, because it is clear that foreign language knowledge cannot be maintained unless it is regularly put to use by the individual.

9.4 Final Remarks

Nearing the end of this project is a bittersweet feeling. We are relieved to publish the results of a successful project, especially given the fact that our data collection largely coincided with the COVID-19 pandemic. We are truly proud that we were able to persevere in the face of such a huge challenge. At the same time, we are sad to close yet another chapter of our lives. The increasing complexity of our globalized world, and the never-ending challenges, always remind us of the importance of research pertaining to the IDs of L2 learners and how teachers' work perspectives and their dispositions can successfully contribute to the learning processes. We came to an end only to start a new project! To be continued…

Appendix A: Constructs in the Student Questionnaire in English and Hungarian

Note: A detailed description of the instruments is also available on the IRIS database: https://www.iris-database.org/

Ideal L2 self
4. I think that English language knowledge will greatly help in my future career.
9. When I think of my future life, I imagine myself using English regularly.
60. When I imagine my future career, I see myself surrounded by people who speak English very well.
66. I like imagining my future self as someone who speaks English very well.
90. I need to know English very well, because of my future plans.

Ought-to L2 self
13. Nobody really cares whether I study English or not.
33. According to my parents, I have to do everything I can to learn English.
43. For the people around me, English proficiency is an important part of general knowledge.
44. English knowledge is essential when it comes to work and jobs.
55. I have to know English in order to be an educated person.
61. If I cannot learn English, it will affect my career negatively.
85. Today it is a must that people know English very well.
88. I feel that others expect me to learn English really well.

L2 learning experience
1. I feel good in the English lessons.
18. I have good experiences from the English lessons.

26. I like the activities that we do in English lessons.
29. I do not have good experiences in the English lessons.
58. The atmosphere is good in my English lessons.

Motivated learning behavior

14. I can honestly say that I do everything I can to master the English language.
35. It is very important for me to speak English.
53. I am determined to learn English very well.
54. Learning English is one of the most important things in my life.
72. I am willing to put an effort into learning English very well.

Autonomous language learning behavior

2. I am trying to look for opportunities to write more in English.
7. I spend more time practicing things in English that I find difficult to understand.
10. I am trying to listen to as much spoken English as possible.
34. I always have a schedule for when to do English homework.
42. I am trying to make myself spend more time learning English.
46. I always have time to learn English in my free time.
51. I take every opportunity to read in English.
82. I am constantly trying to find opportunities to practice my English.
86. I always make plans about how much I am going to practice my English until my next class.

Autonomous use of technology

24. I often use the Internet to improve my English.
64. Sometimes I chat in English on the Internet, and this way I can practice my English.
74. I often read in English because this way I can practice my English.
78. I use international social media sites in English because this way I can practice my English.
80. I often watch content in English because this way I can practice my English.

L2 self-efficacy

92. I am confident that I can do the listening tasks in the English class.
93. I am confident that I can answer questions in English in class.
94. I am confident that I can do the silent reading tasks in English class.
95. I am confident that I can do the writing tasks in the English class.
96. I am confident that I can understand what is said in English in class.
97. I am confident that I can do the speaking tasks in the English class.

Perceived importance of contact

40. I think talking to foreign English speakers is good because I get to know how they live in their country.
48. I believe it is good to speak to foreigners because I can get to know their ways of speaking, their accents and vocabulary.
68. It is a good experience when I have to speak in English with my foreign friends.
89. In my opinion, it is good to speak with foreigners because the more foreigners I meet, the more motivation I have to learn English.
91. In my opinion, it is good to speak with foreigners because if I can't speak as I'd like to, I have more motivation to learn English.

Enjoyment

5. I enjoy talking to others in English during our English lessons.
6. I enjoy the topics that we discuss in English lessons.
23. I enjoy being able to understand English texts in class.
39. I enjoy it when I can successfully complete the tasks during the English lesson.
45. I enjoy the English lessons in school.
76. I enjoy the process of learning English.

Anxiety

11. I am not sure that I will ever understand the logic of the English language.
32. I usually feel unsure when I write in English.
37. I get frustrated if I can't understand an English-language text.
41. I feel very self-conscious about speaking English in front of other students.
57. I'm afraid that my English teacher is ready to correct every mistake I make while speaking English.
75. I get nervous when I don't understand every word that is said to me in English.
79. I feel frustrated about the topics we deal with during English lessons.

Boredom

8. The topics of the English lessons are boring.
17. I get bored by the activities in English lessons.
25. It's boring when I have to talk in English to my classmates during our lessons.
63. Learning English is boring for me.
73. I find the English lessons boring.

Apathy

20. It's hopeless that I will ever accomplish anything in the English lessons.
28. I do not think that the tasks we do in English classes will help me learn English.
62. I feel it's hopeless for me to learn English well in my current group.
71. I feel hopeless about ever mastering English at school.

Hope

3. I hope that I will understand the material in the English lessons.
12. I hope to be successful with my English language knowledge.
21. I feel hopeful about overcoming challenges in the process of learning English.
38. I hope that we will deal with interesting topics in our English classes.
52. I am optimistic about my learning English.
81. I believe that I will be able to keep up with the others during the English lessons.

Pride

27. I am proud of my achievements in English learning.
31. I am proud that I can keep up with the others in the English lessons.
36. I'm proud to show my classmates how good I am at English.
77. I am proud of my English skills.
84. I am proud of myself how well I can use English.

Curiosity

16. In English lessons, we deal with topics that arouse my curiosity.
19. I find the process of learning English interesting.
22. I don't find the things we learn during the English lessons very interesting.
50. During our English lessons, we deal with interesting things that raise my curiosity.
59. The possibility of improving my language knowledge during the English lessons usually makes me enthusiastic.
87. I'm curious to know what my groupmates will say about different topics during the English lessons.

Confusion

15. Complicated grammar structures in English usually confuse me.
56. I find it quite confusing if someone speaks English with a strong accent.

65. Sometimes it is confusing if I do not understand everything when reading English texts.
70. Sometimes I feel confused because I don't understand what is happening in the English lessons.
83. If I listen to an English text and I cannot keep up, I get confused.

Shame
30. I feel ashamed if I get a bad grade in English.
47. I feel ashamed if I can't answer a question during our English lessons.
49. I am ashamed of my English skills.
67. I feel deeply ashamed when I make a mistake in front of my peers in English class.
69. I feel ashamed when I do not understand something during English lessons.

Ideális másodiknyelvi én
4. Szerintem, az angol nyelvtudás nagyban segítené jövőbeli pályafutásomat.
9. Amikor a jövőmre gondolok, az angol nyelv használata fontos része az elképzeléseimnek.
60. Amikor a jövőbeli pályafutásomra gondolok, olyan embernek képzelem el magam, aki jól tud angolul.
66. Szeretem a jövőbeli énemet olyannak elképzelni, aki nagyon jól tud angolul beszélni.
90. A jövőbeli terveim miatt kell, hogy jól tudjak angolul

Szükséges másodiknyelvi én
13. Senki sem törődik azzal, hogy tanulok angolul vagy sem.
33. A szüleim szerint mindent meg kell tegyek, hogy nagyon jól megtanuljak angolul.
43. A körülöttem élő emberek számára az angol nyelv tudása az általános műveltség része.
44. Manapság az ember nem boldogulhat a munka világában angoltudás nélkül.
55. Azért, hogy művelt ember legyek tudnom kell angolul.
61. Ha nem sikerül megtanulnom nagyon jól angolul, az negatív hatással lesz a jövőmre.
85. A mai világban már elvárás, hogy az emberek jól tudjanak angolul.
88. Úgy érzem, mások elvárják tőlem, hogy jól megtanuljak angolul.

Nyelvtanulási tapasztalatok

1. Jól érzem magam az angolórán.
18. Jól élményeim vannak az angolórával kapcsolatban.
26. Tetszenek azok a dolgok, amiket az angolórákon szoktunk csinálni.
29. Nincsenek jó tapasztalataim az angolórával kapcsolatosan. (inv)
58. Az angolórák jó hangulatban telnek.

Motivált nyelvtanulási viselkedés

14. Bátran mondhatom, hogy mindent megteszek azért, hogy nagyon jól megtanuljak angolul.
35. Nagyon fontos számomra, hogy igazán jól megtanuljak angolul.
53. Elszántam magam, hogy nagyon jól megtanuljak angolul.
54. Az angoltanulás az egyik legfontosabb dolog az életemben.
72. Hajlandó vagyok komoly erőfeszítéseket tenni, hogy nagyon jól megtanuljam az angol nyelvet.

Autonóm nyelvtanulási viselkedés

2. Próbálok lehetőségeket keresni arra, hogy minél többet írjak angolul.
7. Több időt fordítok annak a gyakorlására, ami nehezebben megy számomra az angoltanulásban.
10. Törekszem arra, hogy minél több angol nyelvű beszédet halljak.
34. Mindig beosztom, hogy mikor fogom az angol házi feladatot megcsinálni.
42. Igyekszem rávenni magamat, hogy minél több időt fordítsak az angol nyelv tanulására.
46. A szabadidőmből mindig hagyok időt arra, hogy angolul tanuljak.
51. Minden alkalmat megragadok, hogy angolul olvassak.
82. Igyekszem lehetőséget keresni arra, hogy minél többet beszéljek angolul.
86. Mindig megtervezem, hogy mennyit gyakorlom az angolt a következő óráig.

Technológia autonóm használata

24. Gyakran használom az internetet és így az angoltudásom is fejlődik.
64. Szoktam angolul chatelni az interneten és így gyakorlom az angolt.
74. Gyakran olvasok angol nyelvű szövegeket az interneten és így is gyakorolom az angolt.
78. Angolul használok nemzetközi közösségi oldalakat és így fejlődik az angoltudásom.
80. Gyakran nézek angol nyelvű tartalmakat az interneten és így is gyakorolom az angolt.

Énhatékonyság

92. Biztos vagyok benne, hogy ha idegen nyelvű szövegeket hallgatunk az angolórán, meg tudom csinálni az ezzel kapcsolatos feladatokat.
93. Biztos vagyok benne, hogy a nyelvórán feltett kérdésekre tudok angolul válaszolni.
94. Biztos vagyok benne, hogy az angolórán meg tudom csinálni az olvasással kapcsolatos feladatokat.
95. Biztos vagyok benne, hogy az angolórán meg tudom csinálni az írásbeli feladatokat.
96. Biztos vagyok benne, hogy megértem, amit angolul mondanak nekem a nyelvórán.
97. Biztos vagyok benne, hogy az angolórán meg tudom csinálni a szóbeli feladatokat.

Kapcsolat észlelt fontossága

40. Szerintem azért jó külföldiekkel angolul beszélgetni, mert megismerhetem, hogy azokban az országokban hogyan élnek az emberek.
48. Szerintem azért jó külföldiekkel angolul beszélgetni, mert megismerhetem beszédstílusukat, kiejtésüket, szókincsüket.
68. Szerintem jó élmény külföldiekkel való beszélgetésben használni az angol nyelvet.
89. Szerintem azért jó külföldiekkel angolul beszélgetni, mert ha több külföldivel találkozom, több kedvem van angolt tanulni.
91. Szerintem azért jó külföldiekkel angolul beszélgetni, mert ha nem megy a beszéd, akkor elhatározom, hogy jobban fogom tanulni az angolt.

Nyelvtanulás élvezete

5. Élvezem, amikor az angolórán másokkal angolul beszélgethetek.
6. Élvezem azokat a témákat, amikről az angolórákon szó esik.
23. Élvezem, hogy megértem az angol nyelvű szövegeket az órán.
39. Élvezem, amikor sikerül megoldanom a feladatokat az angolórán.
45. Élvezem az angolórákat.
76. Élvezem az angol nyelvtanulás folyamatát.

Szorongás

11. Nem hiszem, hogy valaha képes leszek megérteni az angol nyelv logikáját.
32. Nyugtalanít, ha angolul kell írnom.
37. Frusztrál, ha nem értek meg egy angol szöveget.

41. Zavarba ejtő számomra a többi diák előtt angolul beszélni.
57. Tartok attól, hogy beszéd közben az angoltanár minden hibámat kijavítja.
75. Zavarba jövök, ha nem értek minden egyes szót, amit angolul mondanak nekem.
79. Frusztrálnak azok a témák, amelyekkel az angolórán foglalkozunk.

Unalom

8. Untatnak az angolórán előforduló témák.
17. Untatnak az angolórai feladatok.
25. Unom, ha csoporttársaimmal kell beszélgetni az angolórán.
63. Untat az angol nyelv tanulása.
73. Unalmasnak találom az angolórákat.

Reménytelenség

20. Reménytelennek érzem, hogy sikereket érjek el az angolórán.
28. Nem hiszem, hogy olyan feladatok segítségével amilyeneket az angolórán csinálunk, meg tudok tanulni angolul.
62. Reménytelen, hogy a mostani csoportomban igazán jól megtanuljak angolul.
71. Reménytelennek látom, hogy az iskolában valaha megtanuljak angolul.

Remény

3. Bízom benne, hogy meg fogom érteni az angolórai anyagot.
12. Reményeim szerint sikereket fogok elérni az angoltudásommal.
21. Hiszem, hogy sikerrel fogom venni az angoltanulással kapcsolatos további akadályokat.
38. Azt remélem, hogy a nyelvórákon érdekes témákról lesz szó.
52. Optimistán tekintek az angoltanulásra.
81. Hiszek abban, hogy az angolórán bármiben képes leszek lépést tartani a többiekkel.

Büszkeség

27. Büszke vagyok az angoltanulással kapcsolatos sikereimre.
31. Büszke vagyok rá, hogy lépést tudok tartani a többiekkel az angolórán.
36. Büszkeséggel tölt el az osztálytársaim előtt, hogy milyen jól megy nekem az angol.
77. Büszke vagyok a megszerzett angoltudásomra.
84. Büszke vagyok rá, hogy milyen jól tudom használni az angol nyelvet.

Kíváncsiság

16. Az angolórai témák izgalommal töltenek el.
19. Érdekesnek találom az angoltanulás folyamatát.
22. Az angolórán tanultak nem keltik fel az érdeklődésemet.
50. Az angolórán érdekes dolgokkal foglalkozunk, amik felkeltik a kíváncsiságomat.
59. Az angolórákon többnyire lelkesít, hogy fejleszthetem a nyelvtudásomat.
87. Kíváncsi vagyok, hogy az osztálytársaim mit fognak mondani az angolórán a különböző témákról.

Zavarodottság

15. A bonyolult nyelvtani szerkezetek az angolban általában összezavarnak.
56. Ha valaki erős akcentussal beszél angolul, az eléggé összezavar.
65. Angol nyelvű szövegek olvasásakor néha összezavar, hogy nem értek minden szót.
70. Van, hogy összezavarodok, mert nem értem mi folyik az angolórán.
83. Ha angol szöveget hallgatok, és nem tudom felvenni a ritmust, akkor összezavarodok.

Szégyen

30. Ha rossz jegyet kapok angolórán, szégyellem magam.
47. Szégyellem, ha az angolórán nem tudok egy kérdésre válaszolni.
49. Szégyellem magam az angoltudásom szintje miatt.
67. Úgy érzem, legszívesebben elsüllyednék, ha a többiek előtt hibázok az angolórán.
69. Szégyellem, ha nem értem az angolórai anyagot.

Appendix B: Teacher Interview Guide in English and Hungarian

Dear XY! We thank you very much for volunteering for this interview and helping the work of our research team. I am ZW, I work at ELTE, at the English Department of Applied Linguistics, and our research group would like to gather information about the experience and opinions of language teachers for our research project, in which we analyze high school students' individual learning differences when it comes to language learning. The interview will only be used for research purposes, with the data being collected and analyzed. Naturally research participants will remain completely anonymous and no identifying characteristics of yours will be made public. During the interview we will be interested in your personal opinions, thus there are no wrong or right answers. The interview will take around 35–40 minutes and if you give your consent to having our conversation recorded, then we can begin right now.

Firstly, let's talk about the language teaching experience that you have gained so far in your work.

- As standard procedure I must ask you about your age and how long you have been teaching. How long have you been teaching English specifically?
- Besides English, do you teach any other languages? If so, then which one(s)?
- What type of language teaching degree do you have?
- What type of institutions have you taught English in? And for how long?
- Which age group of students have you taught before and nowadays?

Now let me ask you a few questions about your language lessons.
First some questions about your planning.

- What aspects do you take into consideration when beginning work with a group in a new school year? How do you prepare for different groups?

- When planning classes, what differences do you take into consideration that are unrelated to language proficiency?
- During the school year, what aspects are the most important to you when it comes to planning your classes?
- To what extent do your plans get realized compared to the yearly syllabus in your opinion?

Now a few questions about classroom work.
- What sort of materials do you use during classes?
- What is your method for choosing which type of tasks to use in specific groups?
- What are your favorite task types? What do you like about them?
- Which types of tasks do you avoid? Why do you avoid them?
- In your opinion, what is the students' favorite type of task? How much do you take it into consideration?
- In your opinion, which type of task(s) do the children dislike? How much do you take it into consideration?
- Can you precisely recall the tasks that you used during your last English lesson and what the students did during those tasks?
- How do you differentiate in a language class? What personal differences do you take into consideration? Aside from language knowledge, do you consider any other personal factors?
- How do you help students, or a student, if they fall behind or get stuck in an activity or when doing a task? What do you do when the whole group gets stuck in learning something?

I would like to ask a few questions about language learners and the role of the teacher.
- Describe who you think is a successful language learner.
- What emotions do you see on students in relation to language learning? What signs make you say this?
- Why is it important or unimportant how students feel about language learning in your opinion?
- What is the teacher's role when it comes to the students' emotions during classes?
- What types of emotions do you experience during classes?
- How do the emotions of your students affect you?
- How do your emotions affect your students?
- How motivated do your students appear to be? What signs make you say this?
- How could the students be motivated more when they are un(der)motivated?
- How important do you consider self-confidence as a factor when it comes to success in language learning?

- What is the role of the language teacher when it comes to the self-confidence of students?
- What does students taking responsibility in their own language learning mean to you? How much are your students able to accomplish that?
- What role do you have in your students' learning how to study and improve their language proficiency on their own?

Finally, I would like to ask a few questions about language learning outside school.

- How important is it in the language classes for students to have a connection to English outside lessons?
- How does a connection to English outside classes affect the process of language learning?
- How do you prepare your students for the use of learning English outside class?
- What benefits do you expect from study trips abroad for the 9th and 11th grader students?

Is there anything else you would like to add?
We are very grateful that you have volunteered for this interview!

Kedves XY! Nagyon köszönjük, hogy vállalkoztál erre a beszélgetésre és ezzel segíted a kutatócsoportunk munkáját. ZW vagyok, az ELTE-n dolgozom az Angol Alkalmazott Nyelvészeti Tanszéken, kollégáimmal a nyelvtanárok tapasztalataival és véleményével kapcsolatos információkat szeretnénk gyűjteni egy olyan kutatási projekthez, melyben a középiskolások nyelvtanuláshoz kapcsolódó egyéni különbségeit vizsgáljuk. Az interjút kutatási célokra fogjuk felhasználni, az adatokat összegezve elemezzük. Természetesen a kutatásban teljesen név nélkül szerepelsz és semmilyen azonosító jellemzőt nem fogok nyilvánosságra hozni. Az interjú során a személyes véleményedre vagyunk kíváncsiak, nem „jó" válaszokat szeretnénk hallani, mert ilyen válaszok nincsenek. Az interjú körülbelül 35–40 perc lesz, és ha beleegyezel, hogy felvegyem a beszélgetésünket, akkor kezdhetjük is.

Először arról beszélnénk, hogy milyen nyelvtanítási tapasztalatokat szereztél eddigi munkádban.

- A mintaleírás miatt meg kell kérdeznem, hogy hány éves vagy és mióta tanítasz? Mióta tanítasz angolt?
- Angolon kívül tanítasz-e még más nyelvet? Ha igen, mit?
- Milyen nyelvtanári végzettséggel rendelkezel?
- Milyen iskolatípusokban tanítottál angolt? Hol mennyi ideig?
- Milyen életkorú/évfolyamú gyerekeknek tanítottál angolt? És most milyen életkorú/évfolyamú gyerekeket tanítasz?

Most a nyelvóráidról teszünk fel néhány kérdést.

Először a tervezéssel kapcsolatban szeretnék néhány kérdést feltenni.

- Milyen tényezőket veszel figyelembe, amikor egy csoporttal megkezded a munkát az új tanévben? Hogyan készülsz fel a különböző csoportjaidra?
- Milyen csoportok közti különbségeket veszel figyelembe a nyelvi szinten kívül a tervezésnél?
- A tanév során milyen tényezőket veszel leginkább figyelembe az órák tervezése során?
- Mit mondanál, mennyire valósulnak meg az előzetes terveid általában az éves tanmenettel kapcsolatban? És az óratervekkel kapcsolatban?

Most az osztálytermi munkával kapcsolatosan lesz néhány kérdésem.

- Milyen tananyagokat használsz a tanórákon?
- Hogyan választod ki, hogy milyen feladatokat használsz egy adott csoportban?
- Mik a kedvenc feladataid? Miért kedveled ezeket?
- Milyen feladatokat kerülsz? Miért kerülöd őket?
- Szerinted a gyerekeknek melyek a kedvenc feladatai? Mennyire veszed ezt figyelembe?
- Szerinted a gyerekek mely feladatokat nem kedvelik? Mennyire veszed ezt figyelembe?
- Fel tudnád idézni, hogy konkrétan milyen feladatokat használtál a legutóbbi angolórádon és milyen tevékenységeket végeztek ezek során a tanulók?
- Hogyan differenciálsz a nyelvórán? Milyen egyéni különbségeket veszel figyelembe? A nyelvtudáson kívül más egyéni különbséget figyelembe veszel?
- Hogyan segíted a tanulókat, vagy egy tanulót, ha az órán elakad egy tevékenység során, vagy egy feladat megoldásában? Mit teszel, ha az egész csoport elakad valami miatt a tanulásban?

Most a nyelvtanulókkal és a tanár szerepével kapcsolatban szeretnék feltenni kérdéseket.

- Milyen szerinted egy sikeres nyelvtanuló?
- Milyen érzelmeket látsz a tanulókon a nyelvórákon a nyelvtanulással kapcsolatosan? Milyen jelekből következtetsz erre?
- Szerinted miért fontos vagy miért nem fontos, hogy a tanulók milyen nyelvtanulással kapcsolatos érzelmeket élnek át a tanórán?
- Mi a tanárnak a feladata a tanulók által az órán átélt érzelmekkel kapcsolatban?
- Te általában hogyan érzed magad a nyelvórán?
- Hogyan hatnak a tanulók által átélt érzelmek rád?
- Hogyan hat a te érzelmi állapotod a tanulókra?

- Mennyire látod a tanulókat motiváltnak általában? Milyen jelekből ítéled ezt meg?
- Hogyan lehetne még inkább motiválni a tanulókat, amikor kevésbé motiváltak?
- Mennyire gondolod fontos tényezőnek a tanulók magabiztosságát a nyelvtanulás sikerében?
- Milyen szerepe van a nyelvtanárnak a tanulók magabiztosságával kapcsolatban?
- Mit jelent neked az, hogy a tanulók vállaljanak felelősséget saját nyelvtanulásukért? A te tanulóid mennyire képesek erre?
- Milyen szereped van szerinted neked abban, hogy a tanulók megtanuljanak tanulni és önállóan is képesek legyenek fejleszteni nyelvtudásukat?

Végül az iskolán kívüli nyelvtanulásról is szeretnék feltenni pár kérdést.

- A nyelvóra szempontjából miért fontos vagy miért nem fontos, hogy a nyelvtanulóknak legyen kapcsolata az angol nyelvvel nyelvórán kívül is?
- Hogyan hat szerinted a nyelvtanulás folyamatára az angol nyelvvel való tanórán kívüli kapcsolat?
- Hogyan készíted fel tanulóidat az iskolán kívüli nyelvtanulásra, nyelvhasználatra?
- Milyen hozadékokat vársz a 9. és 11. osztályos tanulók külföldi tanulmányútjaitól?

Van még esetleg valami, amit szívesen elmondanál?
Köszönjük szépen, hogy vállalkoztál erre az interjúra!

Appendix C: Paired Samples t-tests

Table Appendix C1: Paired samples t-tests

Paired Samples Test

	Paired Differences			95% Confidence Interval of the Difference		t	df	Significance	
	Mean	Std. Deviation	Std. Error Mean	Lower	Upper			One-Sided p	Two-Sided p
Pair 1 hope – enjoyment	.29109	.55752	.01643	.25886	.32332	17.721	1151	<.001	<.001
Pair 2 enjoyment – pride	.18766	.75393	.02221	.14408	.23124	8.448	1151	<.001	<.001
Pair 3 pride – curiosity	.33335	.92148	.02715	.28008	.38662	12.278	1151	<.001	<.001
Pair 4 curiosity – shame	.78181	1.22030	.03595	.71127	.85236	21.745	1151	<.001	<.001
Pair 5 shame – anxiety	.08367	.75457	.02223	.04005	.12729	3.763	1151	<.001	<.001
Pair 6 anxiety – confusion	.08064	.70853	.02088	.03968	.12160	3.863	1151	<.001	<.001
Pair 7 confusion – boredom	.50412	1.09930	.03239	.44058	.56767	15.565	1151	<.001	<.001
Pair 8 boredom – apathy	.15699	.73073	.02153	.11475	.19923	7.292	1151	<.001	<.001

References

Act no. 190/2011 on public education (n.d.) *Jogtár* [Law Library]. Retrieved March 10, 2021, from https://net.jogtar.hu/jogszabaly?docid=a1100190.tv.

Act no. 59/2022 on the amendment of certain laws related to higher education, vocational education, and adult education (2022) *Magyar Közlöny, 209*, 9007–9036. Retrieved March 24, 2023, from http://www.kozlonyok.hu/nkonline/MKPDF/hiteles/MK22209.pdf.

Act no. 52/2023 on the new career management system for teachers (2023) *Magyar Közlöny, 100*, 4994–5085. Retrieved July 18, 2023, from https://magyarkozlony.hu/dokumentumok/8615f0642888805693ff027c1cee219e6243dcd6/megtekintes.

Aida, Y. (1994) Examination of Horwitz, Horwitz, and Cope's construct of foreign language anxiety: The case of students of Japanese. *The Modern Language Journal* 78 (2), 155–168. https://doi.org/10.1111/j.1540-4781.1994.tb02026.x.

Albert, Á. (2022) *Investigating the Role of Affective Factors in Second Language Learning Tasks*. Springer.

Albert, Á. and Piniel, K. (2021) Changes in students' motivation, autonomy, self-efficacy, and emotions across a school year: Examining possible effects of switching to online education. In G. Tankó and K. Csizér (eds) *DEAL 2021: Current Explorations in English Applied Linguistics* (pp. 265–298). Faculty of Humanities, Eötvös Loránd University.

Albert, Á. and Csizér, K. (2022) Investigating individual differences with qualitative research methods: Results of a meta-analysis of leading applied linguistics journals. *Studies in Second Language Learning and Teaching* 12 (2), 303–335. https://doi.org/10.14746/ssllt.2022.12.2.6.

Albert, Á., Tankó, G. and Piniel, K. (2018a) A tanulók válaszai a 7. évfolyamon [Answers of grade 7 students]. In E. Öveges and K. Csizér (eds) *Vizsgálat a köznevelésben folyó idegennyelv-oktatás kereteiről és hatékonyságáról* (pp. 52–89). Hungarian Educational Authority. https://www.oktatas.hu/pub_bin/dload/sajtoszoba/nyelvoktatas_kutatasi_jelentes_2018.pdf.

Albert, Á., Tankó, G. and Piniel, K. (2018b) A tanulók válaszai a 11. évfolyamon [Answers of grade 11 students]. In E. Öveges and K. Csizér (eds) *Vizsgálat a köznevelésben folyó idegennyelv-oktatás kereteiről és hatékonyságáról* (pp. 90–160). Hungarian Educational Authority. https://www.oktatas.hu/pub_bin/dload/sajtoszoba/nyelvoktatas_kutatasi_jelentes_2018.pdf.

Albert, Á., Csizér, K. and Piniel, K. (2018c) The relationship between foreign language learning autonomy and emotions: The results of a nationwide study in Hungary. Autonomy in language learning and teaching: The case of target language skills and subsystems. Conference presentation in Konin, Poland.

Albert, Á., Piniel, K. and Lajtai, Á. (2019) Középiskolás diákok angolórákkal kapcsolatos érzelmei egy kérdőíves felmérés tükrében [Investigating high school students' emotions in connection with their English classes with the help of a questionnaire study]. *Modern Nyelvoktatás* 25 (2), 27–41.

Albert, Á., Piniel, K. and Lajtai, Á. (2020) Investigating high school students' emotions in connection with their EFL classes: A questionnaire study. In A. Fekete, M. Lehmann and K. Simon (eds) *UPRT 2019: Empirical Studies in English Applied Linguistics in Honour of József Horváth* (pp. 2–21). Lingua Franca Csoport.

Albert, Á., Dóczi, B., Piniel, K. and Csizér, K. (2022) The contribution of motivation and emotions to language learning autonomy in the Hungarian secondary school classroom: The results of a questionnaire study. In V. De Wilde and C. Goriot (eds) *Second Language Learning before Adulthood: Individual Differences in Children and Aadolescents* (pp. 155–175). De Gruyter Mouton.

Al-Hoorie, H.A. (2018) The L2 motivational self system: A meta-analysis. *Studies in Second Language Learning and Teaching* 8 (4), 721–754. https://doi.org/10.14746/ssllt.2018.8.4.2.

Allport, W.G. (1954) *The Nature of Prejudice*. Addison-Wesley.

Antalné Szabó, Á., Hámori, V., Kimmel, M., Kotschy, B., Móri, Á., Szőke-Milinte, E. and Wölfling, Z. (2014) Útmutató a pedagógusok minősítési rendszeréhez [Guide to pedagogues' qualification system]. Hungarian Educational Authority.

Arguel, A., Lockyer, L., Kennedy, G., Lodge, J.M. and Pachman, M. (2019) Seeking optimal confusion: A review on epistemic emotion management in interactive digital learning environments. *Interactive Learning Environments* 27 (2), 200–210.

Bandura, A. (1993) Perceived self-efficacy in cognitive development and functioning. *Educational Psychologist* 28, 117–148. https://doi.org/10.1207/s15326985ep2802_3.

Bandura, A. (1995) Exercise of personal and collective efficacy in changing societies. In A. Bandura (ed.) *Self-Efficacy in Changing Societies* (pp. 1–45). Cambridge University Press.

Bandura, A. (1997) *Self-Efficacy: The Exercise of Control*. Freeman.

Bárdos, J. (2009) Tanárképzési kontextusok különös tekintettel az angolra [Contexts of teacher training with special regard to English]. In T. Frank and K. Károly (eds) *Anglisztika és amerikanisztika: Magyar kutatások az ezredfordulón* (pp. 33–49). Tinta Könyvkiadó.

Benson, P. (2001) *Teaching and Researching Learner Autonomy in Language Learning*. Longman.

Benson, P. (2007) Autonomy in language teaching and learning. *Language Teaching* 40 (1), 21–40. https://doi.org/10.1017/S0261444806003958.

Benson, P. (2011) What is new in autonomy? *The Language Teacher* 35 (4), 15–18. https://doi.org/10.37546/JALTTLT35.4-4.

Benson, P. (2013) *Teaching and Researching: Autonomy in Language Learning*. Routledge.

Boo, Z., Dörnyei, Z. and Ryan, S. (2015) L2 motivation research 2005–2014: Understanding a publication surge and a changing landscape. *System* 55, 147–157. https://doi.org/10.1016/j.system.2015.10.006.

Borg, S. (2003) Teacher cognition in language teaching: A review of research on what language teachers think, know, believe, and do. *Language Teaching* 36 (2), 81–19. https://doi.org/10.1017/S0261444803001903.

Botes, E., Dewaele, J.-M. and Greiff, S. (2020a) The foreign language classroom anxiety scale and academic achievement: An overview of the prevailing literature and a meta-analysis. *Journal for the Psychology of Language Learning* 2 (1), 26–56.

Botes, E., Dewaele, J.-M. and Greiff, S. (2020b) The power to improve: Effects of multilingualism and perceived proficiency on enjoyment and anxiety in foreign language learning. *European Journal of Applied Linguistics* 8 (2), 279–306. https://doi.org/10.1515/eujal-2020-0003.

Botes, E., Dewaele, J.-M. and Greiff, S. (2022) Taking stock: A meta-analysis of the effects of foreign language enjoyment. *Studies in Second Language Learning and Teaching* 12 (2), 205–232. https://doi.org/10.14746/ssllt.2022.12.2.3.

Boudreau, C., MacIntyre, P.D. and Dewaele, J.-M. (2018) Enjoyment and anxiety in second language communication: An idiodynamic approach. *Studies in Second Language Learning and Teaching* 8 (1), 149–170. https://doi.org/10.14746/ssllt.2018.8.1.7.

Celce-Murcia, M. and Olshtain, E. (2000) *Discourse and Context in Language Teaching: A Guide for Language Teachers*. Cambridge University Press.

Charmaz, K. (2006) *Constructing Grounded Theory: A Practical Guide through Qualitative Analysis*. Sage.

Chastain, K. (1975) Affective and ability factors in second language acquisition. *Language Learning* 25 (1), 153–161.

Central Intelligence Agency (2023) The world factbook. https://www.cia.gov/the-world-factbook/countries/hungary/.

Clément, R. (1980) Ethnicity, contact and communicative competence in a second language. In H.M. Giles, W.P. Robinson and P.M. Smith (eds) *Language: Social Psychological Perspectives* (pp. 147–154). Pergamon.

Clément, R. and Kruidenier, B.G. (1983) Orientation in second language acquisition: I. The effects of ethnicity, milieu, and target language on their emergence. *Language Learning* 33, 273–291.

Clément, R., Gardner, R.C. and Smythe, P.C. (1977) Motivational variables in second language acquisition: A study of francophones learning English. *Canadian Journal of Behavioral Science* 9 (2), 123–133. https://doi.org/10.1037/h0081614.

Clément, R., Dörnyei, Z. and Noels, K. (1994) Motivation, self-confidence, and group cohesion in the foreign language classroom. *Language Learning* 44 (3), 417–448. https://doi.org/10.1111/j.1467-1770.1994.tb01113.x.

Clément, R., Noels, K.A. and Deneault, B. (2001) Interethnic contact, identity, and psychological adjustment: The mediating and moderating roles of communication. *Journal of Social Issues* 57 (3), 559–577.

Cohen, J. (1988) *Statistical Power Analysis for the Behavioral Sciences* (2nd edn). Lawrence Erlbaum.

Cohen, L., Manion, L. and Morrison, K. (2018) *Research Methods in Education* (8th edn). Routledge.

Columbia Encyclopedia (6th edn) (2019) https://www.encyclopedia.com.

Cook, T. (2006) An investigation of shame and anxiety in learning English as a second language. Unpublished doctoral dissertation, University of Southern California.

Council of Europe (2001) *Common European Framework of Reference for Languages: Learning, Teaching, Assessment. Companion Volume with New Descriptions*. Strasbourg Cedex. Retrieved from https://rm.coe.int/cefr-companion-volumewith-new-descriptors2018/1680787989.

Creswell, J.W. and Clark, V.L.P. (2018) *Designing and Conducting Mixed Methods Research* (3rd edn). Sage.

Crosier, D. and Parveva, T. (2013) *The Bologna Process: Its Impact on Higher Education Development in Europe and Beyond*. UNESCO.

Crowther, D., Kim, S., Lee, J., Lim, J. and Loewen, S. (2021) Methodological synthesis of cluster analysis in second language research. *Language Learning* 71 (1), 99–130. https://doi.org/10.1111/lang.12428.

Csíkszentmihályi, M. (1975) *Beyond Boredom and Anxiety: Experiencing Flow in Work and Play*. Jossey-Bass Publishers.

Csíkszentmihályi, M. (1990) *Flow: The Psychology of Optimal Experience*. Harper Perennial.

Csíkszentmihályi, M., Abuhamdeh, S. and Nakamura, J. (2005) Flow. In A. Elliot and C. Dweck (eds) *Handbook of Competence and Motivation* (pp. 598–623). Guilford Press.

Csizér, K. (2018) Some components of language learning experiences: An interview study with English teachers in Hungary. In M. Lehmann, R. Lugossy, M. Nikolov and G. Szabó (eds) *UPRT2017: Empirical Studies in Applied Linguistics* (pp. 1–14). University of Pécs.

Csizér, K. (2019a) The language learning experiences and their perceived impact on teaching: An interview study with English teachers in Hungary. In M. Sato and S. Loewen (eds) *Evidence-Based Second Language Pedagogy: A Collection of Instructed Second Language Acquisition Studies* (pp. 314–330). Routledge.

Csizér, K. (2019b) The L2 motivational self system. In M. Lamb, K. Csizér, A. Henry and S. Ryan (eds) *The Palgrave Handbook of Motivation for Language Learning* (pp. 71–93). Palgrave Macmillan.

Csizér, K. (2020a) *Second Language Learning Motivation in a European Context: The Case of Hungary*. Springer Nature.

Csizér, K. (2020b) *Az angoltanárok motivációja: Egy feltáró kutatás eredményei* [The Motivation of English Teachers: The Results of an Exploratory Study]. Akadémiai Kiadó. Available online at https://real-d.mtak.hu/1284/7/dc_1700_19_doktori_mu.pdf.

Csizér, K. and Dörnyei, Z. (2005) Language learners' motivational profiles and their motivated learning behavior. *Language Learning* 55 (4), 613–659. https://doi.org/10.1111/j.0023-8333.2005.00319.x.

Csizér, K. and Kormos, J. (2008a) The relationship of inter-cultural contact and language learning motivation among Hungarian students of English and German. *Journal of Multilingual and Multicultural Development* 29 (1), 30–48. https://doi.org/10.2167/jmmd557.0.

Csizér, K. and Kormos, J. (2008b) The role of intercultural contact in learning German in Hungary: A structural equation modeling approach. *Zeitschrift für Interkulturellen Fremdsprachenunterricht* 13 (2), 14 S.

Csizér, K. and Kormos, J. (2009a) Learning experiences, selves and motivated learning behaviour: A comparative analysis of structural models for Hungarian secondary and university learners of English. In Z. Dörnyei and E. Ushioda (eds) *Motivation, Language Identity and the L2 Self* (pp. 98–119). Multilingual Matters.

Csizér, K. and Kormos, J. (2009b) Modeling the role of intercultural contact in the motivation of learning English as a foreign language. *Applied Linguistics* 30 (2), 166–185. https://doi.org/10.1093/applin/amn025.

Csizér, K. and Lukács, G. (2010) The comparative analysis of motivation, attitudes and selves: The case of English and German in Hungary. *System* 38 (1), 1–13. https://doi.org/10.1016/j.system.2009.12.001.

Csizér, K. and Kormos, J. (2012) A nyelvtanulási autonómia, az önszabályozó stratégiák és a motiváció kapcsolatának vizsgálata [The investigation of language learning autonomy, self-regulatory strategies, and motivation in Hungarian]. *Magyar Pedagógia* 112, 3–17.

Csizér, K. and Galántai, D. (2012) A tanári és szülői szerepek alakulása a középiskolások idegen nyelvi motivációjának alakításában: Egy strukturális modell tanulságai [The role of parents and teachers in shaping secondary school students' L2 motivation: The results of structural equation modelling]. In A. Németh (ed.) *A neveléstudományi doktori iskola programjai: Tudományos arculat, kutatási eredmények* (pp. 171–178). Eötvös Kiadó.

Csizér, K. and Jamieson, J. (2013) Cluster analysis. In C.A. Chapell (ed.) *The Encyclopedia of Applied Linguistics*. [Online] Blackwell Publishing. https://doi.org/10.1002/9781405198431.wbeal0138.

Csizér, K. and Kormos, J. (2014) The ideal L2 self, self-regulatory strategies and autonomous learning: A comparison of different groups of English learners. In K. Csizér and M. Magid (eds) *The Impact of Self-concept on Language Learning* (pp. 73–86). Multilingual Matters.

Csizér, K. and Kálmán, Cs. (2019) A study of retrospective and concurrent foreign language learning experiences: A comparative interview study in Hungary. *Studies in Second Language Learning and Teaching* 9 (1), 225–246.

Csizér, K. and Öveges, E. (2019) Idegennyelv-tanulási motivációs tényezők és a nyelvi vizsgák Magyarországon: összefüggések vizsgálata egy kérdőíves kutatás segítségével [Motivation to learn a foreign language and language exams in Hungary: Studying their relationships with the help of a questionnaire study]. *Modern Nyelvoktatás* 25, 86–101.

Csizér, K. and Illés, É. (2020) Helping to maximize learners' motivation for second language learning. *Language Teaching Research Quarterly* 19, 19–31.

Csizér, K. and Öveges, E. (2020) Nyelvtanulási autonómia és nyelvi tervezés: egy vegyes módszerű kutatás eredményei [Language learning autonomy and language planning: Results of a mixed methods study]. *Modern Nyelvoktatás* 36, 44–58.

Csizér, K. and Albert, Á. (2022) Trait and state perspectives of individual difference research. In T. Gregersen and S. Mercer (eds) *The Routledge Handbook of the Psychology of Language Learning and Teaching* (pp. 339–349). Routledge.

Csizér, K. and Albert, Á. (2024a) Gender-related differences in the effects of motivation, self-efficacy, and emotions on autonomous use of technology in second language learning. *The Asia-Pacific Education Researcher.* https://doi.org/10.1007/s40299-023-00808-z.

Csizér, K. and Albert, Á. (2024b) The relationship of emotions, motivation and language learning autonomy: Differences in Hungarian secondary schools. *Porta Linguarum Revista Interuniversitaria de Didáctica de las Lenguas Extranjeras* 9, 31–47. https://doi.org/10.30827/portalin.viIX.29890.

Csizér, K., Öveges, E. and Lajtai, Á. (2020) The relationship between foreign language learning motivation and language exams: The results of a questionnaire study. In A. Fekete, M. Lehmann and K. Simon (eds) *UPRT 2019: Empirical Studies in English Applied Linguistics in Honour of József Horváth* (pp. 76–95). Lingua Franca Csoport.

Csizér, K., Albert, Á. and Piniel, K. (2021) The interrelationship of language learning autonomy, self-efficacy, motivation and emotions: The investigation of Hungarian secondary school students. In M. Pawlak (ed.) *Investigating Individual Learner Differences in Second Language Learning* (pp. 1–21). Springer.

Csizér, K., Fekete, I., Szabó, F. and Albert, Á. (2023) Kitartás és érdeklődés a nyelvtanulásban: A grit jelenség vizsgálata Magyarországon angolszakos egyetemisták körében [Perseverance and interest in language learning: The investigation of the notion of grit among English major university students]. *Magyar Pedagógia* 123, 3–17. https://doi.org/10.14232/mped.2023.1.3.

D'Mello, S. and Graesser, A.C. (2014) Confusion. In R. Pekrun and L. Linnenbrink-Garcia (eds) *International Handbook of Emotions in Education* (pp. 299–320). Routledge.

D'Mello, S., Lehman, B., Pekrun, R. and Graesser, A. (2014) Confusion can be beneficial for learning. *Learning and Instruction* 29, 153–170. https://doi.org/10.1016/j.learninstruc.2012.05.003.

De Smet, A., Mettewie, L., Galand, B., Hiligsmann, P. and Van Mensel, L. (2018) Classroom anxiety and enjoyment in CLIL and non-CLIL: Does the target language matter? *Studies in Second Language Learning and Teaching* 8 (1), 47–71. https://doi.org/10.14746/ssllt.2018.8.1.3.

de Zaróba, Y.R. and Catalán, R.M.J. (2009) *Content and Language Integrated Learning: Evidence from Research in Europe.* Multilingual Matters.

Decree no. 20/2012. (VIII.31.) On the operation of educational institutions (n.d.) *Jogtár* [Law Library]. Retrieved March 11, 2021, from https://net.jogtar.hu/jogszabaly?docid=a1200020.emm.

Decree no. 8/2013. (I.30.) On teacher training requirements (2013) *Magyar Közlöny* 15, 979–1324. Retrieved December 23, 2021, from https://magyarkozlony.hu/dokumentumok/7f2de95bc68028c87c367573def263648eead8da/megtekintes.

Decree no. 5/2020. (I.31.) On national core curriculum (2020) *Magyar Közlöny* 17, 290–446. Retrieved February 10, 2021, from https://magyarkozlony.hu/dokumentumok/3288b6548a740b9c8daf918a399a0bed1985db0f/megtekintes.

Decree no. 538/2021. (IX.15.) On teacher education system (2021) *Magyar Közlöny* 170, 8015–8022. Retrieved March 27, 2023, from http://www.kozlonyok.hu/nkonline/index.php?menuindex=200&pageindex=kozltart&ev=2021&szam=170.

Dewaele, J.-M. (2015) On emotions in foreign language learning and use. *The Language Teacher* 39 (3), 13–15.

Dewaele, J.-M. and MacIntyre, P.D. (2014) The two faces of Janus? Anxiety and enjoyment in the foreign language classroom. *Studies in Second Language Learning and Teaching* 4 (2), 237–274. https://doi.org/10.14746/ssllt.2014.4.2.5.

Dewaele, J.-M. and Alfawzan, M. (2018) Does the effect of enjoyment outweigh that of anxiety in foreign language performance? *Studies in Second Language Learning and Teaching* 8 (1), 21–45. https://doi.org/10.14746/ssllt.2018.8.1.2.

Dewaele, J.-M. and Dewaele, L. (2020) Are foreign language learners' enjoyment and anxiety specific to the teacher? An investigation into the dynamics of learners' classroom emotions. *Studies in Second Language Learning and Teaching* 10 (1), 45–65. https://doi.org/10.14746/ssllt.2020.10.1.3.

Dewaele, J.-M., Petrides, K.V. and Furnham, A. (2008) The effects of trait emotional intelligence and sociobiographical variables on communicative anxiety and foreign language anxiety among adult multilinguals: A review and empirical investigation. *Language Learning* 58 (4), 911–960. https://doi.org/10.1111/j.1467-9922.2008.00482.x.

Dewaele, J.-M., MacIntyre, P.D., Boudreau, C. and Dewaele, L. (2016) Do girls have all the fun? Anxiety and enjoyment in the foreign language classroom. *Theory and Practice of Second Language Acquisition* 2 (1), 41–63. https://journals.us.edu.pl/index.php/TAPSLA/article/view/3941/3090.

Dewaele, J.-M., Botes, E. and Greiff, S. (2022) Sources and effects of foreign language enjoyment, anxiety, and boredom: A structural equation modeling approach. *Studies in Second Language Acquisition* 45 (2), 461–479. https://doi.org/10.1017/S0272263122000328.

Dóczi, B. and Csizér, K. (2021) A glimpse into the English classroom: Results of an observation study in Hungarian secondary schools. In G. Tankó and K. Csizér (eds) *DEAL 2021: Current Explorations in English Applied Linguistics* (pp. 107–138). Eötvös Loránd University Faculty of Humanities.

Donovan, L. and MacIntyre, P.D. (2004) Age and sex differences in willingness to communicate, communication apprehension, and self-perceived competence. *Communication Research Reports* 21 (4), 420–427. https://doi.org/10.1080/08824090409360006

Dörnyei, Z. (2001) *Teaching and Researching Motivation*. Longman.

Dörnyei, Z. (2005) *The Psychology of the Language Learner: Individual Differences in Second Language Acquisition*. Lawrence Erlbaum.

Dörnyei, Z. (2007) *Research Methods in Applied Linguistics: Quantitative, Qualitative, and Mixed Methodologies*. Oxford University Press.

Dörnyei, Z. (2009) The L2 motivational self system. In Z. Dörnyei and E. Ushioda (eds) *Motivation, Language Identity and the L2 Self* (pp. 9–42). Multilingual Matters.

Dörnyei, Z. and Kormos, J. (2000) The role of individual and social variables in oral task performance. *Language Teaching Research* 4 (3), 275–300.

Dörnyei, Z. and Ushioda, E. (2011) *Teaching and Researching Motivation* (2nd edn). Longman.

Dörnyei, Z. and Ryan, S. (2015) *The Psychology of the Language Learner Revisited*. Routledge.

Dörnyei, Z. and Ushioda, E. (2021) *Teaching and Researching Motivation* (3rd edn). Longman.

Dörnyei, Z. and Henry, A. (2022) Accounting for long-term motivation and sustained motivated learning: Motivational currents, self-concordant vision, and persistence in language learning. In A.J. Elliot (ed.) *Advances in Motivation Science*. Academic Press.

Dörnyei, Z., Csizér, K. and Németh, N. (2006) *Motivation, Language Attitudes and Globalisation: A Hungarian Perspective*. Multilingual Matters.

Dörnyei, Z., MacIntyre, P.D. and Henry, A. (eds) (2015) *Motivational Dynamics in Language Learning*. Multilingual Matters.

Eccles, J.S. (2009) Who am I and what am I going to do with my life? Personal and collective identities as motivators of action. *Educational Psychologist* 44 (2), 78–89. https://doi.org/10.1080/00461520902832368.

Einhorn, Á. (2007) Az idegen nyelvi érettségi vizsga reformja [The reform of the foreign language school leaving exam]. In I. Vágó (ed.) *Fókuszban a nyelvtanulás* (pp. 73–105). Oktatáskutató és Fejlesztő Intézet.

Ellis, R. (2015) *Understanding Second Language Acquisition* (2nd edn). Oxford.

Elo, S., Kääriäinen, M., Kanste, O., Pölkki, T., Utriainen, K. and Kyngäs, H. (2014) Qualitative content analysis: A focus on trustworthiness. *SAGE Open* 4 (1), 1–10. https://doi.org/10.1177/2158244014522633.

Eurobarometer (2012) *Europeans and their Languages. Special Eurobarometer 286–Wave 71.1.* European Commission. http://ec.europa.eu/public_opinion/archives/eb_special_399_380_en.htm.

European Commission (2005) *A New Framework Strategy for Multilingualism: COM(2005) 596 final.* European Commission.

European Statistics (2016) *Education and Training in Europe: Facts and Figures.* Eurostat. https://ec.europa.eu/eurostat/statistics-explained/index.php?title=Foreign_language_skills_statistics#Number_of_foreign_languages_known.

European Statistics (2021) *Number of Foreign Languages Known (Self-reported) by Age.* Eurostat. https://ec.europa.eu/eurostat/databrowser/view/edat_aes_l22/default/table?lang=en.

Fekete, M. (2020) Digitális átállás – Az első hét tapasztalatai [Digital conversion – Experiences of the first week]. *Iskolakultúra* 30 (9), 77–95. https://doi.org/10.14232/ISKKULT.2020.9.77.

Fekete, I. (2023) *Technology in English Teaching: The Hungarian University Context.* Akadémiai Kiadó. https://doi.org/10.1556/9789634548706.

Fekete, A. and Csépes, I. (2018) B2-es szintű nyelvvizsga bizonyítvány: Útlevél a diplomás élethez, társadalmi mobilitáshoz [B2-level language exam: A passport to a life of a university graduate, social mobility]. *Iskolakultúra* 28 (10–11), 13–24. https://doi.org/10.14232/ISKKULT.2018.10-11.13.

Fekete, T. and Porkoláb, Á. (2020) Karanténpedagógia a magyar közoktatásban – A digitális oktatásra történő átállás eddigi tapasztalatairól [Quarantine pedagogy in Hungarian public education – On the experiences related to the conversion to online teaching thus far]. *Iskolakultúra* 30 (9), 96–112. https://doi.org/10.14232/ISKKULT.2020.9.96.

Field, A. (2018) *Discovering Statistics Using IBM SPSS Statistics* (5th edn). Sage.

Field, J. (2003) *Psycholinguistics: A Resource Book for Students.* Routledge.

Fischer, M. and Öveges, E. (2008) *A Világ – Nyelv pályázati csomag háttere és megvalósítása (2003–2006): Áttekintő tanulmány* [The background and implementation of the World – Language application package (2003–2006): Summary report]. http://www.okm.gov.hu/letolt/vilagnyelv/vny_fischer_oveges_090115.pdf.

Fredrickson, B.L. (2003) The value of positive emotions. *American Scientist* 91 (4), 330–335. https://www.jstor.org/stable/27858244.

Fredrickson, B.L. (2008) Promoting positive affect. In M. Eid and R.J. Larsen (eds) *The Science of Subjective Well-being* (pp. 449–468). Guilford Press.

Fredrickson, B.L. (2013) Updated thinking on positivity ratios. *American Psychologist* 68 (9), 814–822.

Galletta, A. and Cross, W.E. (2013) *Mastering the Semi-structured Interview and Beyond: From Research Design to Analysis and Publication.* New York University Press.

Galmiche, D. (2017) Shame and SLA. *Apples – Journal of Applied Language Studies* 11 (2), 25–53.

Galmiche, D. (2018) The role of shame in language learning. *Journal of Languages, Texts, and Society* 2 (Spring), 99–129.

Gardner, R.C. (1985) *Social Psychology and Second Language Learning: The Role of Attitudes and Motivation.* Edward Arnold.

Ghadyani, F., Tahririan, M.H. and Afzali, K. (2022) An exploratory empirical research on hope for learning English as a foreign language. *Language Teaching Research Quarterly* 27, 24–44.

Gottlieb, J., Oudeyer, P.Y., Lopes, M. and Baranes, A. (2013) Information-seeking, curiosity, and attention: Computational and neural mechanisms. *Trends in Cognitive Sciences* 17 (11), 585–593.

Gregersen, T., MacIntyre, P.D. and Meza, M.D. (2014) The motion of emotion: Idiodynamic case studies of learners' foreign language anxiety. *The Modern Language Journal* 98 (2), 574–588.

Guba, E.G. (1981) Criteria for assessing the trustworthiness of naturalistic inquiries. *Educational Technology Research & Development* 29, 75–91.

Hajdu, T., Hermann, Z., Horn, D. and Varga, J. (2019) *A közoktatás indikátorrendszere* [The Indicator System of Public Education]. Közgazdaság - és Regionális Tudományi Kutatóközpont, Közgazdaság-tudományi Intézet.

Henry, A. (2017) L2 motivation and multilingual identities. *The Modern Language Journal* 101 (3), 548–565.

Henry, A. and Lamb, M. (2019) L2 motivation and digital technologies. In M. Lamb, K. Csizér, A. Henry and S. Ryan (eds) *The Palgrave Handbook of Motivation for Language Learning* (pp. 599–620). Palgrave Macmillan.

Henry, A., Sundqvist, P. and Thorsen, C. (2019) *Motivational Practice: Insights from the Classroom*. Studentlitteratur.

Higgins, E.T. (1987) Self-discrepancy: A theory of relating self and affect. *Psychological Review* 94 (3), 319–340.

Hiver, P. (2016) The triumph over experience: Hope and hardiness in novice L2 teachers. In P.D. MacIntyre, T. Gregersen and S. Mercer (eds) *Positive Psychology in SLA* (pp. 168–192). Multilingual Matters.

Hoekstra, R., Vugteveen, J., Warrens, M.J. and Kruyen, P.M. (2018) An empirical analysis of alleged misunderstandings of coefficient alpha. *International Journal of Social Research Methodology* 22 (4), 351–364. https://doi.org/10.1080/13645579.2018.1547523.

Horváth, S. (2020) A pedagógus életpályamodell vizsgálata [The examination of the teacher career model]. Unpublished doctoral dissertation, University of Kaposvár.

Horwitz, E.K., Horwitz, M.B. and Cope, J. (1986) Foreign language classroom anxiety. *The Modern Language Journal* 70 (2), 125–132. https://doi.org/10.2307/327317.

Horwitz, E.K., Horwitz, M.B. and Cope, J.A. (1991) Foreign language classroom anxiety. In E.K. Horwitz and D.J. Young (eds) *Language Anxiety: From Theory and Research to Classroom Implications* (pp. 27–36). Prentice Hall.

Howitt, D. (2016) *Introduction to Qualitative Research Methods in Psychology*. Pearson.

Hungarian Central Statistical Office (2019) *Gazetteer of Hungary, 1 January 2019*. Hungarian Central Statistical Office.

Hungarian Central Statistical Office (2021) *A Magyarországra tett külföldi többnapos utazások megoszlása a felkeresett turisztikai régió és országok szerint* [Distribution of foreigners' multiple day trips to Hungary according to the visited touristic region and countries]. https://www.ksh.hu/stadat_files/tur/hu/tur0009.html.

Hungarian Central Statistical Office (n.d.a) Regional atlas – Counties. https://www.ksh.hu/regionalatlas_counties.

Hungarian Central Statistical Office (n.d.b) Regional atlas – Regions. https://www.ksh.hu/regionalatlas_regions.

Hungarian Educational Authority (2021) *Hivatalos tankönyvjegyzék* [Official List of Textbooks]. Oktatas. https://www.oktatas.hu/kozneveles/tankonyv/jegyzek_es_rendeles/tankonyvjegyzek_2021_2022.

Hungarian Educational Authority (n.d.a) *Élő idegen nyelv* [Modern Foreign Language]. Oktatas. https://www.oktatas.hu/pub_bin/dload/kozoktatas/erettsegi/vizsgakovetelmenyek2017/elo_idegen_nyelv_vk.pdf.

Hungarian Educational Authority (n.d.b) *Felsőoktatási statisztikák* [*Higher Education Statistics*]. Oktatas. https://www.oktatas.hu/felsooktatas/kozerdeku_adatok/felsooktatasi_adatok_kozzetetele/felsooktatasi_statisztikak.
Hungarian Educational Authority (n.d.c) *Közérdekű adatok* [*Data of General Interest*]. Oktatas. https://www.oktatas.hu/kozneveles/kozerdekuadatok.
Illés, É. (2012) Learner autonomy revisited. *ELT Journal* 66 (4), 505–513.
Illés, É. (2020) *Understanding Context in Language Use and Teaching*. Routledge.
Illés, É. and Csizér, K. (2018) A nyelvtanárok válaszai [The language teachers' responses]. In E. Öveges and K. Csizér (eds) *Vizsgálat a köznevelésben folyó idegennyelv-oktatás kereteiről és hatékonyságáról* (pp. 161–188). Hungarian Educational Authority. https://www.oktatas.hu/pub_bin/dload/sajtoszoba/nyelvoktatas_kutatasi_jelentes_2018.pdf
Islam, M., Lamb, M. and Chambers, G. (2013) The L2 motivational self system and national interest: A Pakistani perspective. *System* 41, 231–244. https://doi.org/10.1016/j.system.2013.01.025.
Iwaniec, J. (2019) Language learning motivation and gender: The case of Poland. *International Journal of Applied Linguistics* 29, 130–143. https://doi.org/10.1111/ijal.12251.
Izard, C.E. (2007) Basic emotions, natural kinds, emotion schemas, and a new paradigm. *Perspectives on Psychological Science* 2 (3), 260–280. https://doi.org/10.1111/j.1745-6916.2007.00044.x.
Izard, C.E. (2010) The many meanings/aspects of emotion: Definitions, functions, activation, and regulation. *Emotion Review* 2 (4), 363–370. https://doi.org/10.1177/1754073910374661.
Jensen, S.H. (2017) Gaming as an English language learning resource among young children in Denmark. *Calico Journal* 34 (1), 1–19. https://doi.org/10.1558/cj.29519.
Jin, Y. and Zhang, L.J. (2021) The dimensions of foreign language classroom enjoyment and their effect on foreign language achievement. *International Journal of Bilingual Education and Bilingualism* 24 (7), 948–962. https://doi.org/10.1080/13670050.2018.1526253.
Kálmán, C. and Tiboldi, T. (2018) A szaktanácsadók válaszai [The consultants' responses]. In E. Öveges and K. Csizér (eds) *Vizsgálat a köznevelésben folyó idegennyelv-oktatás kereteiről és hatékonyságáról* (pp. 189–220). Hungarian Educational Authority. https://www.oktatas.hu/pub_bin/dload/sajtoszoba/nyelvoktatas_kutatasi_jelentes_2018.pdf.
Kapitánffy, J. (2001) Az idegen nyelvek oktatásának fejlesztése a közoktatásban. Az Oktatási Minisztérium fejlesztési stratégiája [The development of foreign language teaching in public education: The policy strategies of the Ministry of Education]. *Iskolakultúra* 8, 71–74.
Keegan, K. (2017) Identifying and building grit in language learners. *English Teaching Forum* 55 (3), 2–9.
Keltner, D., Oatley, K. and Jenkins, J.M. (2014) *Understanding Emotions* (3rd edn). Wiley.
Kissau, S.P., Quach Kolano, L. and Wang, C. (2010) Perceptions of gender differences in high school students' motivation to learn Spanish. *Foreign Language Annals* 43 (3), 703–721. https://doi.org/10.1111/j.1944-9720.2010.01110.x.
Kitano, K. (2001) Anxiety in the college Japanese language classroom. *The Modern Language Journal* 85 (4), 549–566. https://doi.org/10.1111/0026-7902.00125.
Kleinmann, H. (1977) Avoidance behavior in adult second language acquisition. *Language Learning* 27 (1), 93–107. https://doi.org/10.1111/j.1467-1770.1977.tb00294.x.
Kontra, M. (2016) Ups and downs in English language teacher education in Hungary in the last half century. *Working Papers in Language Pedagogy* 10, 1–16.
Kormos, J. and Dörnyei, Z. (2004) The interaction of linguistic and motivational variables in second language task performance. *Zeitschrift für Interkulturellen Fremdsprachenunterricht* 9, 2.
Kormos, J. and Csizér, K. (2007) An interview study of inter-ethnic contact and its role in language learning in a foreign language environment. *System* 35, 241–258. https://doi.org/10.1016/j.system.2006.10.010

Kormos, J. and Csizér, K. (2008) Age-related differences in the motivation of learning English as a foreign language: Attitudes, selves, and motivated learning behaviour. *Language Learning* 58 (2), 327–355. https://doi.org/10.1111/j.1467-9922.2008.00443.x.

Kormos, J. and Csizér, K. (2014) The interaction of motivation, self-regulatory strategies, and autonomous learner behavior in different learner groups. *TESOL Quarterly* 48 (2), 275–299. https://doi.org/10.1002/tesq.129.

Kóródi, K., Jagodics, B. and Szabó, É. (2020) Az észlelt tanári énhatékonyságot befolyásoló tényezők vizsgálata a kényszerű digitális oktatás időszakában: A Tanári Énhatékonyság kérdőív és a Relatív Énhatékonyság Kérdőív pszichometriai vizsgálata [Examining the factors influencing self-perceived teacher efficacy during the period of forced digital teaching: A psychometric examination of the teacher self-efficacy scale and the relative self-efficacy scale]. *Iskolakultúra* 30 (10), 38–52. https://doi.org/10.14232/ISKKULT.2020.10.38.

Krashen, S.D. (1976) Formal and informal linguistic environments in language acquisition and language learning. *TESOL Quarterly* 10 (2), 157–168. https://doi.org/10.2307/3585637.

Kruk, M., Pawlak, M. and Zawodniak, J. (2021) Another look at boredom in language instruction: The role of the predictable and the unexpected. *Studies in Second Language Learning and Teaching* 11 (1), 15-40. https://doi.org/10.14746/ssllt.2021.11.1.2.

Kruk, M., Pawlak, M., Elahi Shirvan, M., Taherian, T. and Yazdanmehr, E. (2022) Potential sources of foreign language learning boredom: A Q methodology study. *Studies in Second Language Learning and Teaching* 12 (1), 37–58. https://doi.org/10.14746/ssllt.2022.12.1.3.

Kubanyiova, M. (2009) Possible selves in language teacher development. In Z. Dörnyei and E. Ushioda (eds) *Motivation, Language Identity and the L2 Self* (pp. 314–332). Multilingual Matters.

Kubanyiova, M. (2015) The role of teachers' future self guides in creating L2 development opportunities in teacher-led classroom discourse: Reclaiming the relevance of language teacher cognition. *Modern Language Journal* 99 (3), 565–584. https://doi.org/10.1111/modl.12244.

Kubanyiova, M. (2020) Language teacher education in the age of ambiguity: Educating responsive meaning makers in the world. *Language Teaching Research* 24 (1), 49–59. https://doi.org/10.1177/1362168818777533.

Lamb, M. (2012) A self-system perspective on young adolescents' motivation to learn English in urban and rural settings. *Language Learning* 62 (4), 997–1023. https://doi.org/10.1111/j.1467-9922.2012.00719.x.

Lamb, M., Csizér, K., Henry, A. and Ryan, S. (eds) (2019a) *The Palgrave Handbook of Motivation for Language Learning*. Palgrave Macmillan.

Lamb, M., Csizér, K., Henry, A. and Ryan, S. (2019b) Introduction. In M. Lamb, K. Csizér, A. Henry and S. Ryan (eds) *The Palgrave Handbook of Motivation for Language Learning* (pp. 1–17). Palgrave Macmillan.

Lazarus, R.S. (1991) *Emotion and Adaptation*. Oxford University Press.

Li, C. and Li, W. (2023) Anxiety, enjoyment, and boredom in language learning amongst junior secondary students in rural China: How do they contribute to L2 achievement? *Studies in Second Language Acquisition* 45 (1), 93–108. https://doi.org/10.1017/S0272263122000031.

Li, C., Dewaele, J.-M. and Jiang, G. (2020) The complex relationship between classroom emotions and EFL achievement in China. *Applied Linguistics Review* 11 (3), 485–510. https://doi.org/10.1515/applirev-2018-0043.

Litman, J.A. and Spielberger, C.D. (2003) Measuring epistemic curiosity and its diversive and specific components. *Journal of Personality Assessment* 80 (1), 75–86. https://doi.org/10.1207/s15327752jpa8001_16.

Little, D. (1999) Learner autonomy is more than a Western cultural construct. In S. Cotterall and D. Crabbe (eds) *Learner Autonomy in Language Learning: Defining the Field and Effecting Change* (pp. 11–18). Peter Lang.

Little, D., Dam, L. and Legenhausen, L. (2017) *Language Learner Autonomy: Theory, Research and Practice*. Multilingual Matters.

Liu, F. (2021) The role of EFL teachers' praise and love in preventing students' hopelessness. *Frontiers in Psychology* 12. https://doi.org/10.3389/fpsyg.2021.800798.

Liyanage, I. and Canagarajah, S. (2019) Shame in English language teaching: Desirable pedagogical possibilities for Kiribati in neoliberal times. *TESOL Quarterly* 53 (2), 430–455. https://doi.org/10.1002/tesq.494.

Long, M. (2014) *Second Language Acquisition and Task-based Language Teaching*. Wiley-Blackwell.

Lortie, D.C. (1975) *Schoolteacher: A Sociological Study*. University of Chicago Press.

MacIntyre, P.D. and Gardner, R.C. (1989) Anxiety and second-language learning: Toward a theoretical clarification. *Language Learning* 39 (2), 251–275. https://doi.org/10.1111/j.1467-1770.1989.tb00423.x.

MacIntyre, P.D. and Gardner, R.C. (1994) The subtle effects of language anxiety on cognitive processing in the second language. *Language Learning* 44 (2), 283–305. https://doi.org/10.1111/j.1467-1770.1994.tb01103.x.

MacIntyre, P.D. and Gregersen, T. (2012) Emotions that facilitate language learning: The positive-broadening power of the imagination. *Studies in Second Language Learning and Teaching* 2 (2), 193–213. https://doi.org/10.14746/ssllt.2012.2.2.4.

MacIntyre, P.D. and Vincze, L. (2017) Positive and negative emotions underlie motivation for L2 learning. *Studies in Second Language Learning and Teaching* 7 (1), 61–88. https://doi.org/10.14746/ssllt.2017.7.1.4.

MacIntyre, P.D., Clément, R., Dörnyei, Z. and Noels, K.A. (1998) Conceptualizing willingness to communicate in a L2: A situational model of L2 confidence and affiliation. *Modern Language Journal* 82 (4), 545–562. https://doi.org/10.1111/j.1540-4781.1998.tb05543.x.

MacIntyre, P.D., Gregersen, T. and Mercer, S. (eds) (2016) *Positive Psychology in SLA*. Multilingual Matters.

MacIntyre, P.D., Gregersen, T. and Mercer, S. (2020) Language teachers' coping strategies during the Covid-19 conversion to online teaching: Correlations with stress, wellbeing and negative emotions. *System* 94. https://doi.org/10.1016/j.system.2020.102352.

Mahmoodzadeh, M. and Khajavy, G.H. (2019) Towards conceptualizing language learning curiosity in SLA: An empirical study. *Journal of Psycholinguistic Research* 48, 333–351. https://doi.org/10.1007/s10936-018-9606-3.

Markus, H. and Nurius, P. (1986) Possible selves. *American Psychologist* 41 (9), 954–969. https://doi.org/10.1037/0003-066X.41.9.954.

Maykut, P. and Morehouse, R. (1994) *Beginning Qualitative Research. A Philosophic and Practical Guide*. Falmer Press.

Medgyes, P. (1992) Angol – A kommunikáció pótnyelve: Körkép az angol nyelv magyarországi oktatásáról és terjedéséről [English – The auxiliary language of communication: A panoramic view of the education and spread of the English language in Hungary]. *Magyar Pedagógia* 92 (4), 263–283.

Medgyes, P. (2011) *Aranykor: A nyelvoktatás két évtizede 1989–2009* [Golden Age: Two Decades of Language Instruction 1989–2009]. Nemzeti Tankönyvkiadó.

Medgyes, P. and Öveges, E. (2004) Paved with good intentions: Foreign language policy in Hungary. In C. Dobos, Á. Kis, Y. Lengyel, G. Székely and S. Tóth (eds) *Mindent fordítunk és mindenki fordít – Értékek teremtése és közvetítése a nyelvészetben* (pp. 279–290). SZAK Kiadó.

Mercer, S. and MacIntyre, P.D. (2014) Introducing positive psychology to SLA. *Studies in Second Language Learning and Teaching* 4 (2), 153–172. https://doi.org/10.14746/ssllt.2014.4.2.2.

Mills, N. (2014) Self-efficacy in second language acquisition. In S. Mercer and M. Williams (eds) *Multiple Perspectives on the Self in SLA* (pp. 6–22). Multilingual Matters.

Mills, N., Pajares, F. and Herron, C. (2007) Self-efficacy of college intermediate French students: Relation to achievement and motivation. *Language Learning* 57 (3), 417–442. https://doi.org/10.1111/j.1467-9922.2007.00421.x.

Ministry of Human Capacities (2020) *Statistical Yearbook of Public Education 2018/2019* [Köznevelési statisztikai évkönyv 2018/2019]. Ministry of Human Capacities. https://2015-2019.kormany.hu/download/7/6e/d1000/K%C3%B6znevel%C3%A9si%20statisztikai%20%C3%A9vk%C3%B6nyv_2018-2019.pdf.

Mirhosseini, S.-A. (2020). *Doing Qualitative Research in Language Education*. Palgrave Macmillan.

Muñoz, C. (2020) Boys like games and girls like movies: Age and gender differences in out-of-school contact with English. *Revista Española de Lingüística Aplicada/Spanish Journal of Applied Linguistics* 33 (1), 171–201.

Nikolov, M. (2003) Angolul és németül tanuló diákok nyelvtanulási attitűdjei és motivációja [Attitudes and motivation of students learning English and German]. *Iskolakultúra* 13 (8), 61–73.

Noels, K.A. (2001a) New orientations in language learning motivation: Toward a model of intrinsic extrinsic, and integrative orientations and motivations. In Z. Dörnyei and R. Schmidt (eds) *Motivation and Second Language Acquisition* (pp. 43–68). The University of Hawai'i, Second Language & Curriculum Center.

Noels, K.A. (2001b) Learning Spanish as a second language: Learners' orientations and perceptions of their teachers' communication style. *Language Learning* 51 (1), 107–144. https://doi.org/10.1111/0023-8333.00149.

Noels, K.A., Pelletier, L.G., Clément, R. and Vallerand, R.J. (2003) Why are you learning a second language? Motivational orientations and self-determination theory. *Language Learning* 53 (S1), 33–64. https://doi.org/10.1111/1467-9922.53223.

Noels, K.A., Chaffee, K.E., Lou, N.M. and Dincer, A. (2016) Self-determination, engagement, and identity in learning German: Some directions in the psychology of language learning motivation. *Fremdsprachen Lehren und Lernen* 45 (2), 12–29.

Oatley, K. (2004) *Emotions: A Brief History*. Blackwell Publishing.

Omaggio Hadley, A. (1993) *Teaching Language in Context* (2nd edn). Heinle & Heinle.

Organisation for Economic Co-operation and Development (2018a) *Education at a Glance 2018: OECD Indicators*. OECD.

Organisation for Economic Co-operation and Development (2018b) *OECD Regions and Cities at a Glance 2018 – Hungary*. OECD. https://www.oecd.org/cfe/HUNGARY-Regions-and-Cities-2018.pdf.

Organisation for Economic Co-operation and Development (2020) *OECD Regions and Cities at a Glance 2020*. OECD. https://doi.org/10.1787/959d5ba0-en.

Öveges, E. (2013) Idegennyelv-oktatás a köznevelésben – Változások az új szabályozók tükrében [Foreign language teaching in public eduction: Changes and new policies]. *Modern Nyelvoktatás* 19 (3), 16–25.

Öveges, E. (2017) Year of intensive language learning, a special program to rocket Hungarian students' foreign language proficiency: A success story? *Sustainable Multilingualism* 10 (1), 150–174. https://doi.org/10.1515/sm-2017-0008.

Öveges, E. (2018) Az iskolai nyelvoktatás keretei [The frameworks of institutional language learning]. In E. Öveges and K. Csizér (eds) *Vizsgálat a köznevelésben folyó idegennyelv-oktatás kereteiről és hatékonyságáról* [*An Investigation into the Frameworks and Efficiency of L2 Instruction in Public Education*] (pp. 14–29). Hungarian Educational Authority. https://www.oktatas.hu/pub_bin/dload/sajtoszoba/nyelvoktatas_kutatasi_jelentes_2018.pdf.

Öveges, E. and Csizér, K. (eds) (2018) *Vizsgálat a köznevelésben folyó idegennyelv-oktatás kereteiről és hatékonyságáról* [*An Investigation into the Frameworks and Efficiency of L2 Instruction in Public Education*]. Hungarian Educational Authority. https://www.oktatas.hu/pub_bin/dload/sajtoszoba/nyelvoktatas_kutatasi_jelentes_2018.pdf.

Oxford, R. (2015) Emotion as the amplifier and the primary motive: Some theories of emotion with relevance to language learning. *Studies in Second Language Learning and Teaching* 5 (3), 371–393. https://doi.org/10.14746/ssllt.2015.5.3.2.

Paksi, B., Veroszta, Z., Schmidt, A., Magi, A., Vörös, A., Endrődi-Kovács, V. and Felvinczi, K. (2015) *Pedagógus-pálya-motiváció: Egy kutatás eredményei* [Pedagogue-Career-Motivation: Results of an Inquiry]. Hungarian Educational Authority.

Pavelescu, L.M. and Petrić, B. (2018) Love and enjoyment in context: Four case studies of adolescent EFL learners. *Studies in Second Language Learning and Teaching* 8 (1), 73–101. https://doi.org/10.14746/ssllt.2018.8.1.4.

Pawlak, M., Zawodniak, J. and Kruk, M. (2020a) *Boredom in the Foreign Language Classroom: A Micro-Perspective.* Springer Nature.

Pawlak, M., Kruk, M., Zawodniak, J. and Pasikowski, S. (2020b) Investigating factors responsible for boredom in English classes: The case of advanced learners. *System* 91. https://doi.org/10.1016/j.system.2020.102259.

Pawlak, M., Derakhshan, A., Mehdizadeh, M. and Kruk, M. (2021) Boredom in online English language classes: Mediating variables and coping strategies. *Language Teaching Research.* https://doi.org/10.1177/13621688211064944.

Pawlak, M., Kruk, M. and Zawodniak, J. (2022a) Investigating individual trajectories in experiencing boredom in the language classroom: The case of 11 Polish students of English. *Language Teaching Research* 26 (4), 598–616. https://doi.org/10.1177/1362168820914004.

Pawlak, M., Kruk, M., Zawodniak, J. and Pasikowski, S. (2022b) Examining the underlying structure of after-class boredom experienced by English majors. *System* 106. https://doi.org/10.1016/j.system.2022.102769.

Pekrun, R. (2006) The control-value theory of achievement emotions: Assumptions, corollaries, and implications for educational research and practice. *Educational Psychology Review* 18 (4), 315–341. https://doi.org/10.1007/s10648-006-9029-9.

Pekrun, R. (2014) *Emotions and Learning.* IAE, IBE and UNESCO. http://www.iaoed.org/downloads/edu-practices_24_eng.pdf.

Pekrun, R., Götz, T., Titz, W. and Perry, R.P. (2002) Academic emotions in students' self-regulated learning and achievement: A program of quantitative and qualitative research. *Educational Psychologist* 37 (2), 91–106. https://doi.org/10.1207/S15326985EP3702_4.

Pekrun, R., Frenzel, A.C., Goetz, T. and Perry, R.P. (2007) The control-value theory of achievement emotions: An integrative approach to emotions in education. In P.A. Schutz and R. Pekrun (eds) *Emotion in Education* (pp. 13–36). Academic Press.

Pekrun, R., Goetz, T., Frenzel, A.C., Barchfeld, P. and Perry, R.P. (2011) Measuring emotions in students' learning and performance: The Achievement Emotions Questionnaire (AEQ). *Contemporary Educational Psychology* 36 (1), 36–48. https://doi.org/10.1016/j.cedpsych.2010.10.002.

Pekrun, R., Marsh, H.W., Elliot, A.J., Stockinger, K., Perry, R.P., Vogl, E., Goetz, T., van Tilburg, W.A.B, Lüdtke, O. and Vispoel, W.P. (2023) A three-dimensional taxonomy of achievement emotions. *Journal of Personality and Social Psychology* 124 (1), 145–178. https://doi.org/10.1037/pspp0000448.

Pettigrew, T.F. (1998) Intergroup contact theory. *Annual Review of Psychology* 49, 65–85.

Pettigrew, T.F. and Tropp, L.R. (2006) A meta-analytic test of intergroup contact theory. *Journal of Personality and Social Psychology* 90 (5), 751–783. https://doi.org/10.1037/0022-3514.90.5.751.

Piniel, K. and Csizér, K. (2013) L2 motivation, anxiety and self-efficacy: The interrelationship of individual variables in the secondary school context. *Studies in Second Language Learning and Teaching* 3 (4), 523–546. https://doi.org/10.14746/ssllt.2013.3.4.5.

Piniel, K. and Csizér, K. (2015) Changes in motivation, anxiety and self-efficacy during the course of an academic writing seminar. In Z. Dörnyei, P.D. MacIntyre and A. Henry (eds) *Motivational Dynamics in Language Learning* (pp. 164–194). Multilingual Matters.

Piniel, K. and Albert, Á. (2018) Advanced learners' foreign language-related emotions across the four skills. *Studies in Second Language Learning and Teaching* 8 (1), 127–147. http://doi.org/10.14746/ssllt.2018.8.1.6.

Piniel, K. and Zólyomi, A. (2022) Gender differences in foreign language classroom anxiety: Results of a meta-analysis. *Studies in Second Language Learning and Teaching* 12 (2), 173–203. https://doi.org/10.14746/ssllt.2022.12.2.2.

Piniel, K. and Albert, Á. (in press) Changes in language learners' affect: A complex dynamic systems theory perspective. *Language Learning*.

Pishghadam, R., Zabetipour, M. and Aminzadeh, A. (2016) Examining emotions in English language learning classes: A case of EFL emotions. *Issues in Educational Research* 26 (3), 508–527. https://search.informit.org/doi/10.3316/ielapa.509386612482268.

Rea, L.M. and Parker, R.A. (2014) *Designing and Conducting Survey Research: A Comprehensive Guide*. Jossey-Bass.

Reeve, J. (2009) *Understanding Motivation and Emotion*. Wiley.

Renninger, K.A. (2009) Interest and identity development in instruction: An inductive model. *Educational Psychologist* 44 (2), 105–118. https://doi.org/10.1080/00461520902832392.

Resnik, P. and Schallmoser, C. (2019) Enjoyment as a key to success? Links between e-tandem language learning and tertiary students' foreign language enjoyment. *Studies in Second Language Learning and Teaching* 9 (3), 541–564. https://doi.org/10.14746/ssllt.2019.9.3.6.

Ross, A.S. and Stracke, E. (2016) Learner perceptions and experiences of pride in second language education. *Australian Review of Applied Linguistics* 39 (3), 272–291. https://doi.org/10.1075/aral.39.3.04ros.

Ross, A.S. and Rivers, D.J. (2018) Emotional experiences beyond the classroom: Interactions with the social world. *Studies in Second Language Learning and Teaching* 8 (1), 103–126. https://doi.org/10.14746/ssllt.2018.8.1.5.

Russell, J.A. (1980) A circumplex model of affect. *Journal of Personality and Social Psychology* 39 (6), 1161–1178. https://doi.org/10.1037/h0077714.

Ryan, R.M. and Deci, E.L. (2000) Self-determination theory and the facilitation of intrinsic motivation, social development, and well-being. *American Psychologist* 55 (1), 68–78.

Ryan, R.M. and Deci, E.L. (2020) Intrinsic and extrinsic motivation from a self-determination theory perspective: Definitions, theory, practices, and future directions. *Contemporary Educational Psychology* 61. https://doi.org/10.1016/j.cedpsych.2020.101860.

Ryan, S. (2019) Motivation as an individual difference. In M. Lamb, K. Csizér, A. Henry and S. Ryan (eds) *The Palgrave Handbook of Motivation for Language Learning* (pp. 163–182). Palgrave Macmillan.

Sági, M. (2015) Első reakciók a pedagógus előmeneteli rendszer bevezetésére [First reactions toward the introduction of the pedagogue career advancement system]. In M. Sági (ed.) *A pedagógushivatás megerősítésének néhány aspektusa* (pp. 10–33). Oktatáskutató és Fejlesztő Intézet.

Sahakyan, T., Lamb, M. and Chambers, G. (2018) Language teacher motivation: From the ideal to the feasible self. In S. Mercer and A. Kostoulas (eds) *Language Teacher Psychology* (pp. 53–70). Multilingual Matters.

Saito, K., Dewaele, J.-M., Abe, M. and In'nami, Y. (2018) Motivation, emotion, learning experience, and second language comprehensibility development in classroom settings: A cross-sectional and longitudinal study. *Language Learning* 68 (3), 709–743. https://doi.org/10.1111/lang.12297.

Şakrak-Ekin, G. and Balcikanli, C. (2019) Does autonomy really matter in language learning? *Journal of Language and Education* 5, 98–111. https://doi.org/10.17323/jle.2019.8762.

Saldaña, J. (2013) *The Coding Manual for Qualitative Researchers* (2nd edn). Sage.

Sampasivam, S. and Clément, R. (2014) The dynamics of second language confidence: Contact and interaction. In S. Mercer and M. Williams (eds) *Multiple Perspectives on the Self* (pp. 23–40). Multilingual Matters.

Sáska, G. (2015) Az elmúlt két évtized pedagógusképzési reformküzdelmei, kreditekben elbeszélve [Struggles for reforms in teachers' training over the past twenty years as explained by credits]. *Magyar Tudomány* 176 (7), 819–827. http://epa.oszk.hu/00600/00691/00142/pdf/EPA00691_mtud_2015_07_0819-0827.pdf.

Sayer, P. and Ban, R. (2014) Young EFL students' engagements with English outside the classroom. *ELT Journal* 68 (3), 321–329. https://doi.org/10.1093/elt/ccu013.

Schutz, P. and Zembylas, M. (eds) (2009) *Advances in Teacher Emotion Research: The Impact on Teachers' Lives.* Springer.

Scrivener, J. (2011) *Learning Teaching: The Essential Guide to English Language Teaching* (3rd edn). Macmillan.

Seidlhofer, B. (2011) *Understanding English as a Lingua Franca.* Oxford University Press.

Shao, K., Pekrun, R. and Nicholson, L.J. (2019) Emotions in classroom language learning: What can we learn from achievement emotion research? *System* 86, 102–121. https://doi.org/10.1016/j.system.2019.102121.

Shao, K., Pekrun, R., Marsh, H.W. and Loderer, K. (2020) Control-value appraisals, achievement emotions, and foreign language performance: A latent interaction analysis. *Learning and Instruction* 69, 101356. https://doi.org/10.1016/j.learninstruc.2020.101356.

Shin, S., Mercer, S., Babic, S., Sulis, G., Mairitsch, A., King, J. and Jin, J. (2021) Riding the happiness curve: The wellbeing of mid-career phase language teachers. *Language Learning Journal* 51 (2), 1–13.

Silvia, P.J. (2010) Confusion and interest: The role of knowledge emotions in aesthetic experience. *Psychology of Aesthetics Creativity and the Arts* 4, 75–80. https://doi.org/10.1037/a0017081.

Sisk, V., Burgoyne, A., Sun, J., Butler, J. and Macnamara, B. (2018) To what extent and under which circumstances are growth mind-sets important to academic achievement? Two meta-analyses. *Psychological Science* 29 (4), 549–571. https://doi.org/10.1177/0956797617739704.

Smid, D. (2022) *Toward an Understanding of Pre-service English Teachers' Motivation: The Case of Hungary.* Akadémiai Kiadó. https://doi.org/10.1556/9789634548188.

Smid, D. and Zólyomi, A. (2021) An interview study on Hungarian high school English teachers' beliefs about learning English. In G. Tankó and K. Csizér (eds) *DEAL 2021: Current Explorations in English Applied Linguistics* (pp. 139–162). Faculty of Humanities, Eötvös Loránd University.

Snyder, C.R., Harris, C., Anderson, J.R., Holleran, S.A., Irving, L.M., Sigmon, S.T., Yoshinobu, L., Gibb, J., Langelle, C. and Harney, P. (1991) The will and the ways: Development and validation of an individual-differences measure of hope. *Journal of Personality and Social Psychology* 60 (4), 570–585. https://doi.org/10.1037/0022-3514.60.4.570.

Sparks, R.L. and Ganschow, L. (1991) Foreign language learning differences: Affective or native language aptitude differences? *Modern Language Journal* 75 (1), 3–16. https://doi.org/10.2307/329830.

Sulis, G., Mercer, S., Babic, S. and Mairitsch, A. (2023) *Language Teacher Wellbeing Across the Career Span.* Multilingual Matters.

Swain, M. (2013) The inseparability of cognition and emotion in second language learning. *Language Teaching* 46 (2), 195–207. https://doi.org/10.1017/S0261444811000486.

Tartsayné Németh, N., Tiboldi, T. and Katona, L. (2018) Az intézményvezetők válaszai [The school leaders' responses]. In E. Öveges and K. Csizér (eds) *Vizsgálat a köznevelésben folyó idegennyelv-oktatás kereteiről és hatékonyságáról* (pp. 29–51). Hungarian Educational Authority. https://www.oktatas.hu/pub_bin/dload/sajtoszoba/nyelvoktatas_kutatasi_jelentes_2018.pdf.

Teimouri, Y. (2017) L2 selves, emotions, and motivated behaviors. *Studies in Second Language Acquisition* 39 (4), 681–709. https://doi.org/10.1017/S0272263116000243.

Teimouri, Y. (2018) Differential roles of shame and guilt in L2 learning: How bad is bad? *The Modern Language Journal* 102 (4), 632–652. https://doi.org/10.1111/modl.12511.

Teimouri, Y., Goetze, J. and Plonsky, L. (2019) Second language anxiety and achievement: A meta-analysis. *Studies in Second Language Acquisition* 41 (2), 363–387. https://doi.org/10.1017/S0272263118000311.

Teimouri, Y., Plonsky, L. and Tabandeh, F. (2020) L2 grit: Passion and perseverance for second-language learning. *Language Teaching Research*. https://doi.org/10.1177/1362168820921895.

Thompson, A.S. and Vásquez, C. (2015) Exploring motivational profiles through language learning narratives. *Modern Language Journal* 99 (1), 158–174. https://doi.org/10.1111/modl.12187.

Thorsen, C., Henry, A. and Cliffordson, C. (2017) The case of a missing person? The current L2 self and the L2 motivational self system. *International Journal of Bilingual Education and Bilingualism* 23 (5), 584–600. https://doi.org/10.1080/13670050.2017.1388356.

Tracy, J.L. and Robins, R.W. (2007) The psychological structure of pride: A tale of two facets. *Journal of Personality and Social Psychology* 92 (3), 506–525. https://doi.org/10.1037/0022-3514.92.3.506.

Tracy, S.J. (2020) *Qualitative Research Methods: Collecting Evidence, Crafting Analysis, Communicating Impact*. Wiley Blackwell.

Tsang, A. and Dewaele, J.-M. (2023) The relationships between young FL learners' classroom emotions (anxiety, boredom, & enjoyment), engagement, and FL proficiency. *Applied Linguistics Review*. https://doi.org/10.1515/applirev-2022-0077.

Tseng, W.-T., Dörnyei, Z. and Schmitt, N. (2006) A new approach to assessing strategic learning: The case of self-regulation in vocabulary acquisition. *Applied Linguistics* 27 (1), 78–102. https://doi.org/10.1093/applin/ami046.

United Nations World Tourism Organisation (2021) *International Tourism Highlights, 2020 Edition*. UNWTO. https://doi.org/10.18111/9789284422456.

Ushioda, E. (2017) The impact of global English on motivation to learn other languages: Toward an ideal multilingual self. *Modern Language Journal* 101 (3), 469–482. https://doi.org/10.1111/modl.12413.

Vágó, I. (1999) Az élő idegen nyelvek oktatása – Egy modernizációs sikertörténet [Teaching foreign language: The success story of modernization efforts]. In I. Vágó (ed.) *Tartalmi változások a közoktatásban a 90-es években* (pp. 135–173). Okker Kiadó.

Világ – Nyelv: Az Oktatási Minisztérium stratégiája az idegennyelv-tudás fejlesztéséhez [The strategy of the Ministry of Education to develop foreign language knowledge]. (2003) *Modern Nyelvoktatás* 9 (1), 3–13.

Vodanovich, S.J., Kass, S.J., Andrasik, F., Gerber, W.-D., Niederberger, U. and Breaux, C. (2011) Culture and gender differences in boredom proneness. *North American Journal of Psychology* 13 (2), 221–230.

Wallace, M. (1998) *Action Research for Language Teachers*. Cambridge University Press.

Williams, M., Burden, R.L. and Lanvers, U. (2002) 'French is the language of love and stuff': Student perceptions of issues related to motivation in learning a foreign language. *British Educational Research Journal* 28 (4), 503–528. https://doi.org/10.1080/01411920220000580.

World Bank. (n.d.) Urban population (% of total population) – Hungary. Retrieved December 23, 2021, from https://data.worldbank.org/indicator/SP.URB.TOTL.IN.ZS?locations=HU&most_recent_value_desc=true.

Yashima, T. (2000) Orientations and motivation in foreign language learning: A study of Japanese college students. *JACET Bulletin* 31, 121–133.

Yim, O., Clément, R. and MacIntyre, P.D. (2019) The contexts of SLA motivation: Linking ideologies to situational variations. In M. Lamb, K. Csizér, A. Henry and S. Ryan (eds) *The Palgrave Handbook of Motivation for Language Learning* (pp. 225–244). Palgrave Macmillan.

You, C.J., Dörnyei, Z. and Csizér, K. (2016) Motivation, vision, and gender: A survey of learners of English in China. *Language Learning* 66 (1), 94–123. https://doi.org/10.1111/lang.12140.

Yun, S., Hiver, P. and Al-Hoorie, A. (2018) Academic buoyancy: Exploring learners' everyday resilience in the language classroom. *Studies in Second Language Acquisition* 40 (4), 805–830. https://doi.org/10.1017/S0272263118000037.

Zawodniak, J., Kruk, M. and Chumas, J. (2017) Towards conceptualizing boredom as an emotion in the EFL academic context. *Konin Language Studies* 5 (4), 425–441. https://doi.org/10.30438/ksj.2017.5.4.3.

Zhang, L.J. (2001) ESL students' classroom anxiety. *Teaching and Learning* 21 (2), 51–62.

Zhao, X. and Chen, W. (2014) Correlation between learning motivation and learner autonomy for non-English majors. *World Transactions on Engineering & Technology Education* 12 (3), 374–379.

Zólyomi, A. (2022) Exploring Hungarian secondary school English teachers' beliefs about differentiated instruction. *Language Teaching Research*. https://doi.org/10.1177/13621688221114780.

Index

Achievement emotions 25, 35, 84
Affective processes 25
Allport, W.G. 19–20
ANOVA 46, 58, 60, 62, 79, 81, 85–6, 90–1, 93–4, 108
Anxiety 25–7, 29–31, 33–7, 44, 47, 51–6, 58–9, 61–4, 66, 69–71, 81, 86, 91–3, 95, 104, 108, 112–14, 119, 127, 131, 143
Apathy 26–7, 29–30, 37, 44, 47, 51–4, 56–61, 63–5, 69, 81–2, 86–8, 91–4, 113–14, 132, 143
Attitude 16, 19, 20, 36, 39, 50, 65, 69
Autonomy 1, 14, 18, 20–1, 34, 36–7, 39, 42–5, 47–52, 54–61, 63–5, 67, 74–8, 84–9, 91, 93–8, 101–2, 105, 108–13, 115, 117–20, 122–3, 125–8
Autonomous learning behavior 21, 37, 47, 51, 54–6, 58–9, 61, 63–4, 74–6, 81, 84–5, 87–9, 91, 94, 105, 108–10, 117–20, 123
Autonomous use of technology 37, 43, 47, 51, 54–6, 58–9, 61, 63–4, 81, 84–5, 87–9, 91–2, 94–5, 98, 105, 108–10, 112, 118, 120, 130

Bandura, A. 1, 33, 82, 111–12
Benson, P. 21, 55, 57, 84, 108–9
Borg, S. 18
Botes, E. 30, 35–6
Broaden-and-build theory 22, 92
Boredom 21, 26–9, 35–7, 44, 47, 51–61, 63–5, 69, 81–2, 86–9, 91–5, 113–14, 131, 143

Central Hungary 3–4, 62–3, 106, 110, 114, 123
Clément, R. 19, 33–4, 52, 79
Cluster analysis 46, 78, 80, 84
Cohen, J. 46, 51, 54, 56, 58, 60, 62, 64–5, 80, 83, 87, 97, 99, 101–2
Cognitive processes 22–3, 67

Confusion 25, 27–9, 44, 47, 51–4, 56, 58–64, 81, 86, 91–3, 95, 113–14, 119, 132, 143
Contact 11, 18–20, 33–4, 43, 47–8, 50–1, 53–4, 56, 58–9, 61, 63–4, 78–80, 86–9, 91, 94–5, 106–7, 115, 127, 131
COVID-19 45, 64–5, 107, 109, 114, 121, 124, 128
Cronbach's alpha 16, 42, 46–7
Cross-tabulation 46, 96–8, 100–3
Curiosity 25, 27, 30–1, 43, 47, 51–6, 58–61, 63–5, 81, 83–4, 86–90, 93–5, 113–15, 117–18, 120, 127, 132, 143
Csíkszentmihályi, M. 29–31, 53, 82

Dewaele, J.-M. 22, 26–7, 30, 35–6, 54–5, 65, 104, 113
Disposition 1, 16–17, 20, 22, 39, 46, 50, 65, 118–20, 125, 128
Dörnyei, Z. xi, 1–2, 12, 15–16, 31, 33–4, 38, 40, 42, 46–7, 50, 52, 55, 62, 67–8, 76, 78, 87, 106–7, 110–11, 121, 124, 127

Eastern Hungary 6–7, 41, 62–3, 114
Effect size 46, 51, 54–5, 58, 60, 62, 64, 83
Emotion 1, 14, 21–32, 34–7, 39, 42–3, 45, 47–54, 56–65, 68–72, 78, 80–5, 90, 92, 100–1, 104–5, 107, 109–18, 120, 122–3, 125–7, 139
Enjoyment 24–7, 30–2, 34–7, 43, 47, 51–61, 63–5, 67, 69, 81–4, 86–90, 92–5, 99, 101, 104, 113–15, 120, 127–8, 131, 143
Epistemic emotion 25, 29, 53, 113, 118
Ethical considerations 48
Extracurricular activities 106, 124

Fekete, I. 7, 65
Fredrickson, B.L. 22, 34, 70, 82, 92, 94

Gender 27–8, 30–1, 40–2, 53–5, 106, 108–9, 111, 113

Henry, A. 16–17, 68, 76, 86–7, 123–4, 126–7
Hope 25–7, 31–2, 35, 43, 47, 51–2, 54, 56–9, 61, 63–4, 69, 81–4, 86, 90, 92, 94–5, 99, 101, 104–5, 113–15, 119–20, 127, 132, 143
Horwitz, E.K. 27, 55, 70
Horwitz, M.B. 27, 55, 70
Hungary xi, 1–14, 16–17, 20–1, 27, 38–40, 50, 52, 56–7, 60, 64–5, 78, 80–1, 106, 110, 112, 117, 120, 123–4
Hungarian context 1, 15–16, 120, 28–30, 33–4, 36, 84, 111, 122–3, 125–6

Ideal L2 self 16–17, 31, 34–5, 42, 47, 51–2, 54, 56–9, 61, 63–4, 78–80, 86, 91–2, 94, 106–7, 129
Illés, É. 7–10, 20–1, 44, 57, 80, 84, 87, 109, 126, 128
Individual difference (ID) 1, 38
Instruction 2, 5, 7–8, 10, 14, 39, 49, 62, 66, 68, 106, 110

Kormos, J. xi, 1, 16, 20–1, 33, 37–8, 42–3, 52, 76, 78, 80, 84, 89, 98, 108, 110–11
Kruk, M. 26
Kubanyiova, M. 18, 44

Lamb, M. 15, 17, 19, 127
Language exam 7, 62, 72–3, 81, 124
Language learning experiences 23, 43, 47, 75
Little, D. 20–1, 84
L2 motivational self system 15–18, 31, 34, 78, 105
L2 self-efficacy 51–2, 54, 56–9, 61–4, 81–2, 85–6, 91, 94–5, 130

MacIntyre, P.D. 19, 22, 26–7, 30, 34, 36, 53–5, 65, 70, 84, 95, 100, 104, 112–13, 126
Medgyes, P. 5, 11, 38
Mills, N. 52, 55, 57, 82
Motivation 1, 14–17, 19, 21, 26, 28, 31, 33–6, 38, 42, 45, 47–53, 58, 60, 62, 67, 69, 72, 78–85, 89, 91, 93–102, 105–11, 113, 115, 118–20, 122–3, 125–7, 131
Motivated learning behavior 16, 20, 34, 37, 42, 47, 50–1, 54–9, 61, 63–4, 81–4, 86–9, 91–2, 94, 106–8, 110, 115, 120, 127, 130

Negative emotions 22, 25, 34–5, 37, 42–3, 47, 49, 52–3, 57, 60, 62, 69–72, 78, 81–2, 84–5, 91–7, 99–104, 108, 111, 113–15, 119, 122–3, 125–6, 128
Noels, K.A. 16, 19, 31, 53, 126

OECD 3–4, 13, 62
Ought-to L2 self 16, 42, 47, 50–1, 54, 56–61, 63–4, 78–81, 86, 91, 94–5, 106–7, 129

Pawlak, M. 26, 28, 45, 53, 58, 65, 82
Pekrun, R. 25–6, 29, 31–2, 43, 53, 65, 84, 94, 113, 117, 122
Perceived importance of contact 19–20, 43, 47, 50–1, 53–4, 56, 58–9, 61, 63–4, 78–80, 86–7, 91, 94–5, 131
Piloting 42, 49
Piniel, K. xi, 17, 26–7, 30, 33, 39, 44, 55, 65, 80, 111, 113, 122, 124
Policy 8, 10, 39
Positive emotions 1, 22, 30, 32, 34–5, 42–3, 47, 52–3, 57, 60, 62, 68–70, 72, 78, 81–2, 84–5, 90–3, 95–101, 103–5, 108, 111, 113–17, 119, 122, 126, 128
Pride 25–7, 32, 35, 43, 47, 51–4, 56–61, 63–5, 69, 81–4, 86, 90, 92–5, 99, 101–2, 104, 113–15, 119, 127, 132, 143
Principal components analysis 46–7
Proficiency 2, 4–8, 10, 14, 30, 36, 42, 129, 139–40
Public education 5–14, 30, 62, 106, 118

Quality control 2, 48–9

Regression analyses 36, 46, 83, 87, 108, 110, 115, 120
Reliability analysis 47

School-leaving exam 7–8
Self-confidence 9, 19, 32–3, 48–9, 72–3, 105, 111–12, 122, 126, 139–40
Self-efficacy beliefs 33, 44, 47, 52, 54–5, 57, 62, 82, 87, 89, 92, 95, 110–12, 120
Shame 25–8, 32, 35, 44, 47, 51–4, 56–9, 61, 63–4, 81, 84, 86, 91–3, 95, 108, 112–15, 119, 133, 143
Social emotion 25
Student profiles 78–9, 81, 83–6, 88, 125

T-test 46, 50–3, 56–7, 143
Topic emotion 25
Trait and state 27

Validity 2, 49, 55, 62

Western Hungary 3, 41, 63
Willingness to communicate (WTC) 19

For Product Safety Concerns and Information please contact our EU Authorised Representative:

Easy Access System Europe

Mustamäe tee 50

10621 Tallinn

Estonia

gpsr.requests@easproject.com

www.ingramcontent.com/pod-product-compliance
Lightning Source LLC
Chambersburg PA
CBHW052049300426
44117CB00012B/2036